MIGRATION, MISSION, AND MINISTRY

An Introduction

Editors

Robert Chao Romero

Stephen E. Burris

Urban Loft Publishers | Skyforest, CA

Migration, Mission, and Ministry
An Introduction

Urban Loft Publishers
P.O. Box 6
Skyforest, CA 92385
www.urbanloftpublishers.com

Senior Editors: Stephen Burris & Kendi Howells Douglas
Copy Editor: Marla Black
Cover Design: Elisabeth Arnold
Interior Typesetting: Elisabeth Arnold

ISBN-13: 978-1-949625-16-5

Made in the U.S

TABLE OF CONTENTS

Chapter Three

A Spirituality of Migration 75

Daniel G. Groody, CSC

Chapter Four

A Christian Ethic of Immigration 93

Kristin E. Heyer

Chapter Five

El Espíritu Migratorio: Toward a Prophetic Pneumatology in the World Christian Movement..115

Pablo A. Jiménez, Emmett G. Price III, and Peter Goodwin Heltzel

SECTION TWO

History and Anthropology 143

Chapter Six

United States Immigration History 145

Robert Chao Romero

Chapter Seven

Using Anthropology to Better Understand Immigrants 163

Doug Priest

CONTRIBUTORS

Editors

Stephen E. Burris is a pastor, teacher, author, and is the Senior Research Missiology and Senior Editor at Urban Loft Publishers specializing in world Christianity and urban-focused kingdom growth. He is the founding editor of *The International Journal of Urban Transformation*. He has edited or co-edited several books including, *River of God: An Introduction to World Mission*. He was the founding editor of the journal *New Urban World* where his contributions include "Seeds of Shalom," "Mission and Money," and "The Academic Dilemma of the Urban Mission Educator." He is a charter member of the International Society for Urban Mission, now the Urban Shalom Society.

Robert Chau Romero, PhD, JD, is an associate professor in the UCLA departments of Chicana/o Studies and Central America Studies, and Asian American Studies. He received his Ph.D. from UCLA in Latin American History and his Juris Doctor from U.C. Berkeley. Romero is the author of *Brown Church: Five Centuries of Latina/o Social Justice, Theology, and Identity*, and *The Chinese in Mexico, 1882-1940*. *The Chinese in Mexico* received the Latina/o Studies book award from the Latin American Studies Association, and *Brown Church* received the IVP Readers' Choice Award for the category of academic title.

Contributors

HyeRan Kim-Cragg, ThD, holds the inaugural professorship in preaching and serves as Graduate Studies Director at Emmanuel College of Victoria University in the University of Toronto. She has published 12 books and her most recent is *Postcolonial Preaching: Creating a Ripple Effect* (Lexington, 2021).

Michael D. Crane, PhD, has spent most of his life in East and Southeast Asia. He and his family live in a global city in Asia where Michael serves on faculty with a local seminary and teaches as an adjunct for Gateway Seminary in California. Michael is a director of Radius Global Cities Network, an urban research think tank serving the global church. In addition to a number of articles and book chapters, Michael has written *Sowing Seeds of Change: Cultivating Transformation in the City* (Urban Loft, 2015) and *City Shaped Churches: Planting Churches in a Global Era* (Urban Loft, 2018).

Ricardo L. Franco, LSW, DMin, is an independent scholar and licensed social worker who uses his pastoral and social work experience and his theological training to research practices of Latinx immigrant spirituality. He is a supervisor of contextual education at Boston University School of Theology.

Daniel G. Groody, CSC, PhD, is Associate Professor of Theology and Global Affairs and director of the Global Leadership Program at the Kellogg Institute for International Studies and the Keough School of Global Affairs at the University of Notre Dame.

Peter Goodwin Heltzel, PhD, is Visiting Researcher at Boston University School of Theology. He is the author of *Jesus and Justice: Evangelicals, Race and American Politics; Resurrection City: A Theology of Improvisation; and Faith-Rooted Organizing: Mobilizing the Church in Service to the World* with Alexia Salvatierra.

Kristin E. Heyer, PhD, is professor of theological ethics and director of graduate studies in the theology department at Boston College. Her books include *Kinship Across Borders; A Christian Ethic of immigration (2012)* and *Prophetic and Public: the Social Witness of U.S. Catholicism* (2006), both published with Georgetown University Press.

Pablo A. Jiménez, PhD, is Associate Professor of Preaching and Associate Dean of the Latino and Global Ministries Program at Gordon-Conwell Theological Seminary. Prior to joining Gordon-Conwell, Dr. Jiménez served as senior pastor of the Iglesia Cristiana (Discípulos de Cristo) in Espinosa, Dorado, Puerto Rico. Dr. Jiménez previously served as pastor of the CCDC in Sonadora, Guaynabo, Puerto Rico; director of the Rev. Juan Figueroa Umpierre Bible Institute of the CCDC in Puerto Rico; and executive director of the Association for Hispanic Theological Education and manager of the Hispanic Summer Program. Dr. Jiménez is the coauthor of *Pulpito: An Introduction to Hispanic Preaching* with Justo L. González.

vănThanh Nguyễn, SVD, STD, Pontifical Gregorian University, Rome, is Professor of New Testament Studies and the holder of the Francis X. Ford, M.M., Chair of Catholic Missiology at Catholic Theological Union in Chicago, U.S.A. He has authored several books including, *What Does the Bible Say About Strangers, Migrants, and Refugees?*

Peter C. Phan, PhD, DD, University of London, is the Ignacio Ellacuria Chair of Catholic Social Thought at Georgetown University, Washington, DC, USA. He has authored and edited 40 books on systematic theology.

Emmett G. Price III, PhD, is Professor of Worship, Church & Culture and Founding Executive Director of the Institute for the Study of the Black Christian Experience at Gordon-Conwell Theological Seminary. He served as Dean of Chapel (Hamilton Campus, 2016-2020). Dr. Price is the author of *HIP HOP Culture* (ABC-CLIO, 2006), executive editor of the *Encyclopedia of African American Music* (ABC-CLIO, 2011), editor of *The Black Church and Hip Hop Culture: Toward Bridging the Generational Divide* (Scarecrow Press, 2012) and author of the ebook, *There is A Balm in Gilead: A Call to Lament Together* (Hendrickson Publishers, 2020).

Doug Priest, PhD, DD, was raised in Ethiopia and later served seventeen years as a missionary in East Africa and Southeast Asia. For twenty-two years he was the executive director of CMF International. Currently retired, he sits on the Board of Directors of Renewal Neighborhood Ministry working in one of the most under-resourced areas of Indianapolis, primarily with African American and immigrant Latinx populations.

Robert Chau Romero, PhD, JD, is an associate professor in the UCLA departments of Chicana/o Studies and Central America Studies, and Asian American Studies. He received his PhD from UCLA in Latin American History and his Juris Doctor from U.C. Berkeley. Romero is the author of *Brown Church: Five Centuries of Latina/o Social Justice, Theology, and Identity*, and *The Chinese in Mexico, 1882-1940*. The Chinese in Mexico received the Latinx Studies book award from the Latin American Studies Association, and Brown Church received the IVP Readers' Choice Award for the category of academic title.

Alexia Salvatierra, PhD, serves as Assistant Professor of Integral Mission and Global Transformation for the School of Mission and Theology at Fuller Theological Seminary as well as Coordinator of a Professional Certificate program for Hispanic pastors and church leaders at Fuller's Centro Latino. She also coordinates the Ecumenical Collaboration for Asylum Seekers and serves on the leadership team of Matthew 25/Mateo 25 SoCal (a bipartisan Christian network to protect and defend families facing deportation in the name and spirit of Jesus.). She co-founded the New Sanctuary Movement, the national Evangelical Immigration Table, the Guardian Angels project for unaccompanied migrant minors, and Matthew 25/Mateo 25.

Jonathan Y. Tan, PhD, is Archbishop Paul J. Hallinan Professor of Catholic Studies in the Department of Religious Studies at Case Western Reserve University in Cleveland, Ohio, USA. He also serves as Organist and Director of Music at the Church of Our Saviour/La Iglesia de Nuestro Salvador, a bilingual and intercultural urban Episcopal parish church in the Mount Auburn neighborhood of Cincinnati, Ohio, which serves the Guatemalan and Honduran immigrant and refugee communities of Cincinnati, together with the African American and White American communities. He is also the author of *Introducing Asian American Theologies* (Orbis Books, 2008), *Christian Mission among the Peoples of Asia* (Orbis Books, 2014), and *The Federation of Asian Bishops' Conferences (FABC): Bearing Witness to the Gospel and the Reign of God in Asia* (Fortress Press, 2021).

Anh Q. Tran, SJ, PhD, is Associate Professor of Theology at Jesuit School of Theology of Santa Clara University. Specializing in comparative theology/religious studies and Asian Christianity, he is the author of *Gods, Heroes, and Ancestors* (Oxford University Press, 2018), and co-editor of *World Christianity: Perspectives and Insights* (Orbis Books, 2016).

PREFACE

At the 2016 joint meeting of the Association of Professors of Mission (APM) and the American Society of Missiology (ASM), Peter C. Phan of Georgetown University addressed the theme, "Teaching Missiology in and for World Christianity: Content and Pedagogy." Peter Phan, a native of Vietnam, emigrated as a refugee to the U.S.A. in 1975. Dr. Phan's talk struck a chord with Kendi Howells Douglas and me as we listened and as we were in an election cycle in 2016 in the United States with immigration policy red hot. In fact, I was on the edge of my seat waiting for the session to be over so I might introduce myself to Dr. Phan. He was very gracious, and we exchanged information. Kendi Howells Douglas, Mark Krause and I had recently purchased Urban Loft Publishers and we were looking for books to publish and a missiologically based book on immigration was high on our list. Was there a biblical/Christian response? Well, no, not a single response. As you read the following pages you will see that there are many responses. And there are very few issues more divisive today than immigration.

Over the last five years as this book took shape the immigration discussion has only become more heated with walls being built, separation of families at the border, reports of kids in cages, and a host of other issues being reported on a daily basis with not much middle ground upon which to land. Claims, counter claims, and false claims were everywhere. It was in this context that this book was conceived. That night I sent an email to Peter with the genesis of the idea. By noon the next day we had this book scoped out in general terms. Over the next several months we continued to sharpen the focus, putting together a list of topics and possible authors. Dr. Phan has been invaluable in the development of this book.

It was about this time that I was introduced to Dr. Robert Chau Romero. Robert was on the leading edge of much of the immigration conversation, especially in Southern California from his base at UCLA. He was in the middle of important conversations and brought great depth and insight into the development of this book. He agreed to be a co-editor. Robert is a "Chino-Chicano." He was born in East Los Angeles and raised in Hacienda Heights, California. His father is an immigrant from Chihuahua, Mexico, and his mother an immigrant from Hubei, in Central China. He has been mixed race at UCLA for more than two decades. At a lunch meeting with Robert, he laid out the basis of "the grace option." That was it! In the discussions and arguments that I was hearing there was very little "grace" present. As you will see in Robert's chapter "Migration as Grace" a common ground just might be present.

As Christians we must follow the biblical admonition of "speaking the truth in love." Yet in the current climate indecent and defensive attack language seem to be more commone. Yes, the topics are volatile. Yes, emotions are high. Yes, we know many who are directly impacted by the outcomes of these discussions. And, yes, we must speak the truth in love into the conversation. The grace option is a good place to start—and that is where this book starts. Using the parable of the sower as a backdrop we should be sowers of the seeds of *Shalom*. We can make a difference. We must make a difference.

The viewpoints expressed are those of each contributor. They do not necessarily represent the views of other contributors. But all viewpoints should cause us to think, reflect, and examine our viewpoints. These are not simple issues, rather, they are very complex with many moving pieces. It is our hope that this book will contribute to the conversation that rages, on a daily basis, over immigration on a global scale. We hope that you will become uncomfortable, even upset, by what you read on these pages. We also hope that you will be provoked to action. We hope that grace will prevail and that the seeds of *shalom* will sprout and grow.

Stephen E. Burris,

Skyforest, California,

July 2021

Opinions expressed in the following essays reflect the opinion of their authors and are not understood to represent the position of Urban Loft Publishers, its publisher, editors, or any other individual or group.

SECTION ONE

Theology, Spirituality, and Ethic of Migration

CHAPTER ONE

Migration as Grace

Robert Chao Romero

The God of Abraham is the God of radical hospitality. He invites all to the banquet table of the Kingdom of God. Through the teachings and example of Jesus we know that, although God's invitation comes to all, it goes especially to the poorest and most marginalized of society. Then, and only then, does it come to the rest of us. In the language of Latin American liberation theology, it cannot come to us without first going to them.

The radical hospitality of God is expressed by Jesus in the Parable of the Great Banquet. In this parable, Jesus tells of a certain man who invited many guests to a great celebration. The first guests were those of economic means who made excuses and rejected the invitation because of materialistic reasons: they had just bought fields and oxen (Luke 14:18–19 NIV). The third likewise rejected the invitation because he was a newlywed. Jesus then tells us:

> "Then the owner of the house became angry and ordered his servant, 'Go out quickly into the streets and alleys of the town and bring in the poor, the crippled, the blind and the lame.'
>
> 22 "'Sir,' the servant said, 'what you ordered has been done, but there is still room.'
>
> 23 "Then the master told his servant, 'Go out to the roads and country lanes and compel them to come in, so that my house will be full" (Luke 14:21–23)

As this parable teaches, God invites many to the banquet table of the Kingdom of God, but it is especially the poor and disenfranchised who respond to His invitation. Indeed, God is such a gracious host that He desires that His "house be full."

Expressing the hospitality of God, specifically to the "stranger," or, "xenos," Jesus says in Matthew 25 that when we welcome the stranger, we are welcoming Jesus Himself, and we when reject the stranger, we are rejecting Jesus Himself.

> 34 "Then the King will say to those on his right, 'Come, you who are blessed by my Father; take your inheritance, the kingdom prepared for you since the creation of the world. 35 For I was hungry and you gave me something to eat, I was thirsty and you gave me something to drink, *I was a stranger [xenos] and you invited me in*... (Matt. 25:34-35)

> 41 "Then he will say to those on his left, 'Depart from me, you who are cursed, into the eternal fire prepared for the devil and his angels. 42 For I was hungry and you gave me nothing to eat, I was thirsty and you gave me nothing to drink, 43 *I was a stranger and you did not invite me in*... (Matt. 25:41–43)

To paraphrase Mother Teresa, "Jesus appears to us in the distressing disguise of the immigrant."[1] In the language of Latina/o Theology: "Those whom society rejects, God welcomes and calls His very own."[2]

A broad review of Scripture reveals a further, more specific principle with respect to immigration: *"Migration is a source of grace both to migrants and their host country"* Here, I define "grace" not in its limited sense of forgiveness, but in its broader biblical usage as God's unmerited favor. So, to restate the previous

---

[1] Mother Teresa, *In the Heart of the World: Thoughts, Stories and Prayers* (Novato: New World Library, 2010).

[2] Virgilio Elizondo, *Galilean Journey: The Mexican American Promise* (Ossining: Orbis Books, 2005).

principle in light of this definition: Migration is a source of God's unmerited favor to both immigrants and their host countries.

Many biblical narratives bear out this spiritual principle. The call of Abraham is one primary example. God affected the salvation of the world through Abraham's obedience in emigrating from Ur. Through Abraham's faithful act of migration and the process which this set in motion, all the peoples of earth have been, and are being, blessed by him:

> 1 "The Lord had said to Abram, 'Go from your country, your people and your father's household to the land I will show you.
>
> 2 'I will make you into a great nation,
>
> and I will bless you;
>
> I will make your name great, and you will be a blessing.
>
> 3 I will bless those who bless you,
>
> and whoever curses you I will curse;
>
> and all peoples on earth
>
> will be blessed through you.'" (Gen. 12:1–3)

Abraham's moniker, "the Hebrew," found in Genesis 14:13, also reinforces the special nature of his migration call. As used in this passage, "ivri," the root of the Hebrew word for "Hebrew" means literally "to cross over."[3] This appears to be a clear image of migration. Abraham is one who "crosses over" He is the "crosser-over," if you will.

The patriarch Joseph offers another example of God using, in this case a forced migrant, as a source of grace for many. Joseph was slave trafficked to Egypt by his jealous brothers and, through a series of divine interventions, rose to the rank of second in Egypt. Through this position, Joseph saved his whole

---

[3] Rabbi and Rachel Trugman, "Abraham the Hebrew," *Ohr Chadash: New Horizons in Jewish Experience*, accessed June 21, 2016, http://thetrugmans.com/673/abraham-the-hebrew/.

family, Egypt, and Canaan, from famine. Joseph states as much to his brothers in Genesis 50:

> "You intended to harm me [by forcing me to migrate
> through slave trafficking], but God intended it for good to
> accomplish what is now being done, the saving of many
> lives" (Gen. 50:20)

Working in the other direction, the Scriptures also indicate that God provides for the food and other basic needs of immigrants when host countries are faithful to notions of biblical hospitality. In Genesis 12:10, Abram (not yet called Abraham) flees to Egypt to find food and escape famine. In Exodus 2, Moses finds refuge for forty years in the land of Midian and the household of Reuel. In the book of Ruth, we are told that Elimelek and Naomi sought relief from famine in the country of Moab. Subsequently, Ruth emigrates from Moab with Naomi to Bethlehem in search of food, and in the process becomes a mother of the Jewish faith. As stated in Deuteronomy 10:18, "He defends the cause of the fatherless and the widow, and loves the foreigner residing among you, giving them food and clothing."

Finally, the most compelling example of migration as grace in the Bible involves the flight of the baby Jesus and the Holy Family to Egypt:

> When they had gone, an angel of the Lord appeared to
> Joseph in a dream. "Get up," he said, "take the child and
> his mother and escape to Egypt. Stay there until I tell you,
> for Herod is going to search for the child to kill him" 14 So
> he got up, took the child and his mother during the night
> and left for Egypt, 15 where he stayed until the death of
> Herod. (Matt. 2:13–15)

In response to the good news of Jesus' birth, the jealous and narcissistic King Herod turned to violence in order to preserve his own power and authority which were built upon the shallow manipulation of religious identity. In order to maintain his false title as King of the Jews, Herod murdered all the boys in Bethlehem who were two years old and younger, and caused the Holy Family to flee as refugees to Egypt. Fleeing the murderous rage of Herod, the lives of Jesus and his entire family were saved by the hospitality of Egypt, and, according to church tradition, the Holy Family found refuge in Egypt for about three and a half years.

Notably, the flight to Egypt is celebrated to this day by the Orthodox Church. Churches and monasteries have been built to commemorate where Jesus dwelt as a child refugee. For example, the Monastery of al-Muharraq houses what is reported to be the oldest Christian altar in the world—a bed of stone which served as a cradle for the infant Jesus. Coptic Christians see this altar as a fulfillment of the prophecy of Isaiah: "In that day there will be an altar to the Lord in the heart of Egypt, and a pillar to the Lord at its border" (Isa.19:19).

It is worth noting that hospitality to strangers is modeled biblically not only on an individual basis, but also on a systemic, or structural, level. Stated another way, God's grace was extended to immigrants on a structural level through the legal requirements of the Mosaic law. Within an agrarian economy based upon land ownership and kinship networks, immigrants, or ger, were an extremely vulnerable population.[4] Because of their sojourner status, the ger were excluded from owning land and meaningful participation in the agrarian sector. As a result, they were dependent upon the larger Israelite community for food, employment, and protection from discrimination. They worked in lowly positions as day laborers and in temple building/conscription. In times of drought, crop failure, or disease, immigrants were especially vulnerable because they did not own land and lacked a familial socio-economic net to supply their basic needs.

Structural provision for the basic needs of immigrants is reflected in the gleaning laws and special tithes divinely instituted in the Mosaic law. According to Old Testament law, landowners were to leave the grain along the edges of their fields, and the fallen remnants from harvesting, for the ger.

---

[4] M. Daniel Carroll R., *Christians at the Border: Immigration, the Church, and the Bible* (Grand Rapids: Baker Academic, 2008), 102.

> "When you harvest the crops of your land, do not harvest
> the grain along the edges of your fields, and do not pick up
> what the harvesters drop. Leave it for the poor and the
> foreigners living among you. I am the LORD your God"
> (Lev. 23:22)

Moreover, every three years, the entire tithe of produce was to be given to the clergy, immigrants, orphans, and widows, "so they can eat in your cities until they are full" (Deut. 26:12 CEB).

Because of their susceptibility to societal discrimination, the Mosaic law also guarantees what might be labeled civil rights protections for the immigrant community:

> "When an alien lives with you in your land, do not mistreat
> him. The alien living with you must be treated as one of
> your native-born. Love him as yourself, for you were aliens
> in Egypt. I am the LORD your God" (Lev. 19: 33–34)

In striking similarity to modern U.S. constitutional law, the Mosaic law also required equitable treatment between immigrants and native Israelites, and prohibited the application of disparate legal codes for the two groups:

> "You are to have the same law for the foreigner and the
> native-born. I am the LORD your God.':" (Lev. 24:22)

These legal requirements bear a striking resemblance to the Equal Protection Clause of the 14th Amendment to the United States Constitution and represent one of its earliest historical precursors.

Returning to the theme of migration as grace, it is important to highlight that migrants often come to know the love of God through the often difficult, immigration process. This is born out in multitudinous biblical examples, including, as previously discussed, the lives of Abraham, Ruth, and Joseph. Other examples include Hagar, Isaac, Jacob, Moses, Joseph, and Mary. In each instance, these biblical characters experienced the grace and provision of God through the migration process, and the end result was the deepening of their faith and relationship with God. The apostle Paul hints at this spiritually transformative aspect of migration in his famous sermon to the learned Areopagus:

> 26"From one man he made all the nations, that they should inhabit the whole earth [an implicit reference to migration]; and he marked out their appointed times in history and the boundaries of their lands. 27God did this so that they would seek him and perhaps reach out for him and find him, though he is not far from any one of us" (Acts 17: 26–27)

In as much as the Bible uplifts the spiritual principle of migration as grace, it also offers counterexamples in which migration is treated as "ungrace" and condemned by the Scriptural record. The Exodus narrative is particularly illustrative in this regard. Xenophobia in a time of war led the king of Egypt to cruelly enslave the Israelites and relegate them to forced labor:

> "9 He said to his people, 'Look, the Israelite people are more numerous and more powerful than we. 10 Come, let us deal shrewdly with them, or they will increase and, in the event of war, join our enemies and fight against us and escape from the land.' 11 Therefore they set taskmasters over them to oppress them with forced labor. They built supply cities, Pithom and Rameses, for Pharaoh" (Exod. 1:9–11)

When the strategy of oppressive labor proved ineffective to subdue the imagined political threat of the Israelites, Pharaoh then turned to the even more insidious policy of male infanticide:

> "12 But the more they were oppressed, the more they multiplied and spread, so that the Egyptians came to dread the Israelites…
>
> 15 The king of Egypt said to the Hebrew midwives, one of whom was named Shiphrah and the other Puah, 16 'When you act as midwives to the Hebrew women, and see them on the birthstool, if it is a boy, kill him; but if it is a girl, she shall live.':" (Exod.1:12, 15–16)

As a consequence of its oppression of the Israelite community, Egypt experienced divine judgment in the form of the ten plagues and its miraculous military defeat in the Red Sea:

> "[Referring to the divine plagues] Pharaoh's officials said to him, 'How long shall this fellow be a snare to us? Let the people go, so that they may worship the Lord their God; do you not yet understand that Egypt is ruined?':" (Exod. 10:7)

> "So Moses stretched out his hand over the sea, and at dawn the sea returned to its normal depth. As the Egyptians fled before it, the Lord tossed the Egyptians into the sea. The waters returned and covered the chariots and the chariot drivers, the entire army of Pharaoh that had followed them into the sea; not one of them remained" (Exod. 14:27–28)

As reflected by the Exodus account, the abuse of immigrant populations is clearly condemned by the biblical record. God takes it seriously when host countries exploit immigrant communities and treat them with "ungrace."

"Migration as Ungrace": U.S. Immigration History

Unfortunately, much of U.S. immigration history over the past 150 years does not square with biblical understandings of migration as grace. Instead, U.S. immigration law and policy has more often reflected an attitude of migration as *"ungrace."* Anti-Chinese xenophobia produced invidious legislation such as the Chinese Exclusion Act of 1882 which, for the first time in United States history, barred an entire ethnic group from immigration.[5] Racism towards Italians and Eastern Europeans fueled passage of the Emergency Quota Act of 1921, the

---

[5] Alexander Saxton, *The Indispensable Enemy: Labor and the Anti-Chinese Movement in California* (Berkeley: University of California Press, 1975).

Cable Act of 1922, and the Immigration Act of 1924.[6] Together with the Oriental
Exclusion Act of 1924, and the Tydings-McDuffie Act (1934), these laws slowed
immigration from Asia and Southern and Eastern Europe to a trickle, and
expanded migration flows from Northern and Western Europe. Between 1930
and 1935, 345,839 Mexicans were repatriated or deported back to Mexico.[7]
Tragically, Mexican Americans were also not excluded from these deportations.
In California, over 80% of the repatriates were U.S. citizens or legal residents of
the U.S. Moreover, between 1947 and 1954 the Immigration and Nationalization
Service boasted of apprehending more than 1 million unauthorized Mexican
immigrants as part of the notorious "Operation Wetback."[8] Racially
discriminatory quotas favoring northern and western European immigrants and
barring immigrants from Asia, Latin America, Africa, and southern and eastern
Europe were not overturned until the passage of the Immigration Act of 1965.

Regrettably, such mass deportations are not just a thing of the past.
Since 2009, the presidential administration of Barack Obama has destroyed the
family structures of untold numbers of immigrant families through the
deportation of more than 2.5 million individuals. At this rate, President Obama is
on pace to deport more people than the combined total of the 19 presidents who
held office from 1892–2000.[9] From January 2014 to October 2015, moreover,
the United States government deported 83 El Salvadoran, Guatemalan, and
Honduran refugees to their deaths in violation of United Nations protocol.[10]

---

[6] Harvard University Open Collections Program, "Key Dates and Landmarks in United
States Immigration History," accessed June 21, 2016,
http://ocp.hul.harvard.edu/immigration/timeline.html.

[7] Zaragosa Vargas, *Crucible of Struggle: A History of Mexican Americans from the Colonial Period
to the Present Era* (Oxford: Oxford University Press, 2010), 220.

[8] David Gutierrez, *Walls and Mirrors: Mexican Americans, Mexican immigrants, and the Politics of
Ethnicity* (Berkeley: University of California Press, 1995), 142.

[9] Tim Rogers, "Obama has deported more immigrants than any other president. Now
he's running up the score," *Fusion*, January 7, 2016, http://fusion.net/story/252637/obama-
has-deported-more-immigrants-than-any-other-president-now-hes-running-up-the-score/.

[10] Sibylla Brodzinsky and Ed Pilkington, "US government deporting Central American
migrants to their deaths," *The Guardian* (U.S. Edition), October 12, 2015.

Tragically, "ungraceful" anti-immigrant federal and state laws have also proliferated over the past two decades. Examples include California Proposition 187 (1994), the federal Sensenbrenner Immigration Bill (2005), the Hazleton "Illegal Immigration Relief Act" (2006), Arizona SB-1070 (2010), Alabama House Bill 56 (2011), and 162 other anti-immigrant laws passed by state legislatures in 2010 and 2011.[11]

Although held to be largely unconstitutional and never implemented, Proposition 187, the so-called "Save Our State" initiative, barred undocumented immigrants in California from receiving health care, K-12 public education, and other public social services.[12] It also required police, teachers, public school officials, and public healthcare providers to check the immigration status of individuals and report undocumented immigrants to the federal government for deportation.

The Sensenbrenner Bill, passed by the U.S. House of Representatives in 2005, sought to construct a 700-mile fence along the U.S.-Mexico border, eliminate the Diversity Immigrant Visa Program, categorize all forms of unlawful presence and visa overstays as felonies, and arguably made it a crime for churches to minister to undocumented immigrants.[13] In passing the "Illegal Immigration Relief Act" in 2006, the city of Hazleton, Pennsylvania tried to take the issue of undocumented immigration into its own hands by fining landlords who rented to undocumented immigrants and suspending the business licenses of people who hired them.[14]

In its explicit terms, Arizona SB-1070 called for the goal of immigrant "attrition through enforcement." SB-1070 requires police to determine the

---

[11] Ian Gordon and Tasneem Raja, "164 Anti-Immigration Laws Passed Since 2010. A MoJo Analysis," *Mother Jones*, March/April 2012 Issue, http://www.motherjones.com/politics/2012/03/anti-immigration-law-database.

[12] "Prop 187 Approved in California," *Migration News*, 1, no. 11 (December 1994), https://migration.ucdavis.edu/mn/more.php?id=492.

[13] For the full text of the Sensenbrenner Bill, see: https://www.congress.gov/bill/109th-congress/house-bill/4437; Arin Gencer, "Parishioners Fast to Protest Migrant Bill?" *Los Angeles Times*, February 2, 2006.

[14] Lozano v. City of Hazleton, 620 F. 3d 170 (2010).

immigration status of someone arrested or detained if they have "reasonable suspicion" that such individuals are undocumented.[15] Civil rights organizations have criticized the law because of the severe danger it poses for racial profiling.[16] Indeed, in May 2016, Maricopa County Sheriff Joe Arpaio was found in contempt of the Federal District Court for his failure to limit racial profiling in the implementation of Arizona SB-1070.[17]

In stark moral condemnation of Arizona SB-1070, Archbishop Desmond Tutu declared forcefully[18]

> "I am saddened today at the prospect of a young Hispanic immigrant in Arizona going to the grocery store and forgetting to bring her passport and immigration documents with her. I cannot be dispassionate about the fact that the very act of her being in the grocery store will soon be a crime in the state she lives in.
>
> Or that, should a policeman hear her accent and form a "reasonable suspicion" that she is an illegal immigrant, she can—and will—be taken into custody until someone sorts it out, while her children are at home waiting for their dinner…
>
> But a solution that degrades innocent people, or that makes anyone with broken English a suspect, is not a solution. A solution that fails to distinguish between a young child coming over the border in search of his mother and a drug smuggler is not a solution.

---

[15] For the full text of Arizona SB-1070, see: http://www.azleg.gov/alispdfs/council/sb1070-hb2162.pdf.

[16] For example, see, "A National Constitutional Crisis: Arizona's Racial Profiling, Anti-Immigrant Law, SB 1070," *Mexican American Legal Defense and Educational Fund*, accessed June 21, 2016, http://www.maldef.org/about/events/arizonas_racial_profiling_anti-immigrant_law_sb_1070/index.html.

[17] Merrit Kennedy, "In Racial Profiling Lawsuit, Ariz. Judge Rules Sheriff Arpaio In Contempt Of Court," *The Two-Way Breaking News from NPR*, May 14, 2016, http://www.npr.org/sections/thetwo-way/2016/05/14/478050934/in-racial-profiling-lawsuit-ariz-judge-rules-sheriff-arpaio-in-contempt-of-court.

[18] Desmond Tutu, "Arizona: The Wrong Answer," *Huffington Post*, August 7, 2010, http://www.huffingtonpost.com/desmond-tutu/arizona----the-wrong-answ_b_557955.html.

> I am not speaking from an ivory tower. I lived in the South
> Africa that has now thankfully faded into history, where a
> black man or woman could be grabbed off the street and
> thrown in jail for not having his or her documents on their
> person."

Alabama House Bill 56 and Georgia House Bill 87 are like Arizona SB-1070 on steroids. Though partially invalidated by the 11th Circuit Court of Appeals, Alabama HB-56 barred undocumented immigrants from attending college, criminalized the rental of residential property to undocumented immigrants, and prohibited them from applying for or soliciting work. It also required school officials to submit an annual tally of all suspected undocumented K-12 students to the state department of education.[19] Georgia House Bill 87, signed into law by state governor Nathan Deal in May 2011, authorized police officers to question individuals about their immigration status in certain criminal investigations and threatened to fine undocumented immigrants $250,000, or send them to jail for 15 years, for using fake identifications in search of employment.[20] In 2010, the Georgia Board of Regents also passed rules effectively barring undocumented students from all public universities in the state.[21]

Political Scapegoats: Donald Trump, Tea Party

These various anti-immigrant laws and policies of the past decade have occurred within the context of political scapegoating. Since the economic

---

[19] For the full text of Alabama HB-56, see:
https://legiscan.com/AL/text/HB56/id/321074.

[20] For the full text of Georgia HB-87, see:
http://www.legis.ga.gov/Legislation/20112012/116631.pdf.

[21] Casey Tolan, "Undocumented students in Georgia are fighting for equal rights to attend public university," *Fusion*, November 19, 2015,
http://fusion.net/story/234860/undocumented-students-georgia-are-fighting-for-equal-rights-public-university-ban/.

downturn of 2008, undocumented immigrant labor has been scapegoated by the white working-class population and opportunistic politicians eager for election.

Such anti-immigrant rhetoric fueled the rise of the Tea Party and Make America Great Again (M.A.G.A.) movements. White workers have condemned immigrant workers as unfair labor competition and culturally inassimilable; politicians have seized upon this discontent among the electorate, adding that immigrants are also a drain upon state and local economic resources because of their use of social services such as education and healthcare. Campaigning on this anti-immigrant, restrictionist platform, many politicians have been successfully elected to local, state, and federal office over the past decade. Most notably, reality TV personality Donald Trump successfully rode the tidal wave of anti-immigrant sentiment to the office of the presidency. In his now notorious words:

> When Mexico sends its people, they're not sending their best . . . They're bringing drugs. They're bringing crime. They're rapists. And some, I assume, are good people.

> I will build a great wall—and nobody builds walls better than me, believe me—and I'll build them very inexpensively. I will build a great, great wall on our southern border, and I will make Mexico pay for that wall. Mark my words.

> "Donald Trump is calling for a total and complete shutdown of Muslims entering the United States."

Like Pharaoh of old, Donald Trump leveraged the full authority of his office to wreak terror and havoc upon Latino and Muslim immigrants. His new policies led to unconscionable arrests, deportations, and enforcement tactics, including: the separation of children from their parents at the border, and their imprisonment in cages; the deportation of these parents without proper due process, and the placement of their children in U.S. foster care—modern day child trafficking by the U.S. government. The arrest and detention of a 10-year-old girl with cerebral palsy who had just left the hospital after receiving emergency gall bladder surgery; an undocumented mother who was hospitalized with a brain tumor; an undocumented father who was dropping his child off at school, and another who was driving his pregnant wife to the hospital to give birth; and domestic violence victim who was testifying in court.[22]

Equally unconscionable was Trump's repeal of Deferred Action for Childhood Arrivals (D.A.C.A.) which has served as a life raft for more than 800,000 undocumented young adults and their families. This executive action was implemented in 2012 after Congress failed to pass the Dream Act. D.A.C.A. shielded undocumented youth from deportation and granted them a work permit. Though it was imperfect and never intended to be a permanent solution, it gave hope to millions of undocumented youth and their family members.[23]

As a further reflection of its xenophobia, moreover, the Trump administration sought to effectively close off all doors of the United States to refugee and asylum seekers. The "Remain in Mexico" policy effectively ended the possibility of asylum for thousands seeking respite from violence and persecution in Central America.[24] Trump's triplet "Muslim bans" aimed to eliminate travel from seven predominantly Muslim countries, including Iran, Iraq, Libya, Somalia, Sudan, Syria, and Yemen, as well as suspend the entry of refugees from Syria and all other nations of the world.[25]

Migration as Grace: The Vast Economic Contributions of Undocumented Immigrants

Contrary to the claims of the loud chorus of anti-immigrant politicians such as Donald Trump, undocumented immigrants serve as an important source

[22] Robert Chao Romero, *Brown Church: Five Centuries of Latina/o Social Justice, Theology, and Identity* (Downers Grove: InterVarsity Press Academic, 2020), 208.
[23] Ibid, 209.
[24] Terence M. Garrett (2020) COVID-19, wall building, and the effects on Migrant Protection Protocols by the Trump administration: the spectacle of the worsening human rights disaster on the Mexico-U.S. border, Administrative Theory & Praxis, 42:2, 240—248; 243.
[25] Earl M. Maltz, "The Constitution and the Trump Travel Ban," Lewis & Clark Law Review 22, no. 2 (2018): 391–412; 393.

of grace to the United States through their vast economic contributions in the form of labor and taxes.

Undocumented immigrants account for 4.3% of the U.S. labor force—about 6.3 million workers out of 146 million.[26] They are clustered in construction, agriculture, the service sector, and domestic work. Undocumented workers make up:

27% of drywall/ceiling tile installers

21% roofers

20% construction laborers

26% grounds maintenance workers

25% butchers/meat and poultry workers

18% cooks

23% misc. agricultural workers

22% maids and housekeepers

18% sewing machine operators[27]

Note that these are national statistics. In places like California, Texas, New York, and Florida, the percentages are much higher. In California, 1 in 10 workers is undocumented.[28]

To fill our ravenous need for cheap labor, approximately 850,000 undocumented immigrants came to the U.S. on an annual basis from 2000–2005.[29] It is estimated that more than 11 million undocumented immigrants lived in the United States in 2014.[30]

[26] Bill Ong Hing, *Deporting Our Souls: Values, Morality, and Immigration Policy* (Cambridge: Cambridge University Press, 2006), 13–14.

[27] Ibid, 13–14.

[28] Kate Linthicum, "Nearly 1 in 10 California workers is in country illegally, study finds," *Los Angeles Times*, September 3, 2014.

[29] Jeffrey S. Passel and D'Vera Cohn, "U.S. Unauthorized Immigration Flows Are Down Sharply Since Mid-Decade," *Pew Research Center*, last modified September 1, 2010.

[30] Jeffrey S. Passel and D'Vera Cohn, "Unauthorized Immigrant Population Stable for Half A Decade," *Pew Research Center*, last modified July 22, 2015.

It is further estimated moreover that undocumented immigrants contribute hundreds of billions of dollars to the U.S. Gross Domestic Product. In 2006, unauthorized immigrants contributed $428 billion dollars to the nation's $13.6 trillion gross domestic product.[31]

Undocumented immigrants are viewed positively by the federal government because of their multi-billion dollar contributions to Social Security and Medicare.[32] In order to secure employment, many undocumented immigrants provide false social security numbers to their employers. Billions of dollars in payroll taxes are in turn collected by the federal government based upon these false social security numbers—to the tune of $12 billion in 2007 alone. According to Stephen C. Goss, the chief actuary of the Social Security Administration, unauthorized immigrants contributed up to $240 billion to the Social Security trust fund by 2007. Moreover, if not for these monumental tax contributions, the Social Security administration would have experienced payment shortfalls as early as 2009. Ironically, undocumented immigrants support the pensions of droves of Tea Party members who are of retirement age and yet who most vehemently support draconian immigration restrictions and deportations.

Unauthorized immigrants contribute in many significant ways to state economies and state and local tax revenues as well. Immigrants make large economic contributions not only in traditional immigration receiving states such as California and Texas, but even in southern and midwestern states not typically associated with large Latino immigrant populations.

For example, in California, unauthorized immigrants constitute 10% of the total workforce and contribute $130 billion annually to the state Gross

---

[31] Travis Loller, "Many Illegal Immigrants Pay Up At Tax Time," *USA Today*, April 11, 2008.
[32] Edwar Schumacher-Matos, "How Illegal Immigrants Are Helping Social Security," *Washington Post*, September 3, 2010.

Domestic Product.[33] A 2006 study by the Texas Comptroller found that undocumented immigrants contributed $17.7 billion dollars to state GDP and generated $1.58 billion in state revenues.[34] The University of Chicago reported that undocumented immigrants spent $2.89 billion in the Chicago metropolitan area in 2001 and helped support more than 30,000 jobs through their spending.

Even in southern states such as Georgia and Virginia, undocumented immigrants supply hundreds of millions of dollars per year in income, payroll, and property taxes.[35] In 2006, the Georgia Budget and Policy Institute reported that unauthorized immigrants contributed more than $215 million in the form of income and property tax and aggregated sales. The Commonwealth Institute, moreover, calculated that undocumented immigrants provide up to $450 million per year in tax revenue in Virginia and that they represent a critical source of labor in the construction, manufacturing, and leisure and hospitality industries.

More recently, the Congressional Budget Office (CBO) found that undocumented immigrants paid an estimated $10.6 billion in state and local taxes in 2010.[36] These contributions varied state by state, with California receiving more than $2.2 billion and the state of Montana receiving less than $2 million. These state and local tax contributions derive from sales and excise taxes, personal income taxes, and property taxes.

---

[33] Jodie Gummow, "New Study: Undocumented Immigrants in California Contribute $130 Billion To State GDP," *Alternet*, last modified September 4, 2014, http://www.alternet.org/immigration/new-study-undocumented-immigrants-california-contribute-130-billion-state-gdp.

[34] American Immigration Council, "Assessing the Economic Impact of Immigration On A State and Local Level," last modified August 18, 2009, http://www.immigrationpolicy.org/just-facts/assessing-economic-impact-immigration-state-and-local-level.

[35] American Immigration Council, "Assessing the Economic Impact of Immigration."

[36] Institute on Taxation and Economic Policy, "Undocumented Immigrants State and Local Tax Contributions," last modified July 2013, http://www.itep.org/pdf/undocumentedtaxes.pdf.

The legalization of undocumented immigrants, moreover, would result in huge windfalls of state tax revenue.[37] This increase in tax revenue would result, in part, from an increase in wages and taxable income for unauthorized workers. Raúl Hinojosa-Ojeda of the UCLA N.A.I.D. Center projects that legalization would increase state tax revenue by $5.3 billion in California, $540 million in Arizona, $297 million in Colorado, $1.13 billion in Florida, and $4.1 billion in Texas.

A "Mathematics of Injustice": The "grace" provided to us by immigrants goes unrecognized by our broken immigration system

Although an estimated 11 million undocumented immigrants supply upwards of 400 billion dollars per year to the national gross domestic product, and contribute hundreds of billions of dollars more to federal and state coffers through tax contributions, guess how many unskilled labor visas the United States granted to all immigrants from every country in the world in 2010? 4,762. Moreover, even if it wished to grant more than that, it is limited to a maximum of 10,000 unskilled worker visas annually for all nations across the globe.[38] On paper therefore, the U.S. government claims the nation has but a small shortage of unskilled labor which requires supplementation through the awarding of a miniscule number of unskilled labor visas; in reality, however, it depends upon, and exploits, the cheap, supplemental labor of more than 6 million undocumented immigrant workers.

Fairness, indeed, biblical justice, requires that the U.S. government recognize the manifold economic contributions of immigrants by granting them a concomitant number of work visas and/or legal residency status. To refuse to

---

[37] American Immigration Council, "An Immigration Stimulus: The Economic Benefits of a Legalization Program," last modified April 2013, http://www.immigrationpolicy.org/just-facts/immigration-stimulus-economic-benefits-legalization-program.

[38] Jessica Vaughn, "Proposal to Axe Green Cards for Unskilled Workers Considered," *Center for Immigration Studies*, last modified October 28, 2011, http://cis.org/vaughan/green-cards-for-unskilled-workers.

do so is biblical exploitation (Deut. 10:17–19; Exod. 23:9; Matt. 25: 35–40). The failure to provide immigration relief constitutes biblical oppression, for it perpetuates a system in which 11 million immigrants are exploited for their multi-billion dollar economic contributions but denied basic civil and human rights. It is tantamount to slavery—benefiting from the labor of a human being but purposefully denying her/his fundamental humanity. Stated another way, although undocumented immigrants already participate as economic citizens of this nation, they have not been granted the concomitant rights of political citizenship. Even worse, despite their vast economic contributions, undocumented immigrants have been scapegoated for the economic woes of our nation and are being manipulated in the national discourse for short-term political gain.

Conclusion

The Christian community of the United States has a serious moral choice to make with respect to the 11 million undocumented immigrants that God has brought to live with us as neighbors. Will we model to them the radical hospitality of the God of Abraham, or will we reflect to them the oppression of Egypt? Will we be Pharaoh or Jesus? As a reflection of Pharaoh, will we continue to exploit their cheap labor in order to buttress our economy while at the same time scapegoating them as part of an imagined political threat and the "war on terror"? Or, in reflection of Jesus and His radical hospitality, will we humble ourselves to recognize the manifold expressions of grace we receive from them and reciprocate this grace through the compassionate reformation of our immigration laws?

If the Christian community continues in the historical trajectory of the Chinese Exclusion Act, the Emergency Quota Act of 1921, Operation Wetback, Proposition 187, and Arizona SB-1070, then we will be known as Egypt. We will also destroy the witness of Christ which is just now beginning to be rehabilitated through the important work of organizations such as the Evangelical

Immigration Table, Christians for Comprehensive Immigration Reform, and the Christian Community Development Association.

As our other alternative, we can choose to embody God's grace to the immigrant community by drawing from the biblical examples of Abraham, Ruth, Naomi, and Jesus. It is interesting to me that Egypt got a second chance. Although it was condemned in the Exodus narrative for its exploitation of the Israelites, in the book of Matthew we are told:

> "When they had gone, an angel of the Lord appeared to Joseph in a dream. "Get up," he said, "take the child and his mother and escape to Egypt. Stay there until I tell you, for Herod is going to search for the child to kill him" (Matt. 2:13).

Egypt got a second chance to show hospitality—in this case to the refugee Christ-child and the Holy Family. Reversing course from the xenophobic pattern expressed in the Exodus account, Egypt lived out radical hospitality towards Jesus the Messiah, Joseph, and Mary.

If this biblical narrative were to take place in the United States today instead of in Egypt 2,000 years ago, would Jesus and His family be welcome? Or would we pass new immigration laws and policies to deport them? Indeed, this is the exact challenge posed to us by the spiritual principles of Matthew 25 and the various selections of Scripture which have been explored in this essay.

Jesus and His mother now appear to us in the distressing disguise of 11 million undocumented immigrants and refugees from Mexico, El Salvador, Guatemala, Honduras, China, the Philippines, and Syria, as well as from many other countries from throughout the globe. Like Jesus and Herod, many of them, especially those from Central America and Syria, are fleeing violence and bloodshed. Many others are fleeing poverty and social displacement caused by the forces of economic globalization and U.S. international economic policy. For the past 150 years, the United States has treated most immigrants from Mexico, Latin America, and Asia like Pharaoh and the Israelites.

Like Egypt and the Holy Family, the United States now has a second chance. Will we make it right by welcoming, with radical hospitality, the millions of immigrant neighbors who now live in our midst? Will we pass compassionate immigration reform which takes seriously the biblical principle of migration as grace? The choice is ours.

CHAPTER TWO

God The Primordial Migrant: A Systematic Theology of God from the Perspective of Migration

Peter C. Phan

This chapter is an exercise in systematic theology from the experience and perspective of migration and migrants. By "theology" here is meant not simply the quest for understanding the Christian faith in general—to use the eleventh-century theologian St. Anselm of Canterbury's celebrated definition of theology as *fides quaerens intellectum*— but a specific reflection on God as such.[39] "Systematic" refers to the logically coherent, structurally well-ordered, and epistemologically critical nature of this scholarly reflection within theology as an academic discipline. Lastly, "migrant" here refers to people who have changed residence within their countries of birth (Internal Displaced Persons) or across national borders, either voluntarily (migrants in general) or by force (refugees).

"God" here is understood in the Christian sense of the Trinitarian God and refers both to what theologians call the "Economic Trinity," that is, God as present and acting in the world according to God's plan of salvation (from Greek *oikonomia,* literally "plan" or "design") and the "Immanent" or "Transcendent" Trinity, that is, God in God's eternal inner mutual relations ("persons") as

---

[39] See St. Anselm, *Proslogion* II-IV, in: *St. Anselm: Basic Writings,* trans. S. N. Deane (La Salle, Illinois: Open Court, 1962), 7–10. This understanding of theology has been anticipated by St. Augustine.

Father, Son, and Holy Spirit.[40] The question to be considered here then is whether God, as both the Economic Trinity and the Immanent Trinity, displays any of the features generally associated with migrants so that Christians, and migrants in particular, can call upon God as the "Migrant God" It will be argued that the Christian God is the "Beginning" and the "End"—the Alpha and the Omega—of migration, taking the two terms in both their theological and temporal meanings. "Beginning" indicates God as the creative source as well as the primordial initiator of migration, and "End" describes God as both the temporal termination and the final goal of migration. To put it tersely, the God of the Christians is essentially *Deus Migrator* or the "Primordial Migrant" Since the Christian God is the Lord of the Hebrew Scripture, I begin by investigating how the Lord has shown himself to be a migrant with the Jewish people. Next, I argue that the Christian/Trinitarian God is also *Deus Migrator*. I conclude with brief reflections on how God as the Primordial Migrant provides the foundation for the Christian ethics of migration.

The Lord as God Migrating with His People

For the Jewish-Christian faith, the Lord/God's migration in history begins with the story of Israel. There are of course many and diverse ways to narrate this story, ranging from a purely secular to a distinctly religious perspective. In telling the history of ancient Israel it is commonplace for believers to frame it as an encounter between the Lord/God and God's people Israel that is punctuated by a series of paradigmatic events. These events include God's call of Abraham and God's promise to grant him and the other patriarchs land, progeny, and prosperity; the liberation of the Israelites from Egypt under the leadership of Moses; God's covenant with the people of Israel at Mount Sinai; the occupation of the Promised Land by the twelves tribes; the establishment of

---

[40] On this distinction, see Karl Rahner, *The Trinity*, trans. Joseph Donceel (New York: Herder and Herder, 2010) 21–33.

the Davidic monarchy; the destruction and exile of the ten tribes in the north (Israel) to Assyria; the exile of the leaders of the two tribes in the south (Judah) to Babylonia; the return of a number of Israelites from Babylonia to Palestine; national restoration and independence; the domination by the Greeks; the conquest by the Romans; and the Diaspora.

Biblical and Theological Language about God

While all these events, which spanned some eighteen centuries, can be authenticated, at least in their broad outlines, by contemporaneous extra-biblical records and archeological finds, it is their theological interpretations, proposed both within the Tanakh/Old Testament and by post-canonical writers, that are of interest here. One common thread in these interpretations, however divergent among themselves, is that the center and principal agent in the history of Israel is always God, who accompanies God's people throughout their migrations and acts for their salvation. Another shared doctrine is that God, in spite of God's self-revelation to Israel, remains the transcendent, sovereign, and mysterious Lord. Indeed, the name that God reveals to Moses as God's own, namely, YHWH (Exod. 3:14), came to be regarded as early as the Second Temple period following Israel's return from exile in the fifth century BCE so sacred that its public pronunciation was forbidden. This practice powerfully bespeaks of God's permanent mysteriousness, whose name YHWH is not susceptible of a single translation.[41]

As a consequence, the many different names as well as attributes that are ascribed to God in the Bible must not be understood as literalist representations of the divinity. Biblical imagery of God, even anthropomorphic metaphors, do of course tell us something real and true about God and not just

---

[41] YHWH, (*'ehyeh 'ašer 'ehyeh*) can be rendered as "I am that I am," "I am who I am," "I am what I am," "I will be who I will be,?" and "I create what I create.?" In Exodus 3:14 Moses is told by God to tell the Israelites that "I AM?" has sent him to them, with I AM functioning as a personal name. Since YHWH is not to be pronounced, in its place readers are to say: "The Name?" (*shema*) or "The Lord?" (*Adonai*).

our feelings and projections, as Ludwig Feuerbach and Karl Marx would have it. However, biblical language and theological discourse (*theologia*) do not provide empirical descriptions of who and what God is. Rather, as Thomas Aquinas has shown, theological language is analogical, that is, similar-and-different. For instance, the term 'king' as applied to God (e.g., "God is king") and to humans (e.g., "Louis XIV was a king") does not have exactly the same meaning (univocal language), nor a totally different meaning (equivocal language), but a similar-and-different meaning (analogical language). Were God-talk, or theology, univocal language, God's transcendence and infiniteness would be annulled. On the other hand, if it is equivocal language, it would tell nothing about God.[42] Furthermore, since, as the Fourth Lateran Council IV (1215) of the Catholic Church affirms, there is greater dissimilarity than similarity between God and humans, the import of our language about God is more negative than affirmative; thus, our statements about God indicate more our ignorance than our knowledge of God.[43] Ultimately, we know only what God is *not* and not what God is.

To maintain this dialectic between knowledge and ignorance in our statements about God, a triple epistemological movement must be made: First, something is affirmed of God. For instance, "God is wise" (*via affirmationis*). Second, this very statement is simultaneously negated: "God is not wise the way humans are wise" (*via negationis*). Third, both the affirmation and the negation are transcended (*via eminentiae*): "God is infinitely wise" Were we asked what we mean by the third statement, we must confess that we do not really know. We are justified in predicating wisdom of God because it is a perfection, but we only know what God is not, that is, God is not wise the way we know wisdom in our experience. We do not and cannot know what God is, that is, how God is

---

[42] See Thomas Aquinas, *Summa Theologiae*, Part I, question 13, especially article 5. In his *Summa contra Gentiles*, Book I, Question 3, Thomas says: "Concerning God, we cannot know what he is, but only what he is not, and how other things stand in relation to him."

[43] On the Fourth Lateran Council, see Norman P. Tanner, ed., *Decrees of the Ecumenical Councils, Vol I (Nicaea I-Lateran V)* (Washington, D.C, Georgetown University Press, 1990), 232: "For between creator and creature there can be noted no similarity so great that a greater dissimilarity cannot be seen between them."

"infinitely" wise, the term "infinite" being itself negative, namely, non-finite. Thus, our knowledge of God ends in ignorance. It is, to use the celebrated expression of the fifteenth-century theologian, Nicholas of Cusa's, our knowledge of God is *docta ignorantia* [learned ignorance].[44]

It is vitally important to keep in mind all the foregoing observations regarding God's absolute transcendence and the analogical nature of theological language as we reflect on *Deus Migrator*. It must be acknowledged at the outset that among the plethora of names and attributes that the Bible and Christian Tradition predicate of God, none explicitly refers to God as the Migrant. Part of the reasons for this absence is that the notions of "migration" and "migrant" immediately connote weakness, destituteness, vulnerability, and movement, which at first sight seem to contradict the traditional concept of God as the all-powerful, infinitely self-sufficient, all-perfect, and immutable Being.

Yet, a careful—perhaps against the grain—reading of the story of Israel, especially its paradigmatic events enumerated above, shows that God not only commanded the migration of the ancestors of the people of Israel and migrated with God's people throughout their migratory movements but also bears all the marks of a migrant. Of course, in carrying out these reflections, we need to recall the triple movement in our statement about *Deus Migrator*. God *is* a migrant; God is *not* a migrant; and God is *infinitely* a migrant. Ultimately, what is meant by *Deus Migrator* can be grasped not primarily through intellectual apprehension but in the concrete experience of migration and in the effective solidarity with the migrants themselves.

Abraham the Migrant Ancestor

For Jews, Christians, and Muslims, Abram/Abraham, whose life can be reliably placed in the first half of the second millennium BCE and whose stories are narrated in the Book of Genesis 12-25, is revered as the model of faith, trust,

---

[44] See Jasper Hopkins, *Nicholas of Cusa on Learned Ignorance: A Translation and Appreciation of De Docta Ignorantia* (Minneapolis: The Arthur Banning Press, 1985). The theology of God in this tradition is called apophatic or negative theology (*theologia negativa*).

and obedience in God. The greatest test of faith for Abraham is commonly taken to be God's command to Abraham to sacrifice his only son Isaac, who is the fulfillment God's covenantal promise of progeny and land (Gen. 22). Abraham passed the test at Moriah, and, according to Paul, it is this faith that was reckoned to him for righteousness (Rom. 4:3–12; see Gen. 15:6). As a consequence, "the Israel of God," again according to Paul, are those who have faith; these are "Abraham's children," and not the physical progeny of Abraham, Isaac, and Jacob. For the author of the Letter of James, too, Abraham's obedience to God's command to sacrifice his son Isaac makes him the ancestor of Israel, though James, differently from Paul, counts this act of obedience, and not faith alone, as that which makes Abraham righteous and God's friend (James 2:21–24). The Letter to the Hebrews too says that this act of obedience makes Abraham a model of faith (Heb. 11:17–19).[45]

While it is certainly valid to underscore Abraham's obedience to God's command to sacrifice his son as an archetype of faith, it is important to examine what Abraham has become as a result of his faith prior to this event. As the Letter to the Hebrews puts it tersely, "By faith Abraham obeyed when he was called to set out for a place that he was to receive as an inheritance; and he set out, not knowing where he was going. By faith he stayed for a time in the land he

---

[45] Biblical scholars have pointed out that there are three accounts of the call of the patriarch, called Abram in the first two narratives and Abraham in third. In the first (Gen 12), attributed to the so-called Yahwistic author (J), the focus is on Yahweh's promise of the land of Canaan. In the second (Gen 15), attributed to the Elohist source (E), the focus is on God's promise of numerous progeny after God's cutting a covenant with Abram. The third (Gen 17), ascribed to the Priestly source (P), focuses less on land and more on progeny through Sarah, that is, Isaac, and though his change of name from Abram to Abraham, the patriarch becomes not only the progenitor of Israel but also "the ancestor of a multitude of nations?" (Gen 17:4). This story of Abraham of the Hebrew Scriptures is creatively interpreted by the New Testament writers such as Paul for whom God's promise of land and progeny plays no role (Mt 3:9; Jn 8:39); instead, it is Abraham's faith that becomes central, on account of which those who believe, including the Gentiles, are Abraham's true descendants. It is interesting to note that the Qur'an views Abraham as neither Jew nor Christian but as a *hanif*, that is, an Arab monotheist, one who has submitted himself to the one and only God (*muslim*). See Patrick J. Ryan, *Amen: Jews, Christians & Muslims Keep Faith with God* (Washington, D.C.: The Catholic University of America Press, 2018), 44–77.

had been promised, as in a foreign land, living in tents, as did Isaac and Jacob, who were heirs with him of the same promise" (Heb. 11:8–9).[46]

The story of Israel as a nation, properly speaking, began with God's call to Abraham. Though in Genesis 15:7 God is reported to have said to Abraham in Canaan: "I am the LORD who brought you from Ur of the Chaldeans, to give you this land to possess," God's call was first addressed to Abraham not in Ur but in Haran, located today in modern Turkey, about ten miles of the Syrian border, where his father Terah, his wife Sarai/Sarah, and his nephew Lot had settled on their way from Ur to Canaan (Gen. 11:31). It was here that God said to Abraham: "Go from your country and your kindred and your father's house to the land that I will show you" (Gen. 12:1).

Amazingly, God's first act in human history, leaving aside the pre-history in Genesis 1–11, was literally making Abraham into what we call today a "migrant" God's words "Go from your country and your kindred and your father's house to the land that I will show you" no doubt resonate in the depth of the heart of every believing migrant at the beginning of her or his journey. In fact, Abraham's life subsequent to his obedience to God's call until his death was that of a semi-nomadic migrant, constantly on the move, a tent-dweller and not a settler in an urban environment, from Haran to the various cities of Canaan such as Shechem, Bethel, Salem, Hebron, Mamre, Beersheba, etc. to Egypt and then back to Canaan, where the only piece of land Abraham bought was the cave of Machpelah and the adjacent land near Mamre as a burial site for his wife Sarah. Because of his wealth and power Abraham could easily have settled down in any city or in one of the many little kingdoms of his choice and become a permanent and preeminent "citizen" But Abraham intentionally chose a migratory way of life for himself and his family, erecting tents as temporary dwellings, rather than being incorporated into the local communities. This is made clear by his decision to send his servant Eliezer back to Haran to find a wife for his son Isaac among

---

[46] The New Revised Standard Version is used throughout this chapter.

49

his kinfolk (Gen. 24) rather than letting him marry local women and be absorbed into the native population.

Such was Abraham's life-on-the move that he was considered as a resident alien (*gēr*), not a "citizen" (Gen. 15:13; 23:4). By "citizen" is meant not in the modern sense of possessing citizenship in a nation-state, but in the sense of a subject of a city or monarchy. In this sense Abraham was a "citizen" of Ur. "Resident alien" refers to anyone living outside their place of birth, that is, a "stranger," of which there are two kinds. A "sojourner" (*tôšāb*) was a transient, a temporary and dependent inhabitant (Lev. 22:10; 25:6), whereas the "resident alien" (*gēr*) was a more permanent albeit still a foreigner.[47] Abraham and his kinsfolk were resident aliens. When trying to buy the cave of Machpelah as a burial site for his wife Sarah, Abraham said to the Hittites: "I am a stranger and an alien residing among you: give me property among you for a burial place" (Gen. 23:4). Indeed, Abraham as well as Lot was regarded as "alien" by the natives of Canaan, the former in Gen. 21:23 and the latter in Gen. 19:9. Finally, Abraham is the first biblical person to be called a "Hebrew" (Gen. 14:13). "Hebrew," an ethnic term, is a disparaging name used by non-Israelites to designate a group of people known as Habiru/Apiru who were a propertyless, dependent, and immigrant social class.

Thus, according to the Bible, Abraham is the first voluntary migrant in human history. Like millions of migrants today, his father and his family migrated from Ur to Canaan in search of a better life, and not unlike many migrants, they could not reach their country of destination directly and immediately but had to settle down in intermediate places on the way. Later, Abraham himself migrated from Haran to Canaan upon God's promise of the land that later is described as "flowing with milk and honey" (Exod. 3:17), a veritable Promised Land in migrants' imagination. Again, like millions of today migrants, he went in search of food in Egypt when there was famine where he was living (Gen. 12:26).

---

[47] For an explanation of these three terms, see John J. Pilch, *A Cultural Handbook to the Bible* (Grand Rapids, Michigan: Eerdmans, 2012), 59–62.

It was noted above that God's first act in human history is to make a migrant out of Abraham. Moreover, it must also be noted—a fact that has often been missed—that the Lord God not only initiated migration in human history but himself became a migrant. Rather than staying as it were behind in Haran after sending Abraham forth from his father's country, home, and kinfolk, God accompanied Abraham and shared his migration through the many cities of Canaan and even to Egypt. In different localities God came to Abraham in vision (Gen. 15:1), apparition (Gen. 17:1), theophany in a human form (Gen. 18), conversation about his plan to destroy Sodom (Gen. 18:17), and dream (Gen. 20:6). The Lord God accompanied Abraham and made and renewed his covenant with him several times and in different places (Gen. 15; 17).

It is interesting to note that the Lord God also migrated in the company of Sarah's Egyptian maid Hagar when she was sent away after her pregnancy (Gen. 16:7) and later, after the birth of Ishmael, when Hagar and her baby Ishmael were chased away from home by Sarah. They were the first biblical refugees in the strict sense of the term, violently forced to leave their home and wandering in the desert of Beersheba, exposed to thirst, hunger, and death (Gen. 21:16–18). Thus, the Lord God himself became a migrant with and for *all* migrants, and not just God's covenanted people. God heard their weeping, even the boy Ishmael's cries, saw their sufferings, and came to protect and bless them.

God Migrating with Israel, God's People-on-the-Move

The motif of God migrating in the company of God's people is even more pronounced and explicit in the story of God's liberation of the Israelites from Egypt. Socially, politically, and economically, their "exodus" from the land of their slavery was a mass migration, one that is familiar to people of all times trying to escape persecution, oppression, and exploitation. It is most important to note what God said to Moses when he balked at God's order to go to the pharaoh and tell him to let the Israelites go free, due to his lack of qualifications: "I will be with you" (Exod. 3:12). Note that "you" here in Hebrew is plural; that is, God promises to be not only with Moses but also with the entire people of Israel, migrating with them and protecting them with God's "mighty hand and outstretched arm, with a terrifying display of power, and with signs and wonders" (Deut. 26:8). God is always God-with. It is this memory of migration that the Israelites recite when they present their first fruits to God: "A wandering [migrating] Aramean was my ancestor; he went into Egypt and lived there as an alien" (Deut. 26:5).

The Israelites' flight from Egypt and wandering for forty years in the desert is the first biblical mass migration This migration and its surrounding events are presented in Exodus 1–19, which provides a narrative of Egyptian oppression of the Hebrews, the origins and call of Moses as a political and religious leader, the contest with the pharaoh, the ten plagues, the celebration of the Passover, the Hebrews' departure from their land of slavery to Canaan, the "land flowing with milk and honey," the miraculous crossing of the Red Sea/Sea of Reeds, and the establishment of the covenant between God and God's people at Mount Horeb/Sinai. The remaining part of the Book of Exodus further lists the legal and ritualistic laws contained in the Book of Covenant and narrates the construction of the portable shrine called the "Tabernacle" or the "Tent of Meeting," the fabrication of the Ark of the Covenant which contains the two stone tablets, the Israelites' violation of the covenant by worshipping the golden calf, the renewal of the covenant, and the final movements toward the Promised Land.

A majority of scholars do not consider these narratives as historiography in the usual sense of the term, as they lack historical data that would permit the exact dating of the Exodus and the determination of the route of the Israelites' journey to Canaan.[48] However, after the skepticism of several modern historians

---

[48] Most scholars date the Exodus to the middle of the 13th century BCE, likely between 1260-1220, under the Pharaoh Rameses II. As for the Israelites' migration from Egypt to Canaan, there were three possible routes once they were out of the Egyptian eastern borders. The first, easier and quicker, is along the northern Sinai coast (the "Way to the Land of the

against the historicity of the events surrounding the Israelites' migration, many scholars today acknowledge that the narrator of the Exodus shows deep familiarity with many features of contemporaneous Egyptian culture.[49] Of course, these elements of Egyptian coloration do not by themselves prove the authenticity of the Hebrews' migration and related events as narrated, but there is no reason to doubt that there is a substantial historical core to this narrative of the Israelites' migration from the land of their slavery and their initial formation into a nation.

Given the centrality of this migration for our theme, it would be appropriate to explore it in greater detail. How large was this mass migration? Exod. 12:37 states that "the Israelites journeyed from Rameses to Succoth, about six hundred thousand men on foot, besides children. A mixed crowd also went up with them, and livestock in great numbers, both flocks and herds" (see also Num. 11:21). Instead of a round number, Exod. 38:26 and the Book of Numbers give a precise number of 603,550 (Num. 1:46; 2:32), and Num. 3:39 adds 22,000 Levites. According to Exod. 38:26 and Num. 1:46–47, these figures refer to men of military age. If older men, women, children, and the "mixed crowd" are added to these men of military age, the number of migrants could amount to two and a half million.

Such a huge number of people would have made the flight from Egypt and the crossing of the Red Sea a logistically impossible feat and the wanderings in the desert impracticable. Some scholars try to overcome this problem by suggesting that the Hebrew *elef* does not mean "thousand" but "clan" or "squad" (as in Num. 1:16; Judg. 6:15; and 1 Sam. 10:19), reducing the purported number of 600,000 individual young men to 600 clans or squads, with a more likely total

---

Philistines") but was forbidden by God (Ex 13:17). The second, which runs across the barren and waterless desert of Shur in the central part of the Sinai Peninsula (the "Way of Shur"), is impracticable. The third, the most likely, is toward the southern part of the Sinai Peninsula (the "Way of the Sea"), where Mount Sinai/Horeb is located, and from there moves northeast, toward Kadesh-barnea.

[49] For a discussion of these features, see Nahum Sarna, *Exploring Exodus: The Origins of Biblical Israel* (New York: Schocken Books, 1986).

of about 72,000 people. However, this interpretation seems to contradict the explicit affirmation in Exod. 38:24–26 and other passages that the number refers to individuals and not groups. Nevertheless, this number of 600,000 is most likely a hyperbole since the land of Goshen and later the Sinai Peninsula could hardly accommodate such a population. Perhaps one likely reason for the inflation of the number of Hebrew migrants is to express God's absolute power and total victory over the pharaoh. Such number inflation was a common practice among Arabian Bedouins and is found in Assyrian inscriptions and annals to underline the magnitude of the event being described.

As with any group of migrants, the fleeing Israelites experienced doubts about the wisdom of migrating, especially when suffering from hunger, thirst, and physical danger. Then they grew nostalgic of the land of their slavery and fondly recalled sitting by the "fleshpots" and eating "their fill of bread" (Exod. 16:3). Such reaction on the part of migrants is, humanly speaking and apart from the context of faith, fully understandable, especially when facing the possibility of loss of life and an uncertain and risky future. Without leaders such as Moses and Aaron, the Israelites would have gone back to Egypt, just as today, without the support of others, both fellow migrants and the native born, migrants would rather return to their miserable lot in their old countries.

It must be noted that however important the roles of Moses, Aaron, and the people during their migration from Egypt were, the central character of the story is not they but the Lord God, "the God of Abraham, the God of Isaac, and the God of Jacob." Now, during this migration, this God chose to be their God and did so through a covenant. Here, as in the Book of Genesis, this God shows Godself again as the *Deus Migrator* accompanying God's people throughout their wanderings in the wilderness. Though the expression "wilderness wanderings" has become a common shorthand to describe the Hebrew migrants' journey for "forty years" in the Sinai desert as punishment for their unfaithfulness to God, it is rather misleading if it is taken to imply that the journey was an aimless and leaderless meandering. On the contrary, the Hebrews' migration is depicted as totally under the benevolent control of the all-powerful and ever-present God from beginning to end. The Lord God is repeatedly portrayed as a trustworthy guide and a watchful protector of the migrating Israelites, charting the route of their escape, providing them with foods and drinks in miraculous ways, and defending them against their attackers. God's guidance is symbolically represented by "a pillar of cloud by day, to lead them along the way, and in a pillar of fire by night, to give them light, so that they might travel by day and by night" (Exod. 13:21). Sometimes God's guidance of the Hebrew migrants was carried out indirectly, through the mediation of an angel: "I am going to send an angel in front of you, to guard you on the way and to bring you to the place I have prepared" (Exod. 23:20).

The climax of the Israelites' migration is the covenant God established with them by which they became God's "treasured possession out of all the peoples," "a priestly kingdom and a holy nation" (Exod. 19:5–6). God's closeness to God's people is also demonstrated in God's giving them the Torah—not a set of laws but instructions for leading a faithful and holy way of life (Exod. 20–23)—and guaranteeing justice for all. In particular, God enjoins justice for migrants, reminding the Hebrews of their former status as migrants: "You shall not wrong or oppress a resident alien, for you were aliens in the land of Egypt" (Exod. 22:21). Clearly, the foundation for the Hebrews' moral obligation to treat migrants with justice and kindness is their own experiences as migrants in Egypt.

Another way God visibly accompanied God's migrating people is God's abiding in the "sanctuary," for the construction of which God gave explicit and detailed instructions (Exod. 25–27). The sanctuary, the place where God dwells among the Israelites, issues commands to them, and receives their sacrificial worship, is referred to by three Hebrew terms: *mikdash*, literally "sanctuary" or "sacred place;" *mishkan*, literally "tabernacle" or "abode"; and *ohel mo'ed*, literally "tent of meeting" The entire compound of the sanctuary is composed of three parts of descending degrees of holiness and restricted access: (a) the "Holy of

Holies," where the Ark and the Tablets are kept and is accessible only to the High Priest on the Day of Atonement; (b) the "Holy Place," which is the "Tabernacle" proper and houses the "Tent of Meeting" and is accessible only to Moses and the priests; and (c) the surrounding courtyard to which the non-priests are allowed to go. An essential feature of the sanctuary is that it is *mobile*; it is as it were a portable Sinai. It was erected wherever the migrants stopped, and was disassembled whenever they departed, in such way that the "Presence/Glory (*kavod*) of the Lord" (also referred to as *Shekinah* in later rabbinic tradition), symbolized by a cloud covering the sanctuary, migrated with the Israelites, and abided constantly with them (Exod. 40:34).

God-in-Exile with the Exiled Community

The next mass migrations in the history of Israel are the forced deportations, first of the ten tribes in the Northern Kingdom of Israel by the neo-Assyrian empire in 721 BCE, and then of the two remaining tribes in the Southern Kingdom of Judah by the neo-Babylonian empire in 587 BCE. At the death of Solomon in 922 BCE, the Davidic-Solomonic "united kingdom" collapsed. Solomon's son Rehoboam, who was slated to continue the Davidic dynasty, was rejected by the assembly of "all Israel," that is, the northern tribes, at Shechem (1 Kings 12:1) because he refused to abolish Solomon's imposition of forced labor and heavy taxation. Instead, Jeroboam was chosen to establish the Northern Kingdom as politically and religiously independent of Judah.

Of the two kingdoms, which would co-exist alongside each other for about two hundred years, the Northern Kingdom, known as Israel, with the center in Samaria, and with a population of 800,000, was the more powerful and prosperous but politically highly unstable, having nineteen kings, only ten of whom legally succeeded to the throne and seven assassinated. The Southern Kingdom, which was known as Judah, with a much smaller population of 200,000, and developed significantly later than the Northern Kingdom, was politically stable, thanks largely to the legitimacy of the Davidic dynasty, the centrality of the city of Jerusalem, and its Temple as the focus of the nation's political identity and religious life.

The survival of these two tiny kingdoms, which never constituted a united kingdom and indeed often were rivals, depended on their political alliances with the powerful empires of Assyria and Babylonia to the east and Egypt to the south. When the king of Israel, Pekah, attempted to rebel against Assyria and joined Aram (Syria) in an anti-Assyrian coalition, the king of Assyria Tiglath-pileser reduced Israel to a rump state ruled by Hoshea (r. 732–724) and deported 13,529 people to Assyria, marking the beginning of the Diaspora of the ten northern tribes (2 Kings 15:29). When in turn Hoshea ceased to be a compliant vassal, stopped paying tribute, and attempted to enlist the aid of Egypt to throw off the Assyrian domination, the Assyrian monarch Shalmaneser V and his successor Sargon II laid siege to Samaria for three years, destroyed it, and incorporated what remained of the Northern Kingdom into the Assyrian provincial system.

What is of interest to us is that following the Assyrian policies of population deportation to prevent pro-independence revolts, Shalmaneser dispersed the conquered Israelites from Samaria to Gozan on the Upper Habor River, to Halah beyond the Tigris northeast of ancient city of Nineveh, and to towns on the Persian plateau (2 Kings 17:6). The number of the exiles in this forced migration from the Northern Kingdom is not given in the Bible. The Israeli archeologist Israel Finkelstein estimates that only a fifth of its population, about 40,000, were actually deported. Many also fled south to Jerusalem, whose population appears to have expanded fivefold during this period. Furthermore, no reliable historical details are available about the ultimate fate of these ten tribes; numerous, some fantastic, claims have been made as to where they settled permanently.[50] At any rate, however big the number of deportees was, this

---

[50] Peoples who at various times were said to be descendants of the lost tribes include the Nestorians, the Mormons, the Afghans, the Falashas of Ethiopia, the American Indians, and

dispersion or diaspora of the Israelites constitutes a forced migration of immense significance. By 721, with the dispersion of the ten northern tribes, the kingdom of Israel ceased to exist as an independent nation, its towns populated by non-Israelite immigrants brought in from other parts of the Assyrian empire, who were called "Samaritans" and would later be regarded as ethnically non-Jewish and religiously impure.[51]

It is interesting to note that the Bible does not say whether God accompanied these exiles and refugees of the Northern Kingdom when they were deported from their country. Perhaps the reason for this failure to affirm God's presence and migration with the Israelite exiles is that contrary to the liberation of the Hebrews from Egypt, which was an act of God's love and power, the destruction of the Northern Kingdom is seen by the Deuteronomist historian(s) as God's punishment for the apostasy of its kings and people. However, given the Deuteronomist theology that divine punishment is inherently an invitation to repentance, it may be said that God was not absent from the dispersed ten tribes but migrated and dwelled with them since they remained God's own people in virtue of God's eternal and irrevocable covenant with them.

In contrast to the exile of the Israelites of the Northern Kingdom in 721, a more detailed narrative is given of the destruction of the Southern Kingdom of Judah, Jerusalem, the Temple, and the final exile of the Judean people in 586 BCE. According to the historical books such as 1 and 2 Samuel, 1 and 2 Kings, and 1 and 2 Chronicles, David, a shepherd from Bethlehem and anointed by the prophet Samuel to replace Saul, became the king of both Judah and Israel after his victory over Ish-bosheth, one of Saul's surviving sons and the ruler of Israel, at Gibeon. To unify the two kingdoms, David conquered

---

the Japanese. Among the numerous immigrants to the State of Israel since its establishment in 1948 were a few who likewise claimed to be remnants of the Ten Lost Tribes. See Zvi Ben-Dor Benite (2009). *The Ten Lost Tribes: A World History* (Oxford: Oxford University Press, 2009).

[51] See Bustenay Oded, *Mass Deportations and Deportees in the Neo-Assyrian Empire* (Wiesbaden: Dr. Ludwig Reichert Verlag 1979).

Jerusalem, the Jebusite city on the border of Judah and the northern tribes, and made it the capital of the new nation. He also made Jerusalem the religious center by moving the Ark of the Covenant there (1 Sam. 6–10). One of David's most cherished dreams is to build a house for Yahweh, or more precisely, for the Ark of Alliance. As it turns out, God declares through the prophet Nathan that it would not be David but his son Solomon who would build a temple for God. Notably, God's words to David in the Deuteronomist account confirm what is said above about God's migrating with the Hebrews and dwelling in the Tabernacle during their wanderings in the desert: "Are you the one to build me a house to live in? I have not lived in a house since the day I brought up the people of Israel from Egypt to this day, but *I have been moving about in a tent and a tabernacle*" (1 Sam. 7:6, italics added).

Among Solomon's many accomplishments the most prominent, from the religious point of view, is the building of the Temple (1 Kings 5–8). What the Temple represents in terms of God's dwelling with God's people, especially in the context of migration, will be elaborated below. As mentioned above, after Solomon's death, the ten northern tribes seceded from Judah to form the Northern Kingdom of Israel, which came to an end in 721. After the destruction of its northern counterpart, Judah struggled on, entangled in the political ambitions and military conquests of the two empires of Assyria to the east and Egypt to the south. Toward the end of the eighth century, one of its kings, Hezekiah, rebelled against Assyria in an attempt to regain independence. His revolt was ruthlessly quashed by the Assyrian king Sennacherib who destroyed most of the cities and towns of Judah, except Jerusalem in exchange for a heavy tribute (701 BCE).

At the end of the seventh century BCE, Assyria was overthrown by a resurgent Babylonia. In the initial years of this new empire, Judah attempted to assert independence, especially during the reign of the king Josiah (640–609), who carried out a religious reform on the basis of the Deuteronomist theology. After Josiah's untimely death in the battle of Megiddo (609) at the hands of the

Egyptian pharaoh Necho (609), Judah rapidly declined. When, under the kings Jehoiakim and Zedekiah, the country allied itself with Egypt and rebelled against Babylonia, the king of Babylonia Nebuchadnezzar laid siege to Jerusalem in 597 and 586, and in the latter military campaign, destroyed the city, burnt down the Temple, and brought the Davidic dynasty to an end. Moreover, he deported a number of the royal and priestly elites, among whom the king Jehoiachim and the prophet Ezekiel, to Babylon. Others escaped to Egypt, including the prophet Jeremiah, settling in Alexandria and on the island of Elephantine, near Syene (modern Aswan).[52]

This sixth-century BCE migration decimated the leadership of the Judean population, though a significant number of Judeans remained in the country. Due to these migrations, a large proportion of Jews would live outside the land of Israel, constituting the Jewish Diaspora. Now the Torah and other writings of the Hebrew Bible replaced the core institutions to shape the identity of the Jews. As the migration of the Hebrews from Egypt in the thirteenth century had shaped their identity as God's covenanted people and a nation, this migration of the Judeans in the sixth century (leaving aside the migration of the Israelites in the eighth century) contributed greatly to the formation of a new Jewish identity and way of life in the Diaspora in place of the traditional markers of Jewish identity—land, kingship, temple, priesthood, and sacrifices—which had been irretrievably lost. Once again, migration, which now became a permanent feature of Jewish life and history and not simply their sporadic events, played a key role in transforming the religion of Judah into what would later be called Judaism, which would not have come into existence and would not persist and evolve into new forms until today without such migration.[53]

---

[52] Jer 52:28–30 mentions three deportations of Judeans into Babylonia, the largest one consisting of 3,023 Jews who were deported by Nebuchadnezzar, including King Jehoiakim and the prophet Ezekiel, in 597 BCE. Eleven years later, Nebuchadnezzar deported 832 more Judeans. Six years later, the commander of the Babylonia army Nebuzaradan took 745 Judeans into exile at Riblah, bringing the total of Jewish deportees to Babylonia to 4,600.

[53] On the Babylonian Exile, see John J. Ahn and Jill Middlemas, eds., *By the Irrigation Canals of Babylon: Approaches to the Study of the Exile* (London: Bloomsbury T&T Clark, 2012).

It is natural after facing this monumental loss, that Judean migrants would cry out: "By the rivers of Babylon—there we sat down and there we wept, when we remembered Zion" (Ps 137:1). Asked by their captors to play musical instruments and sing songs to entertain them, they hang their harps on the willows and lamented: "How could we sing the Lord's song in a foreign land?" (Ps 137:4). Poignantly, they asked where God was in all their forced migrations and their sojourn in "a foreign land" God's seeming absence was thought to be the result of the destruction of the Temple in Jerusalem. Of this First Temple nothing remains, and what can be known of it is derived from its descriptions in Kings 6–7 and 2 Chronicles 3–4, though the latter text is late and seems to have imported certain features of the Tabernacle and the post-exilic Second Temple. What the Temple represents is stated by Solomon in his dedication prayer: "I have built you an exalted house, a place for you to dwell in forever" (1 Kings 8:13). It is the place where *Deus Migrator* settled down among his people of returning migrants.

How God dwells in the Temple is variously expressed by the Priestly and the Deuteronomic Schools. According to the former, the Temple is the place where God manifests God's *kavod*, translated as "glory," or "majesty," or "glorious substance." *Kavod* is God's shining radiance which overwhelms those who gaze upon it and is shrouded by a cloud. According to the latter, God dwells in the heavenly realm and not in the Temple; the Temple contains not the transcendent God but only God's "name," which can be invoked there. God's "Glory" and "Name" are the two ways the migrating God is said to dwell in the Temple.

As to the presence of the Lord God among his migrating people, according to the prophet Ezekiel's vision, when the Temple was destroyed in 586, God, or the "Presence of the Lord" (the divine *kavod*), left not only the Temple but also the city of Jerusalem on the chariot-throne carried off by the cherubim as they lifted their wings and ascended from the earth (Ezek. 10:18–19). Ezekiel does not say where the Glory of the Lord went, only that God's departure from the Temple and the city was a sign of God's abandonment of the sinful city and the defiled Temple (Ezek. 9:9–10). But it is not far-fetched to argue that if God's presence was not limited to Mount Zion and if God could freely leave God's dwelling there, God could follow the Judeans into exile and protect them. Indeed, this is what biblical history affirms, as God is shown to have guided the exiled people through leaders such as Ezekiel, Deutero-Isaiah, Daniel, Esther, Zerubbabel, Ezra, and Nehemiah.[54]

God the-Returning-Migrant with the Homecoming Community

Most if not all migrants, not only seasonal immigrants but also settlers, nourish the dream of going home, if not for permanent resettlement, then at least for a long visit. For the Jews in Babylonia, homecoming was not inspired by nostalgia for the old country but by God's promise to them through the prophet Ezekiel and the prophet (man or woman) now referred to as Deutero-Isaiah (40-53). Ezekiel, addressing his fellow migrants in Babylonia, narrates his vision of a valley full of dry bones which were brought to life by God's breath. The revival of the dead bones symbolizes the restoration of the Jewish exiles to their own land to form a single nation, no longer divided into the Northern Kingdom (Israel) and the Southern Kingdom (Judah), with David's descendants as their king (Ezek. 37:1–28).[55] The fulfillment of Ezekiel's prophecy began in 539 BCE when King Cyrus allowed Judean migrants to return to Judah with the captured Temple treasures under Zerubbabel's leadership. In 458 BCE, the priest Ezra won the approval of Artaxerxes to bring additional migrants home. The third return of Judean migrants to Jerusalem took place under Nehemiah in 445 BCE.

The prophet Deutero-Isaiah lived in Babylonia a generation after the Babylonian empire destroyed the Judean state and exiled much of its population

---

[54] See Mark J. Boda, Frank Ritchel Ames, John Ahn, and Mark Leuchter, eds., *The Prophets Speak on Forced Migration* (Atlanta: SBL Press, 2015).

[55] This vision will be interpreted in postbiblical times as affirming the literal resurrection of the dead.

(587 BCE). He promised his fellow migrants that the Persian king Cyrus, who he anticipated would defeat Assyria, would allow them to return to their homeland and to rebuild the Temple there. From chapter 49 on, the prophet seems to be living in the land of Judah, where he likely moved as soon as Cyrus allowed the migrants to go home in 539 BCE.

As often happens with returning migrants, reality falls far short of their dreams. Both Ezekiel and Deutero-Isaiah predicted that the return to Judah would usher in the re-establishment of Israel and Judah as one nation under the Davidic dynasty, an era of world peace and prosperity, and the universal acknowledgment by all nations of the rule of God. In fact, however, as the Books of Ezra and Nehemiah show, only a small number of migrants chose to return home; those who prospered remained in Babylonia and vicinity, especially in Nippur. Many prosperous Judean migrants chose to remain in the foreign lands, including Egypt, where life was much more comfortable, and became the nucleus of a large and highly influential Jewish Diaspora community. Furthermore, Judah did not become an independent nation but remained an impoverished and insignificant Persian province of Yehud. The rebuilding of the Temple was not completed until 516 BCE, over twenty years after Cyrus's permission to repatriate, and the construction of Jerusalem's wall under Nehemiah in 445 BCE was fiercely opposed. In addition, there were severe conflicts between those who returned from the Diaspora and those who did not go into exile, the former group, more powerful, cosmopolitan, and educated, styled themselves as the "children of the exile" and contemptuously referred to the latter group as "people of the land" (*am ha'aretz*) whose "Jewishness" was deemed questionable. Again, as often happens in returning migrant communities, there was the issue of authentic national and cultural identity, especially in cases of racially and ethnically mixed marriages.

The most important task of the returnees was to rebuild the Temple, for which Ezekiel provides a lengthy and detailed description (40-48). Ezekiel's earlier visions of God's departure from Jerusalem and the destruction of the

Temple (1–7; 9–11) are complemented by his visions while in exile of the rebuilding of the Temple and the return of God's Presence (40–43). In these visions the prophet was transported back to the site of the Temple and was given to see the future Temple with its walls, gates, courtyards, architectural plan, functionaries, and sacrifices. Furthermore, Ezekiel saw the return of the Presence of God to the Temple through the eastern gate from which it had earlier departed. God said to Ezekiel in the inner court: "This is the place of my throne and the place for the soles of my feet, where I will reside among the people of Israel forever" (43:7). Thus, in this new phase of the history of the covenanted people's migration, God assumed a new role, that of the "Returning Migrant," dwelling with the returning migrants as they rebuilt their nation, their center of worship, and their cultural and religious identity.

God and the Jewish Diaspora among the World Empires

During the Persian period (539–333 BCE), to construct and strengthen a distinctly Jewish community, returning migrants from Babylonia were intensely engaged in collecting, revising, and editing works they considered foundational to their identity as God's covenanted people, such as the writings of the older prophets, works now referred to as Deuteronomistic History, and the Psalter. New works were composed as well, such as 1 and 2 Chronicles, Ezra, Nehemiah, and many others. The Lord God is believed to be present through his Spirit guiding the returning migrants in this process of national and religious reconstruction by means of scriptural composition and canonization.

This two-centuries period was followed by the Hellenistic period (333–63 BCE), which began when Philip of Macedonia, and then his son Alexander the Great, attempted to overthrow the Persian empire as it tried to extend its power into Asia Minor. After his rapid and spectacular conquests, Alexander died in 323 at the age of 32, leaving his far-flung empire, from Greece all the way to India, to be carved out among his satraps, including Ptolemy and Seleucus. The Ptolemies ruled Egypt, Libya and Arabia, and the Seleucids Mesopotamia,

Anatolia, and parts of India. The wars between the Ptolemies and the Seleucids carried enormous consequences for Judea and Jerusalem, which were wedged between the two empires and torn apart by internal pro-Ptolemaic and pro-Seleucid factions.

During this period, migration again played a significant role in expanding the Jewish community. During his first attempts at conquering of the eastern Mediterranean territory, Ptolemy I captured Jerusalem and took many Jews back to Egypt. Later, many Jews migrated there, probably for economic reasons. In Alexandria, Egypt, there was a large Jewish Diaspora community. In the island of Elephantine, the Jews worshiped in a temple of their own though they kept contact with Jerusalem to discuss various religious matters. By the Roman period, there were in Egypt hundreds of thousands of Jews, including many wealthy and influential families. It was in Alexandria that the Hebrew Bible was first translated into Greek, commonly referred to as the Septuagint (LXX), so named after the legend that in 275 BCE, Ptolemy II Philadelphia commissioned 72 Jewish scholars to translate the Hebrew Bible into Greek, a task they completed in 72 days. Thus, it was thanks to Jewish migrants that Judaism was propagated not only geographically, outside the country of its birth, but also culturally, in languages other than Hebrew.

The eventual triumph of the Seleucid dynasty over the Ptolemies in 198 BCE brought about profound changes to Jews of Judea. The Seleucid king Antiochus III allowed Jews to practice their religions, as the Seleucid empire was governed through a network of Greek cities (*polis*) with their political, economic, and cultural systems. Unfortunately, conflicts arose between the Jews and the next Seleucid king, Antiochus IV Epiphanes, when two rival Jews, Jason and Menelaus, curried favor with Antiochus IV for the office of the high priesthood. Jason paid Antiochus to have Jerusalem established as a Greek *polis*, whereas Menelaus sold the golden vessels of the Temple to raise money to pay to Antiochus. When the forces of Jason and Menelaus went to war with each other, Antiochus took this violence to be Judea's revolt, and sent in Syrian troops, who retook the city of Jerusalem and ransacked the Temple. In 167, the Temple was reorganized to accommodate the religious needs of the Syrian-Greek troops and was dedicated to Zeus Olympus, and an altar was set up to offer sacrifices to Zeus. Furthermore, circumcision and the observance of the Sabbath were proscribed. These acts were met with resistance by the Jews, and the Hasmoneans, Mattathias and his three sons, Judas Maccabeus, Jonathan, and Simon, led what is known as the "Maccabean Revolt." In 146, they retook control of the Temple and rededicated it, giving rise to the festival of Hanukkah. It was however not until 142 that Simon could establish national independence, and the Hasmonean family ruled the country as both kings and high priests until the Roman conquest of Judea in 63 BCE. In response to a series of Jewish revolts, the Romans destroyed the Second Temple in 70 CE, and another Jewish, much larger and much longer, migration began.

The God of Jesus Christ: The Primordial Migrant

According to the Christian faith, the Lord God, the *Deus Migrator* of the Jews, came to be present in the flesh, first with the Jews and through them with the whole humanity. Consequently, what is said at some length above about the Lord as the Migrating God is not merely a prologue to our discourse about the Christian God below but applies fully to the Christian God as the *Deus Migrator*.

Admittedly, unlike the Tanakh, the New Testament does not contain a lengthy historical account of God's direct involvement with the development of Christianity. Rather its focus is on the history of Jesus of Nazareth and the working of the Holy Spirit in the church and human history. Central to Christianity is the belief that God, more precisely the Son or Word of God, is incarnated in Jesus. As the Gospel of John affirms, "the Word became flesh and lived among us, and we have seen his glory as of a father's only son, full of grace and truth" (John 1:14). Hence, an adequate theology of the Christian God as a Migrating God is possible only after a full elaboration of Jesus as the "Paradigmatic Migrant" and of the Holy Spirit as the "Power of Migration."

God "Tabernacled" Among Us

The verb "lived" in "lived among us" translates the Greek *eskēnōsen*, literally "tabernacled," an allusion to the wilderness Tabernacle, the precursor of Salomon's Jerusalem Temple, which was destroyed and replaced by the Second Temple. It may also be connected with the Hebrew *shekinah*, a technical term for God's presence among God's people, which in turn is the equivalent of the Tanakh's *kavod*, God's radiant glory. Given the intimate historical connection between the Lord's tabernacle, *shekinah* and *kavod* on the one hand and the Lord's migration with his covenanted people on the other, as has been shown above, it is possible to affirm that there is also an intimate connection between the Christian God, who is confessed to be one God in three personal relations named Father, Son, and Holy Spirit on the one hand and the many migrations of the community of Jesus' disciples on the other.

Here, our task is to construct a theology of the Christian God as *Deus Migrator* or "the Primordial Migrant" or "God-on-the-Move." Of course, as has been argued above, the threefold movement of affirmation-negation-transcendence in God-talk must also be applied: God *is*, is *not*, and is *infinitely* a migrant. With this caution in mind, we can explore how the Christian God can be thought of as the Primordial Migrant. Even though the term "migrant" is not predicated of God in the Bible, there are hints suggesting that God possesses most if not all the characteristics commonly associated with migration and migrants.[56]

God's Immutability and God's Migration

Before broaching a theology of God as *Deus Migrator*, a philosophical objection must be considered. The notion of the Migrating God, however well-founded from the biblical point of view, meets a formidable challenge from the

---

[56] For further reflections on God as a migrant, see Ched Myers, *Our God Is Undocumented: Biblical Faith and Immigration Justice* (Maryknoll, NY: Orbis Books, 2012).

metaphysics of God's immutability. Migration means movement and change. To explain the possibility of change in the world Aristotle argues that in order there to be movement at all, there must be *ho ou kinoumenon kinei* [the Unmoved Mover], *proton kinoun akineton* [the Prime Mover], *protaitios* [the First Cause], that which moves everything in the universe but is itself not moved by any prior mover. This Unmoved or Prime or First Mover/Cause is named God. Subsequently, classical metaphysics of substance argues that God as the Unmoved Mover implies that God is immutable and impassible. Hence, it does not seem correct to speak of God as "migrating" in space and time.

Over against this metaphysics it has been pointed out that it does not follow from the notion of "Unmoved" that God cannot be conceived as living and hence, "moving" since, as Aristotle himself puts it, "life also belongs to God; for the actuality of thought is life, and God is that actuality, and God's essential actuality is life most good and eternal. We say therefore that God is a living being, eternal, most good, so that life and duration continuous and eternal belong to God; for this is God."[57]

Furthermore, it is to be noted that in denying change and suffering in God the intent is to affirm God's absolute perfection or God's eternal and perfect life. What is denied is the idea that there is within God change as increase from imperfection to perfection, from lack to fullness (or as Aristotle puts it, from potency to act), and loss of perfection and fullness. But this denial of change in God does not entail that God cannot and does not "move," "change," and "suffer," not out of necessity or by chance but out of God's own all-powerful will and infinite love.

At any rate, whatever philosophical arguments can be mounted in defense of God's immutability and impassibility, from the point of view of the Christian faith in God's creation of the world and especially in God's incarnation

---

[57] Aristotle, *Metaphysics*, Bk XII,1072b. English translation by W. D. Ross in: *The Complete Works of Aristotle: The Revised Oxford Translation*, ed. Jonathan Barnes (Princeton: Princeton University Press, 1995), 1695.

in Jesus of Nazareth, it is incontrovertible that there are "events" or "movements" in God. These events or movements, while not entailing increase in or loss of divinity and attributing temporality in the sense of successive moments of time in God, do affirm a real movement within God.

God's Three Migratory Acts: Creation, Incarnation, Consummation

From the perspective of the Christian faith, there are three divine acts whereby God as it were freely "leaves" the "home" of Godself (the Immanent Trinity) and "migrates" to another "country" other than Godself, that is, the "world"—human and cosmic—and assumes a new way of existing and doing (the Economic Trinity). These three acts are creation, incarnation, and consummation. Though these acts are performed in common by the one God, they are "proper" to each of the three divine Persons and not merely appropriated to them and thus express their distinctive characteristics: The Father as creator, the Son as incarnated, and the Holy Spirit as consummator, and it is in these proper and distinctive modalities that the divine Persons relate themselves in a different way to humans and humans to them. In other words, humans relate to God the Father as his creatures and sons and daughters; to God the Son as his fellow human beings and brothers and sisters; and to the God the Holy Spirit as the Spirit's transformed and perfected creation.

As these three acts are performed by God in (not before and after) time and in the world, I suggest that they may be interpreted as God's migratory acts by which God goes out of Godself and returning to Godself. This exitus-reditus schema, which has an ancient and venerable pedigree, is commonly used to describe the journey of creatures coming out of God (their origin) and returning to God (their end), especially since Thomas Aquinas made use of it to structure his Summa Theologiae, though without the neo-Platonic emanationist overtones. To describe this process in terms of migration, creatures may be said to have "migrated" out of God, their native country as it were, and are now doing the "returning migration" to God, their real homeland, like the Hebrews migrating out of Egypt and settling in the Promised Land as God's covenanted people, and the Judeans migrating out of Judea, from which they had been exiled, and returning to it to rebuild their national and religious community.

The Creating God as Migrating

However, what has not been done is to reflect on how the Christian God himself is the Deus Migrator/Primordial Migrant, accompanying all migrants and migrating with them in their distinctive roles of Father, Son, and Holy Spirit. Not only do the creatures embark upon the "going-out-and-coming-back" migration but it is also the Trinitarian God himself undertaking the same migratory movement. Indeed, it is only because God migrates that humans can migrate, as it was, as noted above, the Lord God's first words in history that made Abraham into the "First Migrant" God's migration into history is the condition of possibility for human migrations in history. Divine migration and human migration are intrinsically intertwined. God is the beginning and the end of human migration, and humans are the co-migrants with God.

God's creative act can be interpreted as God's migration out of the divine into the non-divine, the "other" of God, a movement that bears all the marks of human migration. In creating that which is other than Godself, God crosses the border between Absolute Spirit and finite matter, migrating from eternity to temporality, from omnipotence into weakness, from self-sufficiency (aseity) to utter dependence, from total omniscience to fearful ignorance, from the complete domination of the divine will over all things to the utter subjection of the same will to the uncontrollability of human freedom, from life to death. In the creative act God experiences for the first time the precarious, marginalized, threatened, and endangered condition of the migrant. Like migrants, God enters a new country, that is, the world, and the native people may not, and as it turned out, not only did not offer him welcome and hospitality but also killed him. God remains a stranger and a resident alien, even though God has every right to be a citizen in that country, since after all God has created that country and all its inhabitants. Like God, migrants risk not only rejection but also death at the hands of the native people and in their tragic condition they know they are not alone and abandoned, since God is their co-migrant.

The Migrating God and the Ethics of Migration

Thus, the migrant is not only the imago Dei, as any other human being equally is, created in the image and likeness of God, which is the ontological ground of human rights. As such, the migrant possesses all the human rights, which must be respected by all.[58] However, as imago Dei, the migrant does not enjoy any stronger claim to human dignity and human rights than the citizens of the host country, or anyone else for that matter.[59] What is distinctive and unique about the migrant is that he or she is the imago Dei Migratoris, the privileged, visible, and public face of the God who chooses, freely and out of love, to migrate from the safety of God's eternal home to the strange and risky land of the human family, in which God is a foreigner needing embrace, protection, and love. Thus, when the migrant is embraced, protected, and loved, the Deus Migrator is embraced, protected, and loved. By the same token, when the migrant as imago Dei Migratoris is rejected, marginalized, declared "illegal," imprisoned, tortured, or killed, it is the original of that image, the Deus Migrator,

---

[58] Of course, not all thinkers ground the human rights in the fact that humans are created in the image and likeness of God. This claim for human rights is unique to the Abrahamic religions.

[59] Daniel G. Groody, one of the few Catholic theologians who have written extensively on the theology of migration and contributed a chapter in this volume, makes an eloquent and forceful case for the migrant's human rights based on the fact that the migrant is the *imago Dei*. Groody elaborates on the need to cross over the four divides separating migration from theology by (1) moving from treating the migrant as a problem to seeing the migrant as the *imago Dei*; (2) joining the He divine with the human by seeing Jesus as *Verbum Dei* (3) uniting the human with the divine in understanding Christian mission as *missio Dei*, and (4) overcoming xenophobia by subordinating nation/country to the kingdom of God by considering the goal of human existence as *visio Dei*. See his "Crossing the Divide: Foundations of a Theology of Migration and Refugees," in *And You Welcome Me: Migration and Catholic Social Teaching*, ed. Donald Kerwin and Jill Marie Gerschutz, 1–30.

who is subjected to the same inhuman and sinful treatment. Thus, the theology of God as Deus Migrator is the foundation for a Christian ethics of migration.

No wonder that in commanding the Israelites to treat migrants justly and kindly Yahweh urges them to remember their former experiences of migration: "You shall not wrong or oppress a resident alien, *for you were aliens in the land of Egypt*" (Exod. 22:21). Again: "You shall not oppress a resident alien; you know the heart of an alien, *for you were aliens in the land of Egypt*" (Ex 23:9). Again: "When an alien resides with you in your land, you shall not oppress the alien. The alien who resides with you shall be to you as the citizen among you; you shall love the alien as yourself, *for you were alien in the land of Egypt*" (Lev. 19:33–34). The italicized words occur like a refrain throughout the Hebrew Scripture and serve as the ethical foundation for Israel's various duties to the strangers and aliens among them.

It is true that these words are addressed not to migrants as such but to *former* migrants who have settled in the new land and are now citizens. But arguably God's command to remember the erstwhile status as migrants applies to both since most often migrants, both voluntary and forced, eventually become citizens. If anything, the obligation is even more stringent for erstwhile migrants, as they are more tempted to forget their past now that they enjoy all the privileges accruing to them as successful citizens. Furthermore, the Israelites-now-citizens may be psychologically inclined to erase their experiences as aliens and slaves in Egypt because they were painful, experiences that Yahweh does not fail to recall to their memory: "I have observed the misery of my people in Egypt. I have heard their cry on account of their taskmasters. Indeed, I know their sufferings" (Exod. 3:7).

Indeed, it is this memory of past sufferings associated with migration that grounds ethical behaviors to migrants. Yahweh reminds the Israelites that they have a connatural empathy with migrants because "you know the heart of an alien" But how can one know the depths of "the heart of an alien" if one does not nurture in one's own heart the memory of oneself as a migrant? It takes one to know one, as the saying goes. Without this memory of oneself as migrant, how can one identify oneself with other migrants and fulfill the Lord's command: "You shall love the alien as yourself"? "Yourself" here is a migrant/alien, not a citizen, or a generic human being. It is oneself as *migrant* that is the measure of one's love toward other migrants, even if legally one is now no longer a migrant. Perhaps the divine command may be paraphrased as: "You shall love the migrant in the measure in which you love yourself *as* a migrant." In other words, being migrant is a *permanent* identity and not a phase of life that can eventually be shed as one acquires a better social status. And it can become permanent—an "indelible character"—to use an expression of Catholic sacramental theology—imprinted in the "heart" only if one always and constantly remembers where one came from.

CHAPTER THREE

A Spirituality of Migration

Daniel G. Groody, CSC

Introduction

On July 16, 1969, a Saturn V rocket took off from Kennedy Space Center in Merritt Island, Florida and launched towards the outer reaches of the heavens. With only a fraction of the power of today's smartphones, and 145,000 lines of computing code, scientists sent three human beings 240,000 miles from home and landed them safely on the ground of our closest celestial neighbor.[60] When commander Neil Armstrong set foot on the lunar surface, he celebrated both an extraordinary scientific achievement and an important step forward for the entire human race. It marked an important milestone on our journey into unknown territory and our exploration of outer space.

Thirty-four years later, scientists achieved another milestone that would change our consciousness forever. This time however it would launch us more deeply into the unknown territory of "inner space" With the help of powerful computation software, they mapped and sequenced the entire DNA molecule. If the "code letters" in this molecule were read at one letter per second, it would take thirty-one years to read. If printed out in a regular font it would yield a stack of paper the size of the Washington Monument. Made up more than 3 billion

---

[60] Today's MacOS runs about 86,000,000 code. For more on Lines of Computer code through the years in NASA missions and smartphones, accessed January, 6, 2018, https://www.itworld.com/article/2725085/big-data/curiosity-about-lines-of-code.html.

"characters," this DNA discovery offers us a genetic blueprint for the growth and development of every human being.[61] It holds within itself the elemental language of the divine creator and the spiritual fabric that is woven into the gift of life.[62]

In light of these extraordinary discoveries, how are we understand our own place in the universe and our journey through time and space? This article is a first word on the mystery of our migration through this world and the spirit that guides our earthly journey. In other words, it is about a spirituality of migration, which seeks to map out some of the contours of the internal journey of the human person and its relation to the external migration of peoples.

This article has three parts. In the first part I will speak about the connection between migration and human identity. Secondly, I will elaborate on the connection between migration and the human heart. And thirdly, I will speak about the connection between a spirituality of migration and the migration of peoples today. While spirituality is a broad, interdisciplinary, and interreligious subject, the specific focus of this article is grounded in a vision of Christian spirituality lived within the community of believers, the Church. As we examine the connection between migration and the human journey, I seek to bring out how migration is not simply a socio-political descriptor of those who are crossing political borders today but a key metaphor for understanding what it means to be human before God and to live out a faith that does justice in the world.

Migration and Human Identity

Although stories of migration capture headlines around the world today, it is, in fact, as old as the ages. Genetic research has not only changed how we

---

[61] National Human Genome Research Institute, accessed January 6, 2018, https://www.genome.gov/10001772/all-about-the--human-genome-project-hgp/.

[62] When the Human Genome project presented a draft of this project in June of 2000, President Bill Clinton remarked, "Without a doubt, this is the most important, most wondrous map ever produced by humankind. Today we are learning the language in which God created life. We are gaining ever more awe for the complexity, the beauty, and the wonder of God's most divine and sacred gift. See Francis S. Collins, *The Language of God: A Scientist Presents Evidence for Belief* (New York: Free Press, 2006), 1–2.

think about ourselves, but it has transformed the way we understand who we are and where we have come from. After the Human Genome Project deciphered the sequence of human DNA in April 2003, a number of studies were initiated that sought to discover the migratory history of humankind.[63] One of those is the Genographic Project, which is a joint study conducted by National Geographic and IBM. Coined as a "landmark study of the human journey," it analyzes DNA samples from indigenous tribes throughout the world and compares them with samples from other people. As a result of this research, we can trace back our own migration history more than 60,000 years. With almost three quarters of a million samples, this study is giving us new insight into the origins of humankind and how migration is literally in our genes.

In addition to our biological and family origins, migration is written into the "national genes" of many countries throughout the world. In recent centuries people have migrated into different territories and manifested a "frontier spirit" that has taken them to uncharted places. It has profoundly shaped the national psyches and cultural spirit of people in countries like New Zealand, Canada, South Africa, Brazil, Argentina, Australia, and the United States.

The U.S. American psyche, in particular, has been shaped by immigration since its origins, arguably more than any country on the planet. It has been a country of immigrants since its earliest days, and its narratives are inextricably woven into its national consciousness. In his book, *The Uprooted*, Oscar Handlin wrote, "I once thought to write a history of immigrants in America. Then I discovered that the immigrants were American history."[64] The first Paleo-Indian settlers migrated from Eurasia along the land bridge on Bearing straits (Beringia) to the Americas. Much later the pilgrims' fathers migrated from England to North America in search of religious freedom; Lewis and Clark migrated from established territories in search of new routes across the

---

[63] For more on this study, see National Geographic, accessed January 6, 2018, https://genographic.nationalgeographic.com/.

[64] Oscar Handlin, *The Uprooted: The Epic Story of the Great Migration that made the American People*, (Boston: Little Brown: 1951), 3.

vast unknown of the American west; pioneers and trailblazers migrated along the Oregon trail in search of a prosperous future. And throughout recent centuries, waves of immigrants have come from around the world to the United States seeking a better life. In the process, the country has become known as a "mixing bowl," a "melting pot," and a "stew pot" of different races, creeds, and cultures.

From these cultures the Great American experiment began. Shaped by migrants from virtually every country around the globe, people journeyed from foreign lands to America in search of new possibilities and new opportunities. The Statue of Liberty has long stood as an iconic representation of the Golden door of America, where at her feet are inscribed these famous words of Emma Lazarus,

> Mother of Exiles. From her beacon-hand
> Glows world-wide welcome; her mild eyes command
> The air-bridged harbor that twin cities frame.
> "Keep, ancient lands, your storied pomp!" cries she
> With silent lips. "Give me your tired, your poor,
> Your huddled masses yearning to breathe free,
> The wretched refuse of your teeming shore.
> Send these, the homeless, tempest-tost to me,
> I lift my lamp beside the golden door!

This experiment, however, was not without its challenges. Despite its persona as a land of opportunity and a promise land for the poor and oppressed, the United States and its citizens have had a deep ambivalence about migration. The history of immigration has always been a mixture of lightness and darkness. In 1630 Puritan refugees like John Winthrop described America as a shining "city upon a hill" and a model of Christian charity. The light reflected against this hill, however, would cast a very long xenophobic shadow. Many immigrants who came to America from Ireland, Germany, Italy, China, the Philippines, Japan, and other countries have known, at different times, the sting of social and political exclusion. The resurgence of nativism and populism in our own times have reemerged in the dark rhetoric and anti-immigrant policies of the Trump administration. Such attitudes dualize the foreigner from the native-born and push them into alienating space of "otherness" Ironically, even though migration is one of the defining aspects of our human identity, it is also one of the most divisive issues in our own day. And while social and political forces tear at the bonds that knit the entire human community together, a spirituality of migration seeks to mend these wounds by tending to the outer movement of peoples through a more intentional journey into the human heart.

Migration and the Human Heart

Although migration is a term that deals with much of what is happening in the "outer world," it also has to do with something that is deeply personal. It involves a journey beyond the mind and into the heart, into the center of a person's being. It seeks to enter into the rich and adventurous terrain of a journey with the God who is both infinite and intimate. The journey moves us into luminous territory, and it eludes the grasp of clear and distinct ideas. Understanding it involves more than the search for certainty but moving into the realm of metaphor. Metaphor is important because it gives us a way of accessing this mystery of understanding who we are before God, who God is for us, and who we are in relationship with each other. One of the most powerful integrating metaphors for this journey is the heart.

In many of the world's religions, especially in Mesoamerica, the heart is the place where the biological and the spiritual are united.[65] The heart, or *corazón* in Spanish, has a totally different connotation in the English language, where it is often separated from knowledge and reduced to sentimentality. For the indigenous people of the Americas, the heart is a physical organ with a mystical quality. It symbolizes the innermost mystery of a person and captures the totality of a human person before God. Moreover, the heart is the source of ultimate

---

[65] In the Nahuatl, the ancient Mexican language, the word for heart is *teyolia*, coming from two indigenous words, *yolia* meaning "the one who animates?" and *yol* meaning "life.?" See especially Miguel León-Portilla, *Aztec Thought and Culture: A Study of the Ancient Nahuatl Mind*, trans. Jack Emory Davis (Norman: University of Oklahoma Press, 1963).

understanding.[66] It integrates and informs all aspects of a person, including the mind, will and emotions. In the heart, sentiments, memories, thoughts, reasoning, and planning are united; it is the biological-symbolic site of wisdom and knowledge and a metaphor for the whole of one's conscious, intelligent, and free personality. The heart is the central metaphor of spiritual transformation because it is the place where the divine and human meet. Moreover, the heart it always searching and is always seeking a greater self-realization. In this sense we can say that the heart is always migrating because it is always seeking to find its true and lasting home.

The notions of the heart and migration figure in both literally and figuratively in the Biblical text because they are central to salvation history. As Diane Bergant puts it,

> [B]iblical language is basically metaphorical in character. Imaginative and paradoxical, it opens us to possibilities of expression and insight that precise philosophical or descriptive discourse cannot provide. It generates impressions rather than propositions. It seeks to capture the power and emotion of the event of God and to draw the hearer (only secondarily the reader) into an experience that transcends both the past and the present, and opens to the future. It is important to understand this dimension of religious language, not only for the sake of a method of interpretation that will reveal original meanings (theological reconstruction), but also for the sake of one that will provide new understandings (constructive theology).[67]

The Scriptures take the metaphor of the heart to an entirely new level. In the Old Testament the expulsion of Adam and Eve from Eden and their border-crossing into the land beyond names the human propensity to move towards a state of sin and disorder (Gen. 3:1–13). In the New Testament God's

---

[66] Jean de Fraine and Albert Vanhoye, "Heart," in *Dictionary of Biblical Theology*, ed. Xavier Leon-Defour (Paris: Desclée Company, 1967), 200–202.
[67] Diane Bergant, "Ruth: The Migrant Who Saved the People," *in Migration, Religious Experience, and Globalization,* edited by Gioacchino Campese and Pietro Ciallella, (New York: Center for Migration Studies), 2003, 49.

migration into our world in the person of Jesus Christ reveals God's response to our wayward journey, and the death and resurrection of Jesus and the sending of the Spirit make possible our return migration to God's kingdom.

From the call of Abraham to the Exodus, from Exile to Return, from the Incarnation to Jesus' Ascension, from Jesus' call to his disciples to "follow him" to his sending them out into all nations, the theme of movement and migration are interwoven into the biblical narrative. As it brings out God's movement into our world in an unmerited gift, Jesus' Life, Death and Resurrection make possible our return migration to a homeland. God's movement to the human race in the Incarnation and His journey into the sinful territory of our broken human existence is one of the central theological starting points that grounds a spirituality of migration. Christian faith holds out the conviction that human beings are created in the image and likeness of God. This perspective takes for granted that this world is not our final destination but a transit country through which we are called to journey as pilgrims in a spirit of faith, hope and love. Along this road we not only see darkly through a mirror (1 Cor. 13:12), but we are also riddled by forces that constantly tear at the fabric that stitches together our relationships with each other in the human community. Sin disfigures the imago Dei, resulting in a fallen world which creates discord in relationships. Grace restores one from a place of estrangement from God to communion with Him and indeed all of creation. Migration is a metaphorical way of speaking about this spiritual process.

The community of believers gathered as the Church live out both the gift and the demand of this journey together through this world. Because of its history, the Church has always seen an integral connection between its own identity and those on the move today. As the United States Conference of Catholic Bishops note in the document, *Strangers No Longer*,

> Our continent has consistently received immigrants,
> refugees, exiles, and the persecuted from other lands.
> Fleeing injustice and oppression and seeking liberty and the
> opportunity to achieve a full life, many have found work,

homes, security, liberty, and growth for themselves and
their families. Our countries share this immigrant
experience, though with different expressions and to
different degrees.[68]

The National Shrine of the Immaculate Conception, located adjacently
to the current offices of the United States Conference of Catholic Bishops, is a
microcosm of the Church's mission to migrants over many generations. This
Basilica, in its varied iconic, pictographic and mosaic expressions, honors the
manifold contribution of immigrants to the Church and society and the various
religious communities that have assisted them in difficult times. In many ways
the Church sees in the migrant not only subjects in need of pastoral care but a
mirror of its own identity as the people of God. Among the nationalities
represented in the Basilica's chapels are African, Austrian, Byzantine-Ruthenian,
Chinese, Cuban, Czech, Filipino, French, German, Guamanian, Indian, Irish,
Italian, Korean, Latin American, Lithuanian, Maltese, Polish, Slovak, Slovenian,
and Vietnamese. Through its diverse array culturally expressive chapels and
oratories, this Basilica embodies the catholicity or universality of the Church in
both its unity and diversity. But it also highlights its prophetic role in facing the
unique social, political, and economic challenges of each generation, particularly
those presented by the enduring and perennial issue of migration.

How then are we to understand the connection between this inner
migration into one's deepest self and the outer migration of peoples? As we
explore this question it helps to connect spirituality with justice. From a Christian
perspective, a spirituality of migration is deeply personal, but it is not
individualistic. It acknowledges that human beings are by nature profoundly
social because they are made in the image and likeness of a God who is
profoundly relational. Because of this, relationships are at the heart of a

---

[68] United States Conference of Catholic Bishops, "Strangers No Longer: Together on a
Journey of Hope," accessed January 6, 2018, http://www.usccb.org/issues-and-
action/human-life-and-dignity/immigration/strangers-no-longer-together-on-the-journey-of-
hope.cfm, no. 15.

spirituality of migration. When relationships are rightly ordered to the Reign of God, peace and justice results. When they become disordered and fragment through sin, however, chaos and injustice results. One of the central aspects of its mission is the work of social justice, which is the task of getting our relationships rightly ordered and rightly integrated.

In Christian theology there are two principal notions of justice: internal justice and external justice.[69] Internal justice deals with one's experience of justification or being put in right relationship with God through the saving work of Jesus Christ. External justice deals with the promotion of good works. Internal justice refers to God's activity within a person; external justice refers to one's response to God's grace. Internal justice relates to the first and the greatest command, to love the Lord God with all one's heart, soul, and mind (Matt. 22:37–38). External justice relates to the second command to love one's neighbor as oneself (Matt. 22:39). It seeks humanizing activity leading to right relationships with oneself, the community, its social structures, and finally to the environment itself.[70] God's justice, in other words, is not principally about vengeance or retribution but about restoring people to right relationship with God, themselves, others, and the environment. The kingdom of God is about bringing these relationships to their full flourishing.

Because each and every person has value in God's kingdom, this means that the economic systems of the world should be ordered to the good of all people and not just the benefit of a privileged few. The current order of things gives us much to think about, especially its asymmetry with the designs of a loving Creator. As of January 2018, the eight richest people in the world have as

---

[69] For more on this topic, see Daniel G. Groody, *Globalization, Spirituality and Justice, rev. ed.,* (Maryknoll, NY: Orbis Books, 2015), 28.

[70] This definition drawn in part from an excellent article by Michael Crosby, "Justice," in *The New Dictionary of Catholic Spirituality*, ed. Michael Downey (Collegeville, MN: Liturgical Press, 1993), 597.

much wealth as the poorest half of the world.[71] These disorders are rooted in unjust structures, but as Vatican II observed, they are also rooted in the disorders of the human heart.[72] From this perspective, migration as a socio-political phenomenon is not a problem in itself, but a symptom and a consequence of much deeper imbalances, which can only be transformed by a more fundamental reordering of the human heart.

A Spirituality of Migration and the Migration of People Today

Despite its connections to our deepest identities, however, migration is one of the most complex and controversial issues of our day. Its scope and scale today is unprecedented, and it touches virtually every aspect of human life. If one accounts for both international and domestic migrants, there are more than a billion migrants in the world.[73] More than 65 million of these are forcibly uprooted. Over 40 million are internally displaced within their own countries, and in excess of 22 million are refugees seeking international protection. If these refugees were settled in one particular place, they would be the 21st largest country in the world, growing at 38,000 people per day or 24 people per minute.[74]

By the time you read these statistics, however, these figures will be obsolete. If past trends are a reliable indication, even more people will be on the move than when this chapter was written. According to the International

---

71 "Policy and Practice," OXFAM, accessed January 6, 2018, http://policy-practice.oxfam.org.uk/publications/an-economy-for-the-99-its-time-to-build-a-human-economy-that-benefits-everyone-620170.

72 Gaudium et Spes, no. , accessed January 6, 2018, http://www.vatican.va/archive/hist_councils/ii_vatican_council/documents/vat-ii_const_19651207_gaudium-et-spes_en.html.

73 For more on global migrant statistics, see International Organization for Migration, accessed January 6, 2018, http://www.iom.sk/en/about-migration/migration-in-the-world.

74 For more on these trends, see "UNHCR, "Global Trends in Forced Displacement in 2015," accessed January 6, 2018, http://www.unhcr.org/statistics/unhcrstats/576408cd7/unhcr-global-trends-2015.html and "UNHCR, "Global Trends in Forced Displacement in 2016," accessed January 6, 2018, http://www.unhcr.org/statistics/unhcrstats/5943e8a34/global-trends-forced-displacement-2016.html.

Organization of Migration, there could be more than 400 million migrants by 2050.[75] This means that despite the shallow and hollow and divisive rhetoric of elected officials, building higher and wider walls will not resolve the issues. In many respects, migration is such a definitive dimension of our life and times that some scholars refer to this point in history as "the age of migration."[76]

When I have asked migrants what they find most difficult about their situation, most of them—despite the grueling physical journeys they take—talk more about the deeper insults to their human worth. They may go without food as they stow away on trains and buses. They may gasp for air as they hide in cargo containers of ships. They may thirst for water as they cross the vast stretches of desert. They may suffer in the mountains amid cold and snow. But as difficult as these hardships are, many migrants often say that no physical suffering is worse than being treated as if they were dogs, as if they were not even human beings, as if they were no one to anyone. In contrast to a world that denies the God-given human dignity of each person, a spirituality of migration seeks to proclaim a God that promotes life and works to build a civilization of love.

Because a spirituality of migration seeks to promote human dignity, it seeks to respond to the personal struggles of migrants. In part this involves addressing the structural issues that impact their situation. The root causes of economic migration stem principally from underdevelopment and unemployment. When family members need food, clothing, shelter and medicine, and the problems of underdevelopment and under and unemployment keep them from finding sufficient employment to make ends meet, one or more members of the family will travel to another place to find work. When they are

---

[75] International Organization of Migration, World Migration Report, News Release, accessed January 6, 2018, https://www.iom.int/files/live/sites/iom/files/Newsrelease/docs/WM2010_FINAL_23_11_2010.pdf.
[76] Stephen Castles and Mark J. Miller. *The Age of Migration : International Population Movements in the Modern World. 5th ed.* (New York: Guilford Press), 2013.

unable to obtain visas because they are unskilled laborers, they often resort to crossing the borders without official documentation.

The significance of a spirituality of migration has taken on a renewed significance under the leadership of Pope Francis, whose first pastoral visit was to the small, Italian Island of Lampedusa. On the shores of the place where thousands die each year in the Mediterranean, he celebrated a mass, in the open air, next to a "boat graveyard," preaching out against the "globalization of indifference" During the liturgy he proclaimed the Gospel from a lectern made from the rudders of a refugee boat and used a chalice make from the shipwrecked wood of a downed refugee vessel.[77] His words, gestures and prayers bring out how, in a world that increasingly ignores and discards refugees as "no bodies," a spirituality of migration not only helps each refugee discover their dignity as "some-body" but also to reveal that they are in fact connected to "every-body.[78]

In the context of my own pastoral work in rural Mexico, I was struck by the number of villages inhabited only by women and children. Most of the men went north looking for work, while most of the women and children stayed behind. In these villages, migration causes the disintegration of families—the most basic cell of society. It is this social disintegration that greatly concerns the Church because its costs to the human family are enormous.

Yet more often than not, people take umbrage with migrants because many of them are in a country without official documentation. Not uncommonly people will say, "I have no problem with immigrants, but just that they have come illegally" Underneath this objection is a valid concern for the rule of law, and often the intended aim is fairness, if not justice. These issues need to be seriously considered and carefully evaluated. Especially when we consider the corrupt judicial systems of some countries, and violent social upheaval that

---

[77] For more on this topic see, Daniel G. Groody, "Cup of Suffering, Chalice of Salvation: Refugees, Lampedusa and the Eucharist?" *Theological Studies*, (December 2017), 960–987.
[78] For more on this topic, see Daniel G. Groody, "Cup of Suffering, Chalice of Salvation?" Refugees, Lampedusa and the Eucharist?" *Theological Studies* (December 2017).

results as a consequence, we come to appreciate why the rule of law is so important. The lawlessness of cartels within Mexico, and the social chaos it has caused, is but one example of what happens when the binding role of a legal system loses its integrity.

A spirituality of migration, however—especially because of its rootedness in the prophetic tradition of the Scriptures--is not satisfied with this analysis. It argues that there is more to the law than a civil ordinance. In other words, there is more at stake in reality than what is on the legal books. From a theological perspective, different laws are at work in the problem of immigration and changing enforcement policies alone is not enough to achieve comprehensive immigration reform. In this regard, Thomas Aquinas distinguished four kinds of laws: natural laws, civil laws, divine laws, and eternal laws.[79] While the political debate deals mostly with civil laws, the Church is concerned with these other laws as well. The Church has concern for the national common good of respective countries, but it is also concerned with the universal common good of all of God's people. With regard to immigration, natural laws deal with parents needing to feed their families; civil laws pertain to ordinances utilized by society for the common good. Divine laws, known through Scripture, relate to the Gospel imperative to provide for the hungry, thirsty, naked, sick, imprisoned and estranged; eternal laws deal with how God keeps the universe in motion. When these laws interrelate in such a way that one form of law connects to the other, justice flourishes. However, when we have

---

[79] Aquinas understood "law?" as "an ordinance of reason for the common good, promulgated by him who has the care of the community?" (ST 1–2, q. 90). The eternal law governs everything in the universe: the divine law corresponds to the Old Law and New Law of the Hebrew Scriptures and New Testament; the natural law deals with ethical norms and human behavior; and the civil law deals with human codes used for social order. For an overview of natural law and its development within Catholic tradition, see Stephen J. Pope, "Natural Law in Catholic Social Teachings," in *Modern Catholic Social Teaching: Commentaries and Interpretations,* ed. Kenneth R. Himes (Washington: Georgetown University, 2005) 41–71. For a more extended treatment, see John Finnis, *Natural Law and Natural Rights* (New York: Oxford University, 2001).

civil laws that exclude the poor without any regard for issues of natural law like underdevelopment, injustice abounds.

A spirituality of migration upholds the ways that laws are used to protect and defend people, but it does not see that law in this sense is an unchecked, unqualified, and absolute right. Because of the role of human dignity in the divine economy of creation, the needs of the poor and vulnerable require special, if not primary, consideration. Arguments about the economic, political, and social implications of migration must first find a reference in the human face of the migrant or else the core issues at stake are easily lost. If we cannot see the human face of the migrant, then nothing else will matter. To put it another way, the Bishops have insisted that the economy be made for human beings and not human beings for the economy. They recognize that one of the fundamental ways through which society must be ordered is according to economic justice, which measures the health of an economy not in terms of financial metrics like Gross National Product or stock prices, but in terms of how the economy affects the quality of life in the community as a whole.[80]

Because we confuse illegality with criminality, we end up wasting the efforts of enforcement officials on those who are looking for work and prosecuting those whose only crime at its core has to do with providing for their families. Why are there people who are scandalized by migrants breaking civil laws but are not proportionally more scandalized by the living and working conditions in which migrants find themselves? This question is connected to a spirituality of migration. The Church teaches that the ideal arrangement is for migrants to stay in their homeland, but when there are not sufficient conditions for a dignified life, the Church argues that migrants have a right to look for work, even if this search entails crossing borders without official documentation.

The deeper challenges of the migration issue, then, are rooted not simply in political issues but spiritual ones as well. Since spirituality has to do

---

[80] Economic Justice for All, no. 14, accessed January 6, 2018, http://www.usccb.org/upload/economic_justice_for_all.pdf.

with what we most value, migration — seen from this spiritual perspective — means moving into a new kind of life and a new way of being in the world. In a context in which so much of the debate around migrants and refugees is governed by fear and "otherness," a spirituality of migration highlights the call to oneness and community. This means that migration is not about "us" citizens and "those" foreigners, but about all of "us" who are pilgrims in this world. As St. Paul described it: "So then you are no longer strangers and aliens, but you are citizens with the saints and also members of the household of God" (Eph. 2:19)

Even so, migration is not just about the journey but the walls we build in the process, and not a few people remain walled in constrictive notions about migration. Those animated by a spirituality of migration seek to break down the walls that divide, alienate, exclude, discriminate, and dehumanize. Some seek to break down these barriers in creative ways along the border. One community decided to have a volleyball game with respective teams on both sides. Another held a picnic and shared food between the holes in the fence. And in various communities, some hold Eucharistic liturgies where the congregation joins the altar together from both sides of the border wall. By doing so they not only proclaim that these walls will come down when Christ comes again, but also that we are already united because of who we are as the Body of Christ.

Migrants and refugees, in summary, often bear the burden of a humanity living in tension between the land of likeness to God (regio similitudinis) which fosters the dignity of every person, and the land of unlikeness to God (regio dissimilitudinis).[81] A spirituality of migration helps the world discover, and more fully develop, its humanity as God intended. This means that the journeying through this world is not simply about moving from one physical place to another but moving closer and closer to the divine image and likeness. In other

---

[81] The concept of *regio dissimilitudinis* has its origin in Platonic thought, but it has parallels in the Scriptures. Mystics like Bernard of Clairvaux and others in the Middle Ages also used the concept when speaking about the movement of people away from the divine image and likeness towards a state of alienation. For more on this topic, see Etienne Gilson, "Regio dissimilitudinis de Platon à Saint Bernard de Clairvaux," *Medieval Studies 9* (1947): 109–17.

words, a spirituality of migration is about the path of redemption that leads one to become more fully who one is created to be: an embodied reflection of the living God.

Conclusion

This article has sought to explore a spirituality of migration as it takes shape on the borderlands between "outer space" and "inner space" While it is a subject that often is defined in social, political, and economic terms, we have seen the many ways in which it is an intrinsic part of our human identity. We have also seen how it is a way of understanding the Christian vision in terms of God's movement to us in mercy and our response in compassion to our neighbor in need. In many different ways a spirituality of migration breaks down the dualism between "us" and "them" because it seeks to move us beyond alienation to a place of communion with God and one another.

Spirituality encompasses all of these aspects because it deals with the totality of our lives before God. St. Thomas Aquinas' whole theological vision, in fact, is framed by the notion that everything comes from God and is called to return to God (*Exitus et Reditus*). In this sense, migration names the dynamic nature of creation: the movement from God the Creator, the movement through this world as a creature, and the return movement to God as a new creation through Christ the mediator.[82] A spirituality of migration then involves our sojourn through this world, which, as the second Vatican council puts it, makes us "pilgrims in a strange land" who are moving towards the fullness of God's kingdom.[83] Because migrants mirror our own journey through this world, they help us see that migration is a way of understanding who we are before God,

---

[82] St. Thomas Aquinas' *Summa Theologiae,* I–II, q. 92.

[83] "Lumen Gentium," accessed January 6, 2018, http://www.vatican.va/archive/hist_councils/ii_vatican_council/documents/vat-ii_const_19641121_lumen-gentium_en.html.

who we are in our relationship to each other, and ultimately where we are going in this journey of life.

CHAPTER FOUR

A Christian Ethic of Immigration

Kristin E. Heyer

The 2017 executive orders that call for a wall at the U.S.-Mexico border, a selective travel ban and that strip federal funding to sanctuary cities threaten to further endanger the lives of vulnerable migrants and asylum seekers.[84] These orders issued by President Donald Trump directly reflect his campaign rhetoric that cast immigrants and refugees as threats to the United States. He campaigned on promises to deport undocumented immigrants and secure the border with Mexico, and anti-immigrant sentiment helped elect Trump: the most consistent chant at his rallies was "Build the wall!:" He moved swiftly to make good on these campaign promises, issuing executive orders that call for a wall at the U.S.-Mexico border, a selective travel ban, and stripping federal funding from sanctuary cities. The orders have unleashed fear in immigrant communities in light of the wider latitude given to enforcement officials. They expand those targeted for deportation to include anyone immigration officers judge to pose a risk to public safety or national security. Immigration agents have stepped up raids on homes and workplaces to arrest hundreds of undocumented immigrants in several major cities across the country. These moves threaten to harm already

---

[84] Portions of this article are adapted from Kristin E. Heyer, *Kinship Across Borders: A Christian Ethic of Immigration* (Washington, D.C: Georgetown University Press, 2012); and "The Politics of Immigration and a Catholic Counternarrative: A Perspective from the United States," in *Mobilizing Public Sociology: Scholars, Activists, and Latin@ Migrants Converse on Common Ground* (Brill, 2017).

vulnerable asylum seekers and divide families of mixed immigration status. They also endanger the nation's deepest values and its standing in the world. In the name of safeguarding national security, further militarization of the border treats symptoms rather than causes of migration. The U.S. government already spends more on federal immigration enforcement than on all other principal federal criminal law enforcement agencies combined. The death toll of migrants crossing the deserts of the Southwest has steadily mounted even as crossings decline.

I have found such politicized characterizations largely out of step with my own personal encounters with immigrants, and so I would like to begin this chapter with some reflections from the border rather than the White House, as my relationships there have been formative for my own research and folks there continue their outreach and advocacy no matter which direction the political winds blow.

The Kino Border Initiative is a binational project of Jesuit Refugee Service, the California and Mexican provinces of Jesuits, the Missionary Sisters of the Eucharist and two bordering dioceses in Ambos Nogales. During my last visit I spoke with recently deported migrants at their aid center. One gentleman had spent twenty-six of his twenty-seven years in central California, brought there as a one-year-old by his uncle. He had worked harvesting pistachios and almonds to support his wife and four US citizen children without trouble, even on the occasions he could not produce a driver's license for a routine stop. In the past two years each such stop landed him in jail—with the third resulting in deportation to Nogales. He expressed dread at starting over in a country foreign to him. Up the road at Casa Nazareth, we sat with deported women planning to reattempt the journey north in spite of the considerable dangers it posed. The women at the shelter were simply desperate to be reunited with their families in the US. One had worked at a Motel 6 in Arizona for many years supporting her two citizen children on her own after her husband left them; describing her initial reason for migrating from Mexico she said, resigned, "at home you either eat or send your children to school." The Nazareth House residents repeatedly broke into tears as they shared the pain of being separated from their children and their experiences in detention.

Closer to home I encountered undocumented college students in California also struggling with impossible choices. One recounted how a month after her high school graduation, ICE agents with loaded guns, bullet-proof vests, and steel-toed boots surrounded her house and nearly pounded down her front door, demanding to see her. As she tells it: "I came out to the front yard where the head agent asked my name while pulling out handcuffs as if standing in front of some criminal. No GPA or letter of recommendation could save me then. I fell to my knees in front of the agent and began pleading with him to let me stay, telling him I was starting college in a month on a special scholarship. He said, "Fine, I will let you go, but only if you tell me where your dad is." When her mortified mother nodded "yes" to go ahead and tell them, the student revealed the information and ICE left to arrest her dad in front of his boss and coworkers and deport him. The student reflects, "I stood in complete disbelief; I had sold my own dad for an education."[85]

Experiences wherein questions of citizenship and enforcement tactics take on flesh and blood have shaped my reflections about the Christian narrative in light of migration and globalization. The number of people displaced by war, intrastate strife, and human rights violations reached 65.3 million globally last year, a ten percent increase over the previous year. This was the highest increase in the number of displaced persons ever recorded for a single year. Ours is an era of migration. In the United States, the total number of undocumented migrants fell to 11.3 million in 2014, its lowest level since 2003, despite rhetoric about people pouring across the Southern border. When residents are confronted with newcomers, some reactions reflect the nation's historic openness to immigrants, and others, its deep ambivalence about "outsiders." Legitimate concerns regarding disproportionate burdens on local services and the need to set

---

[85] Heyer, *Kinship Across Borders,* Introduction.

workable limits understandably persist. At the same time, mounting threats to human dignity indicate the urgency of the system's genuine overhaul.

For our immigrant nation's "celebratory narrative" underscores ideas like hospitality, liberty, and democracy. We recall Emma Lazarus' "give me your tired, your poor, your huddled masses yearning to breathe free." Yet legislative debates about immigration have historically centered around issues of national security, economic instrumentalism, and social costs rather than human rights. Today policy debates remain framed by a law-and-order lens, which casts unauthorized immigrants as willful lawbreakers, posing national security threats. (Trump adopted a "law and order" mantle throughout his campaign). A criminal rhetorical frame facilitates scapegoating immigrants as threats to the rule of law, without evoking skepticism about outdated policies such as the *considerable* mismatch between labor needs and legal avenues for pursuing work. Recent studies indicate immigrants are less likely to commit serious crimes than U.S. citizens and that higher rates of immigration correlate with lower rates of violent and property crime.

The rule of law rightly occupies a privileged place in our country, yet I was struck during my visit to an Operation Streamline hearing in Tucson, AZ by the sharp contrast between our law-and-order rhetoric on the one hand, and the lack of accountability or transparency in Border Patrol procedures on the other—or the lack of due process afforded immigrant detainees. We watched young men and women shackled at the wrist, midsection, and ankles collectively herded through the legal process, lacking sufficient time with an attorney to comprehend what was happening and several lacking adequate translations. Migrants from Honduras flee a home with the world's highest number of homicides per capita where gang members murder with impunity—the threat driving many such migrants is precisely the breakdown of the rule of law at home.

Another common paradigm deems newcomers' economic threats, whether as a net burden on the tax base or competitors for finite social resources and low wage work opportunities, a perception heightened in times of economic downturn. Beyond studies that consistently show immigrant laborers provide a net benefit to the US economy, the detention industry profits off of irregular migrants and confounds the "economic threat" frame. Elements of the "immigration industrial complex," have become a transnational, multibillion-dollar affair.[86] Private companies house nearly half of the nation's immigrant detainees, compared to about 25 percent a decade ago. Share prices for GEO group and Corrections Corporation of America have risen over 100% since election day 2016, given the president's avowed commitment to increase incarceration of immigrants. Their associates have funneled more than $10 million to candidates since 1989 and have spent nearly $25 million on lobbying efforts.[87]

Finally, the Trump Administration connected these economic anxieties with enduring anxieties over cultural and national identity, casting newcomers as threats in this regard. Tapping into the related anti-immigrant sentiment has provoked the demonization of racial, ethnic, and religious minorities. Bias-related hate crimes surged following the election. Whereas appeals to nostalgia or anxieties about rapid cultural and demographic changes may have remained more hidden in the recent past, a resurgence of white nationalism has brought overt racist and xenophobic fears into the open. Representations of the outsider as a social menace have historically been reinvented in moments of national crisis. Such portrayals of immigrants as public charges and a border out of control powerfully shaped recent measures. On the whole each of these frameworks

---

[86] See Tanya Golash-Boza, "The Industrial Complex: Why We Enforce Immigration Policies Destined to Fail," *Sociology Compass* 3.2 (Feb 2009): Immigration 295–309 for a genealogy of this idea, which alludes to the conflation of national security with immigration law enforcement and "the confluence of public and private sector interests in the criminalization of undocumented migration, immigration law enforcement, and the promotion of 'anti-illegal' rhetoric?" (295).

[87] Michael Cohen, "How Private Prisons Have Become the Biggest Lobby No One is Talking About," *Washington Post* (April 28, 2015) available at https://www.washingtonpost.com/posteverything/wp/2015/04/28/how-for-profit-prisons-have-become-the-biggest-lobby-no-one-is-talking-about/?utm_term=.a8e9c928af1e.

reflect legitimate concerns regarding the contemporary status of immigration, but employed on their own, they serve to distort and eclipse fundamental features of the whole picture.

Hence operative lenses shaping the immigration debate can mask realities and can become surrogates for other cultural and political concerns. The voices of reluctant or desperate migrants rarely register in national debates about border control policy or visa quotas. I open with this context in attempt to shed light on the interests and values that drive immigration policy. If fear and profit largely hold sway, de-humanizing newcomers according to these dominant scripts, I suggest the Christian tradition's commitments shape a different story, a (counter)narrative of our common humanity, our kinship, with implications for a just immigration ethic. Christian understandings of what it means to be human radically critique pervasive exploitation and prevailing immigration paradigms. I would like to outline how insights from Scripture and the Catholic social tradition challenge dangerous myths that enable exclusion and abet division.

Certainly, the story of the Jewish and Christian pilgrim communities is one of migration, diaspora, and the call to live accordingly. Indeed, after the commandment to worship one God, no moral imperative is repeated more frequently in the Hebrew Scriptures than the command to care for the stranger.[88] Despite convenient amnesia in our own nation of immigrants, "it was Israel's own bitter experience of displacement that undergirded its ethic of just compassion toward outsiders: 'You shall not wrong or oppress a resident alien, for you were aliens in the land of Egypt.' (Exod. 22:21)."[89] When Joseph, Mary,

---

[88] William O'Neill, S.J., "Rights of Passage: The Ethics of Forced Displacement," *Journal of the Society of Christian Ethics* 127:1 (Spring/Summer 2007). O'Neill cites W. Gunther Plaut, "Jewish Ethics and International Migrations," *International Migration Review: Ethics, Migration and Global Stewardship* 30 (Spring 1996): 18–36 at 20–21. For a comprehensive discussion of New Testament themes related to migration, see Donald Senior, "'Beloved Aliens and Exiles'?" New Testament Perspectives on Migration," Daniel G. Groody and Gioacchino Campese, *A Promised Land, A Perilous Journey: Theological Perspectives in Migration* (Notre Dame, IN: University of Notre Dame Press, 2008) 20–34.

[89] Ched Myers and Matthew Colwell, *Our God is Undocumented* (Maryknoll, NY: Orbis, 2012) 15.

and Jesus flee to Egypt, the émigré Holy Family becomes the archetype for every refugee family.[90] In Matthew's gospel "Jesus begins his early journey as a migrant and a displaced person—Jesus who in this same gospel would radically identify with the 'least' and make hospitality to the stranger a criterion of judgment (Matt. 25:35)."[91] Patterns of migration across scripture do not readily resolve complex modern dilemmas. Yet scripture shapes moral perception. By engaging the voice of scripture in a manner that dislocates dominant frameworks of interpretation we become attuned to how our perspective impacts our moral response and how scripture might enhance our perceptive imagination.

So, if the conventional politics of immigration are driven in large part by instrumental values, how might a scriptural of politics of immigration shape a Christian counternarrative? One of the most persistently recurrent themes in Scripture is justice and compassion for the vulnerable.[92] The Prophets repeatedly connect bringing justice for the poor to experiencing God. Concern for the economically vulnerable echoes throughout the New Testament as well, particularly in the Gospel of Luke, which depicts Jesus being born in a stable among mere shepherds and as inaugurating his public ministry in terms that emphasize his mission to bring good news to the poor and release the oppressed. New Testament scholar Donald Senior notes that in "the overall landscape of the gospel stories, the rich and powerful are often 'in place'—reclining at table, calculating their harvest, standing comfortably in the front of the sanctuary, or seated on the judgment seat passing judgment on the crimes of others. The poor, on the other hand, are often mobile or rootless: the sick coming from the four corners of the compass seeking healing; the crowds desperate to hear Jesus, roaming lost and hungry; the leper crouched outside the door."[93] Senior suggests

---

[90] Pope Pius XII, *Exsul Familia* (On the Spiritual Care to Migrants) (September 30, 1952), in *The Church's Magna Charta for Migrants*, ed. Rev. Giulivo Tessarolo, PSSC (Staten Island, N.Y: St. Charles Seminary, 1962), introduction.
[91] Senior, *"Beloved Aliens and Exiles,"* 23.
[92] William Spohn, *Go and Do Likewise: Jesus and Ethics* (New York: Continuum, 2007) 76.
[93] Senior, *"Beloved Aliens and Exiles,"* 27–8.

the mobility and experiences of migrant people "reveal a profound dimension of all human experience" and "challenge the false ideologies of unlimited resources [or] of unconditional national sovereignty," that "plague our contemporary world and choke its spiritual capacity."[94]

Hence whereas the Scriptures do not provide detailed solutions to contemporary economic and social challenges posed by immigration, "for people who turn to the Scriptures for guidance on how to live and what sort of people to become, it is clear they should show a deep concern" for marginalized persons.[95] Biblical justice—which demands active concern for the vulnerable and prophetic critique of structures of injustice[96]—challenges approaches to immigration driven by market or security concerns alone. A key contribution a scriptural imagination offers, then, is to bring perspectives of the most vulnerable and often silenced into the equation.

In Jesus' parable of the Good Samaritan, he identifies neighbor love and just living with care for the vulnerable stranger among us. Recall Jesus reverses the lawyer's expectations with the story of a perceived enemy's loving response to one in need lying in the ditch. Jewish audiences would have been shocked to hear of a discredited priest and a Samaritan exemplar. In the parable the priest and the Levite notice the wounded man yet "keep their distance to avoid any contact that might defile them" Unlike the Samaritan who sees the man as a fellow human being in distress, the others did not allow themselves to be affected by his plight. By sharp contrast, the Samaritan "apprehends the situation as the man in the ditch experiences it" Typical of Jesus' parables where the "extraordinary keeps breaking out of the ordinary," the Samaritan "surpasses the

---

[94] Ibid. 29.

[95] Christopher Vogt, Liturgy, Discipleship, and Economic Justice," in Mark Alman and Catholic Church, ed., *The Almighty and the Dollar: Reflections on Economic Justice for All* (Anselm Academic, 2012).

[96] John R. Donahue, SJ, "The Bible and Catholic Social Teaching: Will This Engagement Lead to Marriage??" in Kenneth R. Himes, Editor, Lisa Sowle Cahill, Charles E. Curran, David Hollenbach, and Thomas Shannon, Associate Editors, *Modern Catholic Social Teaching: Commentaries and Interpretations* (Washington, DC: Georgetown University Press) 15.

care that would be appropriate for a fellow countryman to aid this stranger, who might belong to his ethnic groups' worst enemies."[97] As William Spohn notes, "Jesus stretches the limits of vision and compassion precisely where fear, enmity and inconvenience want to constrict them."[98]

How might this parable where Jesus exposes the lawyer's categories as "too cramped" shape our imagination about immigration? Posing the lawyer's very question of "who is my neighbor?" erects boundaries between members and outsiders. We quickly remove ourselves from the scene to balance (abstract) obligations. Perceptions of immigrants as threats alone significantly influence immigration analyses. This prior question of perception shapes our assessment: whom do we see as the immigrant? Freeloaders who take advantage of American generosity while taking jobs from U.S. citizens? Men cueing up outside Home Depot? Threats to the neighborhood? Outsiders overcrowding our kids' schools? The women I described at Casa Nazaret? The student whose narrative I recounted? If we "see" the face of immigration as "illegal"—anchor babies, forever foreigners—or if we "see" separated mothers, displaced 3rd generation family farmers, taxpayers, honest workers, we pursue different avenues of analysis. Seeing immigrants' humanity as primary does not resolve conflicting claims over stretched resources or absolve cases of immigrant crime. Yet it does foreclose on death-dealing practices and invite us away from simplistic scapegoating. To get at root causes and complex motives, like the Samaritan, we must identify with and become neighbor to the immigrant.[99]

Taking the victim's side as our own enjoins not only compassion but also liberation. Just as the Good Samaritan promises additional recompense to the innkeeper, Christians are called to enter the world of the neighbor and "leave it in such a way that the neighbor is given freedom along with the very help that

---

[97] Spohn, Go and Do Likewise, 90.
[98] Ibid., 91.
[99] Ibid., 91.

is offered."[100] The "unfreedom" of present and would-be migrants pointedly illustrates the urgency of this responsibility. The radical hospitality that tutors our vision does not reduce the immigration paradigm to charity or largesse, or move it out of the inclusive civic conversation, but requires justice.

Immigrants encounter legion forms of injustice: widespread wage theft of day laborers violates fundamental fairness in exchange (commutative justice). The regional juxtaposition of relative luxury and misery while basic needs go unmet challenges basic notions of distributive justice. The nearly 2,000-mile U.S.-Mexico border, spanning six Mexican and four U.S. states, bisects the sharpest divide in average income on the planet. The impact of free trade agreements and utterly outmoded visa policies impede rather than empower persons' active participation in societal life (social justice). A Christian ethic of immigration demands basic, unmet responsibilities in justice, particularly given the role the United States has played in shaping conditions that directly contribute to irregular migration.[101]

Recent measures perpetuate the myth that responsibility for irregular migration lies with border crossers alone. Transnational actors responsible for violent conflict, economic instability or climate change are eclipsed from view, much less blame. Some have proposed an "instability tax" be levied upon private and governmental entities that destabilize refugee-producing regions—whether hedge funds profiting off of commodity-trading in African minerals or weapons manufacturers profiting from selling arms to the Middle East, or multinationals

---

[100] John R. Donahue, *The Gospel in Parable* (Philadelphia: Fortress Press, 1988) 133. I am indebted to Christopher Vogt's work for this reference.

[101] John J. Hoeffner and Michele R. Pistone, "But the Laborers Are ... Many? Catholic Social Teaching on Business, Labor and Economic Migration," in *And You Welcomed Me* 55–92, at 74. For an excellent discussion of such connections see William R. O'Neill, S.J., "Anamnestic Solidarity: Immigration from the Perspective of Restorative Justice?" paper delivered at the 2009 Catholic Theological Society of America Halifax, Nova Scotia (June 5, 2009). William O'Neill, "Anamnestic Solidarity.?" See also Kristin Heyer, A Response to "Restorative Justice as a Prophetic Path to Peace??" Plenary Address by Stephen J. Pope, *Catholic Theological Society of America Annual Proceedings* 65 (2010).

who profit from degrading or destabilizing poor nations.[102] In terms of the proposed border wall, the inability of small family farmers in Mexico to compete with agricultural subsidies implicates taxpayers to their north. An immigration ethic attentive to structural justice demands the national and global community resist a "crisis management" approach in favor of honest, contextual assessments of what enduring patterns the crises reveal. Justice for immigrants will not be achieved by pursuing market or security interests alone.

Hence attitudes and policies that compel and then punish irregular migration are profoundly at odds with Christian commitments. In particular, the tradition's understanding of human rights and the political community squarely challenges the fact that the vast majority of contributing and vulnerable migrants remain excluded from a viable, timely path to citizenship and its protections.[103] Undocumented immigrants remain deprived of the primary good of membership, in Hannah Arendt's terms, "right to have rights."[104]

Flowing from its Scriptural "optic nerve of compassion," the Catholic social tradition champions robust rights for immigrants in its documents, outreach, witness, and advocacy. The Mexican and US bishops' joint pastoral, "Strangers No Longer: Together on the Journey of Hope," called for the United States and Mexico to address root causes of and legal avenues for migration and to safeguard family unity; by contrast, border enforcement has remained the

---

[102] Ian Almond, "The Migrant Crisis: Time for an Instability Tax??" *Political Theology Today* (September 22, 2015) available at http://www.politicaltheology.com/blog/the-migrant-crisis-time-for-an-instability-tax/.

[103] Pope Pius XII, *Exsul familia (On the Spiritual Care to Migrants)* August 1, 1952 in *The Church's Magna Charta for Migrants*, ed. Giulivo Tessarolo, PSCC (Staten Island, N.Y: St. Charles Seminary, 1962); Pope John XXIII, *Pacem in terris* (April 11, 1963) http://www.vatican.va/holy_father/john_xxiii/encyclicals/documents/hf_j-xxiii_enc_11041963_pacem_en.html; Pope Paul VI, *Populorum progressio* (March 26, 1967) http://www.vatican.va/holy_father/paul_vi/encyclicals/documents/hf_p-vi_enc_26031967_populorum_en.html; Second Vatican Council, *Gaudium et spes*, 69, 71 see also Catechism of Catholic Church, 240.

[104] See Hannah Arendt, *The Origins of Totalitarianism* (New York: Harcourt, Brace & World, 1966), chapter 9.

primary focus in the US context over the subsequent decade.[105] Consequent deportation-by-attrition practices and removal quotas have nevertheless failed to resolve the problem of a significant undocumented presence. The global phenomenon of human mobility has only intensified: today, one person in nine lives in a country where international migrants comprise one-tenth or more of the total population.[106]

A Christian immigration ethic is grounded in its vision of the person as inherently sacred and made for community. All persons are created in the image of God—loved into being by God—and therefore worthy of inherent dignity and respect. Whereas this vision does not compromise autonomy, it understands humans as profoundly interdependent—to be a person is to be in relationship. Hence human rights are claims to goods necessary for each to participate with dignity in community life.[107] Catholic principles of economic and migration ethics protect not only civil and political rights, but also more robust social and economic rights and responsibilities. These establish persons' rights not to migrate (fulfill human rights in their homeland) and to migrate (if they cannot support themselves or their families in their country of origin).[108] This vision of the person is not fundamentally at odds with our national narrative at its best. As Sr. Simone Campbell put it during NETWORK Social Justice Lobby's "Nuns on the Bus" tour, "fear is crippling us and promoting an unpatriotic lie of individualism…after all the Constitution begins 'We the People,' not 'We who got here first,' or 'We the owners of businesses' or even 'We the citizens.'" She

---

[105] United States Conference of Catholic Bishops and *Conferencia del Episcopado Mexicano*, "Strangers No Longer: Together on the Journey of Hope?" (Washington, D.C.: USCCB, 2003).

[106] Forty years ago, the ratio was 1:29; see Aaron Terrazas, *Migration and Development: Policy Perspectives from the United States* (Washington, D.C.: Migration Policy Institute, 2011): 1; available at: http://www.migrationpolicy.org/pubs/migdevpolicy-2011.pdf (accessed July 17, 2012).

[107] Michael J. Himes and Kenneth R. Himes, *Fullness of Faith: The Public Significance of Theology* (New York: Paulist Press, 1993), 46.

[108] See Pope John XXIII, *Pacem in terris* (April 11, 1963) no. 106. All encyclical citations are taken from David J. O'Brien and Thomas A. Shannon, *Catholic Social Thought: The Documentary Heritage* (Maryknoll, NY: Orbis, 1992), unless otherwise indicated. See also "Strangers No Longer," 34–5.

worried the nation would lose its democracy if residents could not return to living in community.

Once people do immigrate, the Catholic tradition profoundly critiques patterns wherein stable receiving countries accept the labor of millions without offering legal protections. Such "shadow" societies risk the creation of a permanent underclass, harming both human dignity and the common good. From Pope Leo XIII's 1891 warnings against employers' exploitation through Pope Francis' condemnations of harmful global economic practices, the protection of human dignity has remained the central criterion of economic justice. The tradition makes clear that "every economic decision and institution must be judged in light of whether it protects or undermines [human dignity] realized in community."[109] Pope John Paul II condemned the exploitation of migrant workers based on the principle that ". . . capital should be at the service of labor and not labor at the service of capital." This idea that the economy should serve the person raises serious concerns not only about the freedom of markets compared to people, but also about the significant financial stakes in the broken immigration system—detained immigrants fill beds, deportations fill private buses.

So, a counter-narrative of economic ethics critiquing global dynamics that allow capital and goods and information to flow freely across borders but not laborers also shapes a Christian ethic of migration. Pope Francis has been outspoken about the dictatorship of faceless economies; his image of humans as commodities in a throwaway culture[110] particularly resonates with vulnerable migrant workers' experiences. The Southern Poverty Law Center's interviews

---

[109] National Council of Catholic Bishops, "Economic Justice for All: Pastoral Letter on Catholic Social Teaching and the U.S. Economy Issued by the National Conference of Catholic Bishops, November 13, 1986?" (Washington, D.C.: the United States Conference of Catholic Bishops Inc., 1986), nos. 1, 14.

[110] Pope Francis, "Address to the New Non-Resident Ambassadors to the Holy See," May 16, 2013 available at http://www.vatican.va/holy_father/francesco/speeches/2013/may/documents/papa-francesco_20130516_nuovi-ambasciatori_en.html (accessed June 1, 2013).

with undocumented women across sectors of the food industry indicate respondents overwhelmingly report feeling like they are "seen by employers as disposable workers with no lasting value, to be squeezed of every last drop of sweat and labor before being cast aside."[111]

The tradition explicitly protects the basic human rights of undocumented migrants in host countries in light of longstanding teachings on human and workers' rights, which do not depend on citizenship status.[112]

With 66 percent of undocumented immigrants in the United States having lived here for over ten years and 2 million undocumented students in our primary and secondary schools, a "double society" increasingly threatens the common good: "... one visible with rights and one invisible without rights."[113] Obstructing viable paths to legalization for the majority of immigrants welcomed in the marketplace but not the voting booth, college campus, or stable workplace risks making permanent this underclass of disenfranchised persons, undermining not only Christian commitments but also significant civic values and interests. Ultimately an approach rooted in human rights championed by Catholic commitments must both reduce the need to migrate, and protect those who find themselves compelled to do so as a last resort.

---

[111] 150 women were interviewed by Southern Poverty Law Center (SPLC) who worked in the U.S. food industry in Arkansas, California, Florida, Iowa, New York, and North Carolina (all without documents at the time or at some point). The interviews were conducted from January—March 2010. See Southern Poverty Law Center, "Injustice on Our Plates: Immigrant Women in the U.S. Food Industry," 23, 63.

[112] Pope John Paul II's *Ecclesia in* America "reiterates the rights of migrants and their families and the respect for human dignity 'even in cases of non-legal immigration.?" *Ecclesia in America* (Washington, D.C> USCCB, 1999), no. 65. Over recent decades social encyclicals have enumerated migrant rights to life and a means of livelihood; decent housing; education of their children; humane working conditions; public profession of religion; and to have such rights recognized and respected by host of government policies. See 1969 Vatican *Instruction on Pastoral Care* (no. 7); 1978 *Letter to Episcopal Conferences* from the Pontifical Commission for the Pastoral Care of Migrant and Itinerant peoples (no. 3); Pope Paul VI, *Octogesima adveniens* (no. 17); Pope John XIII, *Pacem en terris* (no. 106); National Council of Catholic Bishops, *Resolution on the Pastoral Concern of the Church for People on the Move* (Washington, D.C.: USCC, 1976) and endorsed by Pope Paul VI; and "Strangers No Longer," no. 38.

[113] National Conference of Catholic Bishops, *Together a New People, Pastoral Statement on Migration and Refugees*, November 8, 1986, p.10.

Pope Francis has emphasized solidarity with migrants, whether in first visit outside Rome as Pope to the island of **Lampedusa**—a gateway to Europe for Africans fleeing violent conflict and dire poverty—or his lived example returning from Lesbos with refugee families. He has lamented a "globalization of indifference" that leads to the tragedies of migrants' manipulation and their deaths. His attention to the anesthetizing effects of such indifference illuminates the structures and attitudes that harm immigrants in terms of social sin. At the border mass he celebrated in Juárez in 2016, he also spoke of tears that purify our gaze and enable us to see the cycle of sin into which very often we have sunk; tears he said can soften our hardened attitudes opening us to conversion.

Pope Francis reminds us that sin is not merely a private transaction. He highlights the impact of social sins through our participation in harmful structures. Distinct elements of social sin—dehumanizing trends, unjust structures, and harmful ideologies—shape complex dynamics that perpetuate inequalities. Whether in forms of cultural superiority or profiteering, social inducements to personal sin in the immigration context abound. Social sin indicates how powerful narratives casting immigrants as threats or "takers" are connected to collective actions or inaction that impact migration (like votes in a presidential election or Congressional failures to pass comprehensive reform). Portraying immigration through a lens of individual culpability obscures these multileveled dynamics at play. At a more subtle level than overt xenophobia, a consumerist ideology shapes citizens' willingness to underpay or mistreat migrant laborers either directly or through indirect demand for inexpensive goods and services. A preoccupation with *having* over *being* can impede solidarity with immigrants as much as distorted nationalism: it shapes loyalties, frames questions, informs votes.

As unaccompanied women undertake these journeys in increasing number—about half of migrants worldwide are female—they face *unique* threats, from sexual assault by smugglers and officials, to harassment on the job, to manipulation in detention facilities. Less likely to qualify for employment-based immigration than men, the majority of migrant women work in unregulated jobs in the informal sector. Whereas undocumented immigrants earn lower wages than citizens in the same jobs, women routinely earn less than their male counterparts. Undocumented women are often perceived by predators as "perfect victims" of sexual assault: they remain isolated, uninformed about their rights, and are presumed to lack credibility.[114] Women farm workers hide their gender with baggy clothing and bandanas to deter assault: 80% of women of Mexican descent working in California's Central Valley report experiencing sexual harassment as compared to 50% of all women in the U.S. workforce, who experience at least one incident.[115]

Beyond well-founded fears that reporting abuses will risk job loss and family separation via deportation, such women lack access to legal resources and face language barriers and cultural pressures.[116] Many remain indebted to their *coyotes* (smugglers) and because they understand that immigration officials collaborate with law enforcement, they rarely seek help from the latter. Migrant women frequently cite family reunification as their primary motive for migrating. Today more than 16 million people in the United States live in mixed status families (undocumented parent with US citizen children, e.g.). In the aftermath of detention or deportation, families face major economic instability, and children suffer poor health and behavioral outcomes.

In spite of immigrants' courage and resilience, many of these patterns obscure their full humanity as spouses, parents, and children. Families comprise our most intimate relationships such that protracted separation threatens our very human subjectivity. Policies that undermine family unity frustrate this core relationally and harm the common good. Beyond a critique of economic idolatry,

---

[114] Randy Capps, Michael Fix, Jeffrey S. Passel, Jason Ost, and Dan Perez-Lopez, "A Profile of the Low-Wage Immigrant Workforce," Urban Institute, Brief No. 4 (November 2003).

[115] Irma Morales Waugh, "Examining the Sexual Harassment Experiences of Mexican Immigrant Farmworking Women," *Violence Against Women* (January 2010) 8.

[116] Ibid., 42.

the sanctity and social mission of the family indicate how conditions that perpetuate family separation undermine the common good. Christian thought integrates a family's intimate communion with its charge to mutually engage the broader social good.[117] Deprivation of dignified labor opportunities and traumatic enforcement mechanisms signify hostile social forces impeding immigrant families' access to social goods. (These too threaten "family values" despite their narrow construal in standard political and religious rhetoric.).

Talking points that highlight scarce resources, scheming lawbreakers, or demographic threats fail to register the social contexts that compel migration and its harmful consequences: ruptured family lives, border deaths, and gender-based violence. Christian understandings of economics, human rights, and the social mission of the family issue a prophetic immigration ethic. In contrast to the reductive sound bites and fear mongering that dominate our airwaves, pursuing justice in terms of the common good reorients contested political and social questions. A culture in which "good fences make good neighbors" either due to isolationist fears or on our campuses due to intellectual wariness significantly hinders deliberative engagement about common goods. Whereas fear of the other is easily mass-marketed, mutual understanding across difference can be harder to come by and engender. I conclude with two signs of hope in this regard.

First, Pope Francis' ongoing witness to encounter and solidarity. Beyond his powerful personal witness—in addition to the Lesbos and Lampedusa examples, we might recall his washing the feet of Muslim, Hindu, and Copt refugees on Holy Thursday—In his historic address to the U.S. Congress, Pope Francis spoke about immigration in our national context. There he summoned listeners to something seemingly far less radical than civic kinship: the Golden Rule. Identifying as a fellow descendant of immigrants from a shared continent,

---

[117] See, e.g., Pope John Paul II's discussions of the intimate link between family and wider society and an option for the poor in *Familiaris Consortio* (November 22, 1981) http://w2.vatican.va/content/john-paul-ii/en/apost_exhortations/documents/hf_jp-ii_exh_19811122_familiaris-consortio.html.

he asked us to identify with the needs and dreams propelling the immigrants traveling north, asking "Is this not what we want for our own children?:" With characteristic directness and clarity, he concluded, "In a word, if we want security, let us give security; if we want life, let us give life; if we want opportunities, let us provide opportunities. The yardstick we use for others will be the yardstick which time will use for us."[118] Pope Francis' abiding solidarity with immigrants throughout his papacy and his unwavering attention to ideologies that inhibit such kinship offer us a way forward.

Pope Francis' own dialogue with the "existential extremities" paves this way. His expressed preference for a street-bound over a risk-averse and "self-referential" church also provides an apt orientation, for Christian immigration ethics is fraught with risks: its "subversive hospitality" risks making conversation partners uncomfortable (whether in terms of racial dimensions of inhospitality, disrupting privilege, naming sin) and risks accusations of eroding respect for 'rule of law.' Preoccupation with safeguarding against such risks impedes a culture of encounter and ongoing conversion by the suffering and resilience of those at various borders.

Finally, I share testimony from a recent graduate of my former university (Santa Clara), José Arreola, who spoke out courageously on public radio a few summers ago in a series called "My Life is True."

We had to decide whether we were going north or south to get into California. My friend decided it was best to go south, to avoid a big snowstorm up north. But south would take us through Arizona. I really, really didn't want to go through Arizona.

I got more and more nervous. I felt paralyzed. My friend kept asking me what my problem was. Finally, I told him: I'm undocumented. I came to the United States when I was three with my family. And Arizona had just passed a

---

[118] Address of Pope Francis to the Joint Session of the U.S. Congress, September 25, 2015.

law that gave police officers the authority to check peoples' immigration status. If we got stopped in Arizona, I could be detained and deported.

My friend is white. He comes from a really privileged, upper-class background. He attended a private high school, then Santa Clara University, with me. I went on scholarship. Politically, he sees things a little differently than I do. We've had our disagreements.

He was quiet for a while.

Then, he barraged me with questions. I answered the best that I could.

Silence again.

Then he told me about his grandfather, how he hadn't been able to find work in Ireland, so he decided to hop on a fishing boat, and get off in New York. He worked as a janitor, without citizenship. Now his son, my friend's father, is a high-ranking bank executive.

The whole time, through Arizona, my friend drove, like, 50 miles an hour. He didn't even wanna change lanes. He told me he wasn't gonna lose his best friend. He wasn't gonna let that happen.

The immigration debate became real to my friend in the car that day. We had a very different conversation than the one politicians are having right now. The minute actual undocumented immigrants are included, the conversation changes.

Now, I'm completely open about my status. I'm still afraid. Conversations don't always go well. And it's always a risk. But as long as I remain in the shadows, I will never really get to know you, and you will never really know me.[119]

José's courage, together with the resilience of so many others, witnesses to enduring hope. Christians are called to live in anticipation of a new heaven and a new earth and cooperate with the abundance of life already inaugurated. Taking the migrant's side as our own changes our perception with implications for political reforms, ecclesial practices, even university pedagogies. Amid the pervasive misinformation that cloud the exploitation of immigrants, a Catholic ethic of kinship across borders offers guideposts along the journey from exclusion to solidarity. We who are "settled" must remember that even remaining adrift in a sea of indifference is a privilege.

Whereas a Christian immigration ethic requires more than a policy response, it necessarily entails attention to the politically possible in light of the stakes of ongoing suffering. At a concrete level, justice requires, negatively, that countries refrain from creating or substantially contributing to situations that compel people to emigrate and that host countries refrain from exploiting or extorting undocumented laborers. Positively, receiving immigrants fleeing situations of dire economic need, offering citizenship protections to those they do employ, and developing policies that reflect actual labor needs and hiring practices and protect family unity are obligations in justice. Given these demands of justice, the United States has obligations to redress its role in abetting irregular migration and to offer those who live and work within its borders a viable path to earned legalization. Care must be taken that reform efforts do not accomplish greater justice for new immigrants at the expense of low-wage native-born

---

[119] José Arreola, **"Get to Know Me,"** National Public Radio /KQED Radio (Fri, Jul 8, 2011, 7:35 AM). Audio version in Arreola's voice available at http://www.kqed.org/a/perspectives/R201107080735 (accessed July 8, 2011). See also José Antonio Vargas, "My Life as an Undocumented Immigrant," *New York Times* (June 22, 2011) for the Pulitzer Prize winner's revealing narrative about his own life in the United States without legal documents.

workers. Solutions that "raise the floor" for all workers must be sought. An approach rooted in Christian commitments must both reduce the need to migrate and protect those who find themselves compelled to do so as a last resort. Safeguarding justice and compassion for immigrants will require lasting commitment over the long haul no matter the direction political winds blow.

CHAPTER FIVE

El Espíritu Migratorio: Toward a Prophetic Pneumatology in the World Christian Movement

Pablo A. Jiménez, Emmett G. Price III, and Peter Goodwin Heltzel

"God leads me beside still waters…" (Psalm 23:2b)

The U.S. border with Mexico has become a contested zone of state-sanctioned violence, revealing migration as a moral crisis and the vulnerability of poor immigrants from Latinx people countries as a moral crisis. Mass migration because of economic displacement, political instability, and environmental devastation (among other reasons) is changing the face of our cities, churches, and world. In our Age of Migration, it is vital that Christian theologians and ethicists reflect on the personal, spiritual, and social complexities of the lives of the migrants that God has called us to care for as we honestly engage the migratory experiences in our own lives.

The lens of migration provides the opportunity for the development of new collaborative projects in constructive theology in the third millennium. For example, Puerto Rican theologian Elaine Padilla and Vietnamese theologian Peter C. Phan collaborated in co-editing a three-volume work on Theology and Migration in World Christianity (2013–2016), focusing on contemporary issues,

Abrahamic religions, and global migration.[120] God the Migrant ("Deus Migrator"), as Peter C. Phan names God, is leading a missional movement in the world and has called us to be co-workers in God's struggle for faith-rooted justice with love.[121] Since God is on the move, Christians are called to offer our gifts and graces to strengthen the missional witness of a migratory church.

While Peter C. Phan writes as a first-generation Vietnamese migrant to the United States at the end of the Vietnam War, Elaine Padilla writes as a member of the Puerto Rican diaspora. Padilla offers a glimpse of her existential struggle as an exile in her own land, seeking to negotiate two worlds as a Puerto Rican woman who lives in California:

> As a Puerto Rican, I am after all a US-born citizen and can thus claim to be at home anywhere in the United States. Nevertheless, I experience profoundly the sense of being "not-at-home," of being "outside a place" (ek), or of being in "no place." At every first meeting with someone new, I have to provide an explanation of my being, and thus of my home. My accent, my last name, my facial expressions, and body movements, the whole of who I am gives me away. I am Latina, Puerto Rican, Other. I am in exile. But exile is also a posture I choose to take, not only for myself but also on behalf of all those who migrate.[122]

When stating "I am Latina, Puerto Rican, Other. I am in exile," Padilla bravely acknowledges the state of exile that Puerto Ricans and other migrants experience as they struggle to survive. She goes on to contend that exile is a political posture that she has intentionally chosen to take to embody solidarity with "all those who migrate" Prophetic theologies of migration are holistic with both a personal and political dimension.

---

[120] Elaine Padilla and Peter C. Phan, eds. *Contemporary Issues of Migration and Theology* (New York: Palgrave/Macmillan. 2013); *Theologies of Migration in the Abrahamic Religions* (New York: Palgrave/Macmillan, 2014); and *Christianities in Migration* (New York: Palgrave/Macmillan, 2016).
[121] Peter C. Phan, "Deus Migrator – God the Migrant: Migration Theology and Theology of Migration," *Theological Studies* 77/4 (November 2016): 845-868.
[122] Elaine Padilla, "Border-Crossing and Exile: A Latina's Theological Encounter with Shekhinah," *Cross Currents*, 60:4 (December 2010): 526-548, quote on 528.

Building on the solid theoretical foundation laid by Padilla and Phan, we seek to develop a prophetic intercultural pneumatology in world Christian context. When we imagine the Holy Spirit through a migratory lens, *El Espíritu Migratorio* ("the Migratory Spirit") offers an illuminating perspective on the movement of God's Spirit throughout redemptive history and in the mission of the church today. As we develop our constructive pneumatology, we narrow the scope of our chapter by focusing our biblical pneumatology on the book of the Acts of the Apostles and our historical analysis on manifestations of *El Espíritu Migratorio* in three migrations: African/African American; Anglo/Irish; and Latinx/Puerto Rican, drawing out implications for prophetic missiology in the World Christian Movement. *El Espíritu Migratorio* is the merciful presence of God manifest in the lives of migrants in our arduous journey toward justice, love, and life.

El Espíritu Migratorio: A Constructive Proposal

Prophetic pneumatology is a source of spiritual and social renewal in the World Christian movement today. Puerto Rican Pentecostal theologian Eldin Villafañe's landmark book *The Liberating Spirit: Toward a Hispanic American Pentecostal Social Ethic* contends that the Holy Spirit is actively working to manifest the redemption and liberation of Jesus Christ in both the personal and social dimensions of our lives together.[123] A manifesto in *teología evangélica de la liberación* ("Evangelical Theology of Liberation"), Villafañe's *The Liberating Spirit* is emblematic of a vibrant tradition of evangelical liberation theology that our own constructive migratory pneumatology continues.

Building on Villafañe's evangelical liberationist vision, we contend that Spirit-led improvisational collaboration for the common good is integral to

---

[123] Eldin Villafañe, *The Liberating Spirit: Toward a Hispanic American Pentecostal Social Ethic* (Grand Rapids: Eerdmans, 1993); El Espíritu Liberador: Hacia una ética social pentecostal hispanoamericana (Grand Rapids: Nueva Creación/Eerdmans, 1996).

teología evangélica de la liberación. *"Following Jesus who loved the poor, evangelical theologians of liberation proclaim and embody Christ's righteous reign through joining the liberating Spirit in seeking justice, embodying love, and walking humbly with our Lord (Micah 6:8),"* we write in our paradigmatic article "Lean into Liberation Love: The Origins of Evangelical Liberation Theology at Gordon-Conwell's Center for Urban Ministerial Education."[124] As prophetic evangelicals committed to following the leading of the Liberating Spirit, we faithfully and creatively continue this tradition of prophetic intercultural theology in our Age of Migration.

Following Jesus in Spirit-led transformative mission, teología evangélica de la liberación's primary source is Holy Scripture, placing priority on the perspective of poor people.[125] Beginning on the Black and Brown margins of a white-male-led evangelical modernity, we deploy an anti-racist Afro-Latinx liberationist hermeneutic. We see in the Caribbean the mixing of African, Latinx and Indigenous people and cultures, the creole culinary constitution of a prophetic underground Christian alternative to modernity-coloniality and the white religion of "Christendom" that was exported from Europe.

As evangelical theologians of liberation, we affirm that we are saved by grace through faith in Jesus Christ's redemptive death on a Roman cross and his bodily resurrection on the third day, that we should study the Holy Bible without error in Spirit-led cooperative ways, and that we should unite in integral mission through boldly sharing our faith in Jesus Christ with all the people of the world, joining God in the faith-rooted struggle to liberate the "least of these" (Matt. 25:40, 45). In his Parable of the Last Judgment (Matt. 25:31–46), Jesus

---

[124] Peter G. Heltzel, Pablo A. Jiménez and Emmett G. Price III, "Lean into Liberation Love: The Origins of Evangelical Liberation Theology at Gordon-Conwell's Center for Urban Ministerial Education," *Evangelical Theologies of Liberation and Justice,* edited by Mae Elise Cannon and Andrea Smith (Downers Grove: InterVarsity Press, 2019), 195–234, quote on 206.

[125] On the priority of the perspective of the poor, see Alexia Salvatierra and Peter Goodwin Heltzel, *Faith-Rooted Organizing: Mobilizing the Church in Service to the World* (Downers Grove: InterVarsity, 2014), 42–64.

proclaimed "I was a stranger and you welcomed me" (Matt. 25:35c). When we offer compassionate hospitality to migrants, Jesus says that we are caring for him.

"A jazz-inflected theology of migratory mission is an inspiring trajectory for evangelicalism's prophetic, intercultural, gender-just future," we write.[126] Expanding on our earlier call for "a jazz-inflected migratory mission," we now set out to explore the presence and activity of the Holy Spirit in the lives of migrants. We draw on deep and different wells of cultural tradition—African American, Puerto Rican, and Scotch-Irish—as we discuss three migrations to the US (Black, Latinx and Anglo). A prophetic pneumatology of migration offers an important improvisational paradigm for the stouthearted struggle for justice among migrants at our southern border. Before we begin our historic genealogy of the Holy Spirit's presence and activity, we would like to take a look at the Spirit's movement in Acts of the Apostles, which in our pneumatological imagination we could discuss as Acts of the Holy Spirit through the Apostles.

Acts of the Migrating Spirit

> At Pentecost in Jerusalem, the Holy Spirit was "poured out on all flesh" (Acts 2:17; Joel 2:28).

> When the day of Pentecost had come, they were all together in one place. And suddenly from heaven there came a sound like the rush of a violent wind, and it filled the entire house where they were sitting. Divided tongues, as of fire, appeared among them, and a tongue rested on each of them. All of them were filled with the Holy Spirit and began to speak in other languages, as the Spirit gave them ability" (Acts 2:1–4).

Since the word *pneuma* in Greek means both "wind" and "spirit," the "rushing wind" of Pentecost can be understood as the power of the Holy Spirit.

---

[126] Heltzel, Peter Goodwin, Pablo A. Jiménez, and Emmett G. Price III, "Lean into Liberation Love: The Origins of Evangelical Liberation Theology at Gordon-Conwell Center for Urban Ministerial Education." In *Evangelical Theologies of Liberation and Justice*, 233. (Downers Grove, IL: IVP Academic), 2019.

Sounding like a rushing wind, the Spirit of God swept through the followers of Jesus who were miraculously able to speak in different tongues.

When the Jesus people started speaking in different tongues, they were accused of being drunk with wine (Acts 2:13). Peter, the leader of the disciples, responded to the detractors, explaining what they were witnessing was a revelatory manifestation of the promised presence of God. Peter quotes the Joel Promise that proclaims that God's Spirit would fall on "all flesh" and all would hear the praises of God in their "native languages" (Acts 2:17–21). Affirming the gift of diversity, inclusivity and equity, Pentecost's multilingualism meant that everyone understood that they were beloved children of God without social stratification. Being a child of God affirmed equal access to God, equal proximity to God and equal ability to dialogue with God. Pentecost reveals that the Gospel of Jesus Christ is for everyone as instantiated in the universal outpouring of the Holy Spirit.

In addition to quoting the Joel Promise, Peter cites King David's prophecy of the resurrection of Israel's Messiah (Acts 16:10): "He was not abandoned to Hades, nor did his flesh experience corruption" Drawing Messiah Jesus into the royal Davidic line, Peter proclaims: "This Jesus God raised up, and of that all of us are witnesses. Being therefore exalted at the right hand of God, and having received from the Father the promise of the Holy Spirit, he has poured out this that you both see and hear" (Acts 2:32, 33). The Holy Spirit's powerful audio-visual manifestation at Pentecost is rooted in the resurrection of Jesus who sends the Holy Spirit to earth when he ascends into heaven.

At Pentecost, the church is birthed as a Spirit-led movement of love that is diverse in culture, ethnicity, and languages. Since the people gathered in Jerusalem heard God's love in their "native languages," they were energized and equipped to return to their hometowns and share the Gospel with their people. Thus, we see at Pentecost the mobilization of a migratory movement of prophetic mission.

"Jesus the Spirit Baptizer," as Frank Macchia argues, pours out the Spirit upon his followers at Pentecost so they can speak in many languages.[127] The multilingualism of Pentecost reveals Christ's desire for the good news of the Gospel to be proclaimed in all languages and to all peoples. A fulfillment of the Joel Promise, Pentecost also gives people the gift of prophecy. Both foretelling and forthtelling, prophecy proclaims and ignites the new economy that Jesus has proclaimed in his Kingdom teaching.

With the power of the Holy Spirit, Christ's followers go forth to preach, heal, and break-bread with others. At the "Beautiful Gate," a man is healed who shares his healing in Jesus' name with priestly leaders in Jerusalem who get jealous of Christ's followers and throw them in jail. Throughout the book of Acts Christ's followers are persecuted, maimed, and martyred, beginning with Deacon Stephen. Many of the early Christians were oppressed by the opposition because of their bold Christian witness.

When Philip met the Ethiopian Eunuch, who was perplexed upon reading the Isaiah scroll, he helps patiently teaches him how to exegete the passage (Acts 8:26–40). Through the movement of the Migratory Spirit in this moment of evangelistic conversation, the Gospel is taken with the Ethiopian Eunuch to Africa, which becomes the center of the early Christian movement. While the Migratory Spirit guides the evangelists to certain regions, it also blocks them from entering other regions.

On a missionary journey through Phrygia and Galatia, Paul was prevented by the Holy Spirit from entering Bithynia and received God's revelation in a dream that he needed to preach the word in Macedonia.

> They went through the region of Phrygia and Galatia,
> having been forbidden by the Holy Spirit to speak the word
> in Asia. When they had come opposite Mysia, they
> attempted to go into Bithynia, *but the Spirit of Jesus did not
> allow them;* so, passing by Mysia, they went down to Troas.

---

[127] Frank D. Macchia, *Jesus the Spirit Baptizer: Christology in Light of Pentecost* (Grand Rapids: Eerdmans, 2018).

> During the night Paul had a vision: there stood a man of
> Macedonia pleading with him and saying, "Come over to
> Macedonia and help us" When he had seen the vision, we
> immediately tried to cross over to Macedonia, being
> convinced that God had called us to proclaim the good
> news to them. (Acts 16:6–10)

What is the significance of the "Spirit of Jesus" not allowing Paul and the Jesus people from going into Bithynia? "This is the only time that the Holy Spirit is called 'the Spirit of Jesus,' appropriate in light of [Acts] 2:33 where Peter asserts that Jesus, the risen and exalted messianic son of David, has brought about the fulfillment of the promise of the Spirit of prophecy, bestowing God's Spirit upon his disciples. For Luke, Jesus continues to be involved in the life and ministry of his witnesses (cf. 7:56; 9:5)," writes Eckhard J. Schnabel revealing that the presence of the Holy Spirit is the way that Jesus is engaged in the lives of his people.[128] Christ's reign is advanced and expanded through the migratory movement of the Holy Spirit.

As Paul was obedient to go to Macedonia, he was able to discover the church that he loved the most in Philippi and down by the riverside he met Lydia, who converted to Christ and became a generous donor of Paul's ministry: "The Lord opened her heart to listen eagerly to what was said by Paul" (Acts 16:14). Lydia's open heart created a space for the river of God's grace to grow. Paul's obedience to a divine word in a dream ignited a migration of the Holy Spirit crossing rivers that led into the Mediterranean Sea.

Pentecost is the headwaters of rivers of the Spirit that flow east, west, north, and south. Christianity begins as a prophetic movement of God's Spirit that energized the people of God to courageously follow in the footsteps of Jesus. Throughout the history of World Christianity, we see spiritual renewal flow like a river in the spirit of Pentecost. From the Franciscan Movement of the

---

[128] Eckhard J. Schnabel, *Acts: Exegetical Commentary on the New Testament* (Grand Rapids: Zondervan, 2012), 688.

13th century to the Protestant Reformation in the 16th century to the Missionary Movement in the 19th century, God's Spirit is always moving and migrating like a rolling river into new spaces and places. *El Espíritu Migratorio* flows like a river. When it hits banks or high-county, the Migratory Spirit may twist and turn, but it is ever-flowing to the sea.

Migration within the Black Christian Experience (1441–1800)

While *El Espíritu Migratorio* moves among all people, the movement is distinct depending on the people and places through which the Holy Spirit is moving. Among whites of European descent, positions of political power often provided opportunities for them to move freely about the world that is spatially configured around whiteness. Among peoples of color (not European descended whites) movement was often a form of oppression rooted in racism, white supremacy, and colonization. While white Europeans immigrated to the Americas in search of freedom and fortune, most Africans arrived enslaved, kidnapped or both.

In chains and without dignity, these trafficked black bodies were forced to immigrate and work to build the colonies without being paid for their labor. Initiated by the Portuguese in the 15th century, the transatlantic slave trade was a source of great revenue for white-led trading companies owned by white landowners who purchased, traded, and sold black bodies as commodities throughout the Caribbean as well as south, central and north America. In 1441, Portuguese crusaders captured Africans off the coast of Mauritania, beginning the Atlantic slave trade. In *Romanus Pontifex* of 1455, the Pope declared "the Doctrine of Discovery," giving the Spanish explorers the right to own the land that they discovered if there were no Christians already inhabiting the area.[129]

---

[129] On the doctrine of discovery see Steven T. Newcomb, *Pagans in the Promised Land: Decoding the Doctrine of Christian Discovery* (Golden: Fulcrom, 2008); Mark Charles and Soong-Chan Rah, *Unsettling Truths: The Ongoing, Dehumanizing Legacy of the Doctrine of Discovery* (Grand Rapids: InterVarsity Press, 2019).

Christian theology provided the religious legitimation for colonial exploitation, racial oppression, and land ownership.

From the 16th century, well into the 19th century about 10,000,000 living Africans were transported into the Portuguese, British, Spanish, French and Dutch colonies across the western hemisphere.[130] One such African was Olaudah Equiano, born into the Igbo people of the kingdom of Benin (present day Nigeria) around 1745. According to his 1789 autobiography, *The Interesting Narrative of the Life of Olaudah Equiano*, or Gustavus Vassa, Equiano was kidnapped as an adolescent and taken to Barbados, an island in the West Indies colonized by the British before being sold in the colony of Virginia. By the time of the writing of his life story, Equiano was a free man and a Christian. Reflecting on his life experience through the lens of faith, he wrote, "O, ye nominal Christians! Might not an African ask you, learned you this from your God, who says unto you, Do unto all men as you would men should do unto you?"[131] For Africans who were victims of an enforced migration into slavery in the Americas, the only question they have for white Christians is "Would they love them with compassion, dignity, and fidelity through the struggle, including abolish the shackles of slavery that oppressed them?"

During the first and second Great Awakenings (1740–1820), generations of enslaved Africans converted to Christianity adding to the number of freed Black Christians and enslaved Africa Christians who came from the continent of Africa, the Caribbean, or South and Central America. From this heterogenous amalgamation of Afro-Diasporic converts arose the "invisible institution" from whence the prophetic witness of the Black Christian Experience emerged.

In the antebellum South, slaves often gathered in the woods or "down by the riverside," in order to worship God outside of the surveillance of whites. While experiencing the sacraments and rituals they would also plan, with divine

---

[130] Philip D. Curin, *The Atlantic Slave Trade: A Census* (Madison: University of Wisconsin Press, 1972), 88.

[131] Olaudah Equiano, *The Interesting Narrative of the Life of Olaudah Equiano*, or Gustavus Vassa, the African (Public Domain Books, 2006), 32.

blessing, their escape. Through the various elements of slave worship, including but not limited to singing, dancing, recitation of scriptures, and passionate prayer, the wisdom and courage to maintain a sense of hope was often restored and intensified during these riverside gatherings.

For these black believers, the act of worship was as political as it was spiritual, as they invoked the presence of the God who "delivered Daniel," while simultaneously asking the question, "then why not every man?"[132] The lived, enslaved experience of Black Christians call the question of white supremist infused expressions of Christianity as inferences of "neighborly love" and Christ's commandment to "love one another" were not reflected or experienced in real time given Black Christians subjugation in slavery. Just as God had "troubled the water" of the Red Sea, when Israel escaped from Egypt with the assistance of God, enslaved Christians believed that God would trouble the waters once again to free them of bondage in the American system of dehumanization, human trafficking, and systematic oppression.

Freedom was on the mind, heart, and spirit of Ida Bell Wells, who was born into slavery in Holly Springs, Mississippi in 1862. Freed as a result of the Emancipation Proclamation and orphaned at 16 years-old, Wells would emerge as fierce investigative reporter for *Memphis Free Speech* and *Headlight* newspaper which she co-owned. A renown chronicler of lynchings, Wells was forced to migrate North after death threats by white racists escalated beyond the protection of her community. A sister in the struggle whose prophetic ethic was birthed Black Christian Experience, Wells once wrote, "Somebody must show that the Afro-American race is more sinned against than sinning, and it seems to have fallen upon me to do so."[133] Wells, an unnamed founding member of the

---

[132] The negro spiritual "Didn't My Lord Deliver Daniel?" has no known author and has been arranged for choral and instrumental ensembles by many of the leading composers, arrangers, and choral conductors across the world. The refrain to this popular selection in public domain is: "Didn't my Lord deliver Daniel, deliver Daniel, deliver Daniel; didn't my Lord deliver Daniel, an' why not-a every man."

[133] Dickerson, Caitlin, "Ida B. Wells, Who Took on Racism in the Deep South With Powerful Reporting on Lynching?" The New York Times, March 8, 2018.

National Association for the Advancement of Colored People (NAACP) emerged as a leading civil rights and woman's suffrage leader in Chicago, Illinois. Wells was a colleague of Marcus Garvey, Monroe Trotter, Madame C. J. Walker and Frederic Douglass who publicly spoke highly of her on a number of occasions. Both Equiano and Wells are examples of thousands of Black Christians whose lives reflect the move of God while on the move. Within the Black Christian Experience over the centuries, the central quest for liberation is matched with the question of David when he composed the blues-tinged psalm, that begins, "How long, O Lord? Will you forget me forever? How long will you hide your face from me?[134] In the ever-present journey toward justice, love and the sanctity of life, the Holy Spirit has been a fixture. Sometimes noticeable, but always prevalent.

Before leading the Hebrew children into the promise land, Joshua while mourning the death of his mentor and spiritual father, Moses, was instructed, encouraged, and then exhorted to "be strong and courageous."[135] Joshua's adherence to God's words secured the movement of an entire population of people into a new land that had been promised them generations ago. This same strength and courage provided the pathway for Equiano, Wells, and countless others including Harriet Tubman, Sojourner Truth, Richard Allen, Martin Luther King, Jr., William J. Barber, II and so many other courageous women and men convicted by Jesus' great commandment and his great commission to the Church.

The Anglo-Irish Migration and the Stone Campbell Movement (1801–1900)

Called "America's first Pentecost," the Cane Ridge Revival in Kentucky in 1801 was a moment when Americans, black-and-white, female-and-male,

---

[134] Psalm 13 (ESV).
[135] Joshua 1: 6–7; 9.

slave-and-free, gathered together for a week to worship our Lord. Many Irish and British people (including many Scotts) migrated to the United States during the Great Awakening (1790–1820). It was largely British, Irish, and Scottish pastors who were Baptist, Methodist and Presbyterian who collaboratively planned the Cane Ridge Revival. During this period of revivalism, many African Americans converted to Christianity, transforming American Christianity through redirecting it toward a more prophetic destiny.

One of the organizers of the Cane Ridge Revivals, Barton W. Stone, a Presbyterian pastor with Anglican roots, was an ardent abolitionist who shook hands with associates of Alexander Campbell in 1832 to give birth to the Christian Church (Disciples of Christ). The Stone-Campbell Movement revealed both the promise and the problems with the search for truly prophetic, democratic, and multiracial Christian movement in the United States. While Stone fought against slavery, Campbell was an "anti-slavery slave holder," unveiling the moral contradiction at the heart of white American evangelicalism.

Evangelicalism's white supremacy took social form in its anti-Blackness lodged against enslaved Africans and its anti-Indigenous posture manifest its mistreatment of Native Americas. Two years earlier in 1830, President Andrew Jackson enacted the Trail of Tears—the path walked by members of the First Nations who were forcibly removed from the southeastern United States to the lands west of the Mississippi River.[136]

The Stone-Campbell movement found their voice in a deep concern for the unity of the whole church, yet the moral crisis of slavery remained a problem. Alexander Campbell was a young Irish migrant to the United States. Born in the parish of Broughshane, County Antrim, Ireland on September 12, 1788, Alexander Campbell migrated to the United States when he was 21 years old.

---

[136] See John Ehle, *Trail of Tears: The Rise and Fall of the Cherokee Nation* (New York: Anchor Books, 1988); Cf. Stuart Banner, *How the Indians Lost their Land: Law and Power on the Frontier* (Cambridge: Harvard University Press, 2005); Robert Warrior, "Canaanites, Cowboys and Indians," *Natives and Christians*. ed. James Treat (New York: Routledge, 1996), 93–100.

Alexander's father Thomas Campbell (1763–1854) had migrated earlier in 1807. After studying theology at the University of Glasgow in Scotland, Alexander Campbell migrated with his mother Jane Corneigie and his siblings in 1809. Their ship, the Latonia, came into port in New York City on September 29, 1809. They traveled to Philadelphia and were reunited with Thomas Campbell in western Pennsylvania. Starting his preaching ministry in 1810, Alexander was ordained by his father Thomas Campbell at the Brush Run Church on January 1, 1812. A fierce theological debater, Campbell founded a journal called the *Christian Baptist* *in* 1823, but the issue that plagued Campbell and the Restorationist movement was the moral contradiction of slavery.

While publicly arguing against the institution of slavery, Alexander Campbell was a slave owner. In 1827 Campbell purchased two brothers, James and Charley Pool, from a Methodist preacher. When the two enslaved brothers turned twenty-eight years old, Campbell set them free, a practice he would continue with other slaves that he owned. While Campbell spoke out against slavery in the early 1830s, he began to moderate his position in the 1840s and 1850s in order to maintain unity in the growing Stone-Campbell Movement, especially seeking to appease Southern congregations who had slave-holding members. Like many Reformed theologians in the Antebellum Period, including Princeton theologian Charles Hodge (1797–1878), Alexander Campbell stood in the precarious and problematic position of being an anti-slavery salve holder. Seeing the majority of the verses on slavery in the Bible condoning the practice of slavery made Charles Hodge and Alexander Campbell ambivalent about the abolition movement, squelching their moral courage to set their slaves free.

Alexander Campbell argued that the Bible "sanctions the relations of master and slave."[137] While Campbell thought "slavery as practiced in any part of the civilized world is inexpedient," he decided not to become an abolitionist

---

[137] Alexander Campbell, "Our Position to American Slavery—No. 7," *Millennial Harbinger*, Third Series, 2/5 (May 1845), 236–237. *Emphasis Original.*

because he viewed their organizing tactics as militant and divisive.[138] Campbell wrote "I am neither the advocate nor the apologist of American or any other kind of slavery....I have always been anti-slavery, but never an abolitionist."[139] To be an anti-slavery thinker who owns slaves is the height of moral hypocrisy, a plight that Campbell shared with Thomas Jefferson.[140]

Disciples missionary work among Latinxs shares the same inconsistencies. In the early 19th century, Texas was part of Mexico. Illegally, people from the growing United States moved to Texas, changing the population of the territory. These colonists joined forces with Tejanos (which were culturally Mexicans) against Mexican rule, causing the Texas Revolution (1835–36). Texas gained independence but, unable to defend itself against constant attacks by the Mexican Army, sought annexation to the United States. Texas obtained statehood in 1845.

The Disciples movement was well represented among the Texan colonists.[141] However, in the 1860's Disciples began missionary work in Mexico, establishing orphanages and planting congregations. Eventually, this movement also lead to the establishment of the first Spanish-Speaking congregations in Texas around the turn of the century.

These congregations ebbed and flowed depending on two factors. First, on the support of Anglo Disciples pastors and, second, on the migration movement caused by the Mexican Revolution (1910–1920). Pastors who supported ministry with Spanish-speaking people in Texas established missions supported by the Anglo congregations. But whenever these pastors moved to a

---

[138] Alexander Campbell, "View of Slavery," *Millennial Harbinger*, Vol. 2 (1845), 236; Barton W. Stone, "An Humble Address to Christians, on the Colonization of Free People of Color," *The Christian Messenger* 3/8 (June 1829): 198.

[139] Alexander Campbell, "American Slavery," *Millennial Harbinger* (1845): 355.

[140] See Peter Goodwin Heltzel's discussion on Thomas Jefferson and the moral contradiction of American slavery in "Freedom Dreams: Thomas Jefferson, Sojourner Truth, and the Promise of Freedom," Chapter 4 in *Resurrection City: A Theology of Improvisation* (Grand Rapids: Eerdmans, 2015), 73–89.

[141] See Daisy Machado, *Of Borders and Margins: Hispanic Disciples in Texas, 1888–1945* (New York: Oxford University Press, 2003).

new congregation, most of those Spanish-speaking missions closed. That explains why several Latinxs congregations, like the Christian Church in San Benito, opened and closed several times in their early years.

Something similar occurred in the case of the Puerto Rico. The first Disciples missionaries arrived at the Island in 1899 after Spain ceded Puerto Rico and other territories to the United States as a consequence of losing the Hispanic American War of 1898. Like most mainline US denominations, missionary work in Puerto Rico was motivated by the incorporation of the Island to the United States, not by a general interest in evangelizing Spanish-speaking people in the Caribbean.

In an age of egalitarian political values undergirded by an Enlightenment era advocacy of reason and popular education, members of the Stone-Campbell Movement added their perspective to others in the church seeking an end to divisions among Christians, but struggled to overcome the racial divisions between whites and Black, indigenous and the Latinx community. The reason for resistance for true multiracial unity in the Disciples was its formation and complicity within the social sin and idol of what white supremacy.

Whiteness is a fluid category that would gradually expand through the history of migration in the United States. Given America's origins in Europe's colonial expansionism and frontier revivalism, Winthrop D. Jordan argues that after the 1680s 'white' becomes the normative ethnic identity in the United States.[142] Different ethnic groups are designated as white at different moments within American history. For example, when Irish Catholics first arrived in droves during the 1840s as a result of the Irish potato famine, they were not considered white; but with time they, too, would be assimilated into what Matthew Frye Jacobson calls the 'alchemy of whiteness.'[143] Many of the Irish

---

[142] Winthrop D. Jordan, *The White Man's Burden: Historical Origins of Racism in the United States* (London: Oxford University Press, 1974), 52 as quoted by Jennifer Harvey, *Dear White Christians: For Those Still Longing for Racial Reconciliation* (Grand Rapids: Eerdmans, 2014), 51.

[143] Matthew Frye Jacobson, *Whiteness of a Different Color: European Immigrants and the Alchemy of Race* (Cambridge: Harvard University Press, 1998).

men who arrived into ports on the Northeastern Seaboard like New York City, were enlisted in the Union Army, given a rifle and sent south to fight the Confederate Army in the Civil War (1861–1865).

With the Union Army's victory in the Civil War and Abraham Lincoln's Emancipation proclamation that freed enslaved Africans, the Migratory Spirit was manifest as freed African Americans journeyed north to search for a new job, a new life, and a new form of prophetic Christian witness. During the Reconstruction era (1861–1898), the United States faced the challenge of integrating millions of newly liberated African Americans into the political economy. While many African Americans became successful famers, businessmen, and elected officials during this period, white racist vigilantes fought back to shut down their progress, especially down South. In Harlem, Rev. Adam Clayton Powell, Jr. opened the doors of the church for social programs that helped African Americans who migrated to New York City find food, fellowship, and jobs in Central Harlem. East Harlem was a historic Italian neighborhood, but after World War II, it soon became Puerto Rican through a post-war Puerto Rican migration. With Robert Chao Romero, we want to advance the Spirit-shaped holistic vision of the "Brown Church," that includes Puerto Rican Pentecostals.[144]

El Espíritu Migratorio and the Puerto Rican Migration (1940– 1970)

The migration of Puerto Ricans from the island to cities in the United States offers another important example of the *El Espíritu Migratorio* in action. Although some may think that Puerto Rican migration to the United States is a relatively new phenomenon, the first significant waves of migrants from the Island moved to New York in the late 19th century. At the time, Puerto Rican,

---

[144] Robert Chao Romero, *Brown Church* (Downers Grove: InterVarsity Press, 2020).

Dominican and Cuban politicians who advocated independence from Spain organized *La Confederación Antillana* (*The Antillean Confederation*) in New York. Key Puerto Rican leaders, such as Ramón Emeterio Betances, Segundo Ruiz Belvis and Eugenio María de Hostos moved to New York as early as 1869 to work on this important political project.

On August 8, 1899, Hurricane San Ciriaco struck Puerto Rico with winds over 100 miles per hour, causing 3,369 deaths and displacing 250,000 persons. One of the many responses to this tragedy was migration to Hawaii, where around 5,000 Puerto Ricans moved to work on sugar cane and pineapple fields from 1900 to 1905. They moved at a time when United States had not granted citizenship to Puerto Ricans, leaving this immigrant community in legal limbo. Citizenship came in 1917, thanks to the *Jones-Shaforth Act*, better known as the *Jones Act of Puerto Rico*. However, the law did not extend citizenship to Puerto Ricans living in Hawaii. For several years, Hawaiians of Puerto Rican descent lived in legal ambiguity, being considered as citizens for military service, but not for voting.

A Puerto Rican migrant to Hawaii had an enormous impact on the rise of Pentecostalism on the Island of Puerto Rico. A courageous leader in the early Pentecostal movement, Juan L. Lugo,[145] was born in Yauco, Puerto Rico, on October 26, 1890. His family moved to Hawaii in 1900, when he was 10 years old. In 1913, Lugo had a conversion experience and received the baptism in the Holy Spirit shaped by spiritual streams of the Azusa Street Mission and Revival. Filled with the Holy Spirit, Lugo felt called to preach the Gospel as a missionary teacher. Just as Jesus has shared with his disciples that he was *sending them forth* with the power of the Holy Spirit (John 20:21–22), Lugo understood his baptism in the Spirit as empowering him to follow Jesus in the liberating mission of preaching "good news to the poor" (Luke 4:18–19).

---

[145] See the article written by Benjamin Alicea Lugo, a grandson of Juan L. Lugo, titled "El legado de Juan L. Lugo: El Pentecostalismo Puertorriqueño". http://agwebservices.org/Content/RSSResources/El%20legado%20de%20Juan%20L.%20Lugo%20(PDF).pdf (Accessed: September 15, 2019).

With the mentorship of Rev. Francisco Ortiz, Sr., Juan L. Lugo became a candidate for ordained ministry in the Assemblies of God. From Hawaii he moved to California, where he enrolled in a Bible School. Convinced of his call to be a missionary to Puerto Rico, Lugo left California in 1916. After a brief stay in New York, Lugo finally reached Puerto Rico in 1916, where he established congregations for the Assemblies of God. On November 3, 1916, Lugo planted his first Assemblies of God congregation in Ponce, Puerto Rico. Eventually, his missionary work yielded another denomination, *La Iglesia de Dios Pentecostal Movimiento Internacional* or M.I. (*The Pentecostal Church of God, International Movement*), formed by congregations that seceded the Assemblies of God. Lugo also served congregations affiliated to the Church of God (Cleveland) in Puerto Rico.

After bringing the Pentecostal fire to Puerto Rico, Juan L. Lugo shared his Pentecostal spirit with New York City. In 1928 Lugo sent Rev. Thomas Alvarez from Puerto Rico to plant La Iglesia Misionera Pentecostal in Brooklyn. In 1931 Lugo founded "La Sinagoga" Church in East Harlem (Called *El Barrio*). In 1933 a Pentecostal Revival broke out in Puerto Rico, called *El Avivamiento del 33* renewing churches, adding members and challenges to Protestant denominations like the Christian Church (Disciples of Christ) in the United States and Canada. In 1933 a group of Christians were meeting in Calle Comerío Christian Church and the Holy Spirit fell upon them bringing spiritual fervor, evangelistic zeal, and a passion for social transformation.

These courageous Pentecostal Christians would quickly spread their passionate spirituality throughout the Disciples movement in Puerto Rico and plant churches in New York City, like La Hermosa at Duke Ellington Circle, in the intersection of Fifth Avenue and Central Park North. La Hermosa, meaning "The Beautiful Gate" became the mother churches of many Disciples congregations throughout the Northeastern Region.[146] La Hermosa and other

---

[146] Pablo A. Jiménez, "Hispanics in the Movement," in *The Encyclopedia of the Stone-Campbell Movement*, edited by Douglas A. Foster, Paul M. Blowers, Anthony L. Dunnavant, and D. Newell Williams (Grand Rapids: Eerdmans, 2004), 395–399.

Disciples congregations in the New York metro area provided Puerto Ricans a spiritual home where "they can be persons" treated with love and respect.[147] In Puerto Rican congregations, like La Hermosa, Puerto Ricans could sing in Spanish, find jobs, receive legal counsel, make friends, and fall in love.

Within the network of Puerto Rican Disciples congregations, called *La Convención*, there was always a preference for Senior Pastors who were Puerto Rican men who had studied at the Evangelical Seminary of Puerto Rico which was founded in 1919 by missionaries from mainline denominations, including Baptists, Disciples of Christ, Methodists, United Brethren, and Presbyterians. With time, these congregations have become diverse along the lines of the emerging migration patterns to New York City with congregations that include members who are Central Americans, Latin Americans, African Americans and Anglo American.

Within the changing dynamics of the world Christian Movement, Puerto Rico offers an example of "reverse mission" While white missionaries were sent to Puerto Rico in the early 20th century, Puerto Rico became a source of missionaries for Latinx communities in the Northeastern coast of the United States in the second half of the 20th century and early 21st century. The growth of the Puerto Rican missionary movement coincided with an important shift in migrations patterns from the Island to the United States. Four factors contributed to what came to be known as "The Great Migration" of Puerto Ricans to the United States: The Great Depression, World War II, the advent of air travel, and *Operation Bootstrap*.

The Great Depression was a time of economic distress that rocked the United States in the early 1930's. The effects of this season of economic turmoil in Puerto Rico were devastating. Unemployment was rampant and people had little to eat. Understandably, many Puerto Ricans moved to the States, seeking to improve their financial situation.

---

[147] Orlando Costas, *Christ outside of the Gates*, 113.

The United States entered the World War II after the attack on Pearl Harbor, on December 7, 1941. Puerto Rican recruits joined all branches of the US Armed Forces to help advance the U.S. war effort. Many veterans stayed in the US Mainland after the war, while others alternated living in Puerto Rico and the States for months or even years at a time.

Although the *Isla Grande Airport* (now known as the Major Fernando Luis Ribas Dominicci Airport), had been in operation since 1926, in 1945 the Puerto Rican government decided to open a new airport, capable of servicing larger planes. The *Isla Verde International Airport* (now known as the Luis Muñoz Marín International Airport) opened in 1949, serving airlines such as *Pan American World Airways* and *Eastern Air Lines.* Lesser-known carriers, such as *Flying Tigers Airline,* transported seasonal workers to and from the Northeast, where Puerto Ricans provided cheap labor in both urban and rural settings.

The creator of *Operation Bootstrap* (known in Spanish as "Operación Manos a la Obra") was Governor Luis Muñoz Marín. The goal of this initiative was to move the Island away from its agrarian system to an industrial economy, enticing heavy industry—such as oil refineries—to establish operations in Puerto Rico. As part of the program, the Puerto Rican government encouraged displaced farm workers to migrate to the United States.

These four factors—The Great Depression, World War II, the advent of air travel, and *Operation Bootstrap*—explain the growth of the Puerto Rican community during the 1960's and 1970's in the United States, in general, and in the Northeast, in particular. Migration created a distinct Puerto Rican subculture centered in New York. Evangelicalism, Bilingualism, and Salsa music thrived in this community. Second and third generation Puerto Ricans became professionals, earned advanced degrees, and even reached positions in government as we see in the election of Alexandria Ocasio-Cortez as the U.S. Representative for New York's 14th congressional district.

While many migrants who are displaced for humanitarian, political and ecological reasons often end up staying and settling in their host home, Puerto

Ricans are unique because they often embody what Jorge Duany calls a "transient and bidirectional flow" of migration.[148] Instead of "crossing the border" once-and-for-all, they live their lives in continual border crossing back-and-forth. The bidirectional flow has intensified since the aftermath of Hurricane Maria that devastated Puerto Rico in September 2017, as the Puerto Rican diaspora makes frequent trips back to the island to check on loved ones and help in rebuilding efforts and medical missions. Constant movement to-and-from the Island has become a trait of Puerto Rican culture as a whole.

The Puerto Rican Protestant Church, in general, and its Pentecostal movement, in particular, played a key role in the migrant community. Thanks to missionaries such as Juan L. Lugo, Spanish-speaking churches in the Northeastern United States were ready to minister to the incoming migrant waves. Ministers moved from Puerto Rico to the Northeast, establishing new congregations. Puerto Rican Pentecostal ministers, such as Eldin Villafañe, Samuel Cruz, and Samuel Solivan became scholars and helped develop what is now known as Hispanic/Latino or Latinx Theology.

Pentecostalism grew rapidly on the Island and in the Puerto Rican diaspora because Puerto Rican's experiences with the Spirit provided a holistic spirituality that resonated with Puerto Rican's *mestizaje* culture. "Of all Hispanics, the Puerto Rican American is perhaps the most representative of *mestizaje* in the U.S.A. The *mestizaje* of Puerto Ricans is threefold: Spaniard, Amerindian, and African," writes Eldin Villafañe.[149] Puerto Rican's African heritage was central to its explosive growth of Pentecostalism in Puerto Rico. Puerto Rican Pentecostalism grew was "masked Africanism" because Pentecostal worship

---

[148] Jorge Dunay, *The Puerto Rican Nation on the Move: Identities on the Island and in the United States* (Chapel Hill: University of North Carolina Press, 2012), 212 as cited by Elaine Padilla, "The End of Christianity," *Christianities in Migration: The Global Perspective*, edited by Elaine Padilla and Peter C. Phan (New York: Palgrave/Macmillan, 2016), 315.

[149] Villafañe, *The Liberating Spirit*, 58,

resonated with the singing, shouting and music that were existentially familiar to the rituals and cultural forms of their West African religious past.[150]

In sum, Puerto Rican migration is a complex multigenerational, multilingual, and multinational phenomenon, which explains why 5 of the 8 million Puerto Ricans in the world today live in the continental United States, while only 3 million live on the Island. While hurricanes, earthquakes and continual colonial economic exploitation continue to plague the people of Puerto Rico, in the spirit of Pedro Albizu Campos, Puerto Rican and the Puerto Rican Diaspora stands strong. Due to the particular roots of their *mestizaje* ethnicity, Puerto Rican Pentecostal ministers and religious scholars have been in the forefront of faith-rooted organizing, racial reconciliation, and the inclusion of women in ministry.

Latin Jazz as a Sign of a Spirit-led Musical Migratory Missiology

"From the very beginning Christianity was a missionary faith in two ways: apostolic individuals being sent out from a church center *and* migrations of people carrying the cross of Jesus into new cultures and nations," writes Scott W. Sunquist.[151] Just as the early followers of Jesus were *sent out* into new cultures, *El Espíritu Migratorio* has led people to "new cultures and nations," going before them, walking with them, and guiding them toward a prophetic intercultural future. Mission is migratory.

In this chapter, we have sought a process of discerning the movement of the Holy Spirit in the movement of migrants. As Christians have migrated to new countries and cultures, they have played an integral role in the cultivation of a prophetic intercultural vision of Christian faith. With a heart for Christian mission, Pentecostals have seen migrations as a result of socio-economic

---

[150] Samuel Cruz, *Masked Africanisms: Puerto Rican Pentecostalism* (Dubuque, IA: Kendall/Hunt Publishing Company, 2005).

[151] Scott W. Sunquist, *The Unexpected Christian Century: The Reversal and Transformation of Global Christianity, 1900–2000* (Grand Rapids: Baker Books, 2015), 136.

dislocations as a Spirit-sending out to take the Gospel "to the ends of the earth" (Mark 16:15). "If its missionizing heart has driven Pentecostals ever outward from their comfort zones, the result has been literally the globalization of the renewal movement over the last century," writes Amos Yong.[152] Prophetic Pentecostalism at its best seamlessly integrates evangelistic witness with the struggle for freedom amidst the tumultuous mobility of migration.

"Azusa Street was many things, but it was first of all a *Black Church*," writes Dale T. Irvin.[153] Preaching in an old building in Los Angeles, William J. Seymour, a charismatic Black preacher, began a revival that would grow into the Azusa Street Revival and Mission, igniting a global renewal movement; however, the Seymour's successful ministry was resisted by many white Christian leaders including his white teacher Charles Fox Parham who had ties to the KKK. In contrast to what Leslie D. Callahan reveals is Charles Fox Parham's Quest for the Sanctified Body in "Whiteness,"[154] we argue that the migratory spirit moves mightily in the Black and Brown bodies and are committed to their liberation.

Discerning the movement of the Spirit through lens of the Black Christian experience reveals structural inequities that are the result of systemic racism, white supremacy, and European colonization. Music was one way that the Afro-Diaspora resisted racism and colonization. Down in New Orleans, "jazz was born when Creoles and blacks were allowed to integrate in the 1890s and began musically influencing each other."[155] The Creole constitution of Jazz

---

[152] Amos Yong, "The Im/Migrant Spirit: De/Constructing a Pentecostal Theology of Migration," edited by Peter C. Phan and Elaine Padilla, *Theology of Migration in the Abrahamic Religions*, Christianities of the World (New York: Palgrave Macmillan, 2014), 133–53, quote on 135.

[153] Dale T. Irvin, "Meeting Beyond These Shores: Black Pentecostalism, Black Theology, and Global Context," in *Afro-Pentecostalism: Black Pentecostalism and Charismatic Christianity in History and Culture,* edited by Amos Yong and Estrelda Alexander, Religion, Race, and Ethnicity Series (New York: New York University Press, 2011), 233–248, quote on 233. The *Italics* are ours.

[154] Leslie D. Callahan, "Fleshly Manifestations: Charles Fox Parham's Quest for the Sanctified Body," Ph.D. dissertation, Princeton University, 2002).

[155] Peter Goodwin Heltzel, *Resurrection City: A Theology of Improvisation* (Grand Rapids: Eerdmans, 2012), 14.

highlights the Black encounter with Brown folks in the origins of jazz music. Our
mentor in musical migratory missiology is Eldin Villafañe who entered in
dialogue with musical improvisation in his call for a theology of Spirit-led shalom
shaped by the rhythm of "Latin Jazz."

Villafañe suggests that a "jazz-approach" to evangelical theology that
includes an ethic of improvisation provides an important pathway ahead for
liberative theology and practice. In Villfañe's "Salsa Christianity: Reflections on
the Latino Church in the Barrio," he finds a point of contact between the musical
genre of jazz and the Latino Church, representing a mixture of traditions from
different ethnic groups.[156] *El Espíritu Migratorio* created the conditions for Afro-
Diasporic roots of Jazz, bringing together a blending of Black music (slave songs,
spirituals and blues), Latinx music (salsa, samba, and bossa nova) and Anglo
music (European folk music, classical and opera). With their *mestizaje* identity,
Latinx musicians are often able to move fluidly musically through musical form
of jazz forms. If we open our ears, we can hear in "Latin Jazz," rooted in the
struggle of a blues people, the different "cultures and nationalities" of the
Pentecostal Promise. A migratory mission calls us dance to the rhythm of the
river of *El Espíritu Migratorio*.

The Afro-Cuban jazz music of Buena Vista Social Club reveals Black,
Indigenous and Latinx musicians working together to make amazing music. With
a salsa rhythm, blues licks, and Spanish poetic lyrics, Afro-Cuban jazz points
ahead to a more fundamentally just and joyful tomorrow. Latin jazz is a
"prophetic witness," Villafañe writes "to challenge the church to a biblical
posture of 'racial *Shalom*' (peace – with its rich biblical meanings of healing,

---

[156] Eldin Villafañe, "Salsa Christianity: Reflections on the Latino Church in the Barrio."
In *A Prayer for the City: Further Reflections on Urban Ministry* (Austin: Asociación para la Educación
Teológica Hispana, 2001), 35–51. This chapter is based on Eldin Villafañe's keynote address at
an Urban Ministry Symposium at Harvard Divinity School, Cambridge, Massachusetts on
October 15, 1998.

harmony, reconciliation, welfare, wholeness, and justice)."[157] Jazz clubs are transitional spaces, where people of all races can make music, listen to music, and lean into liberating love.

Migratory mission calls the church toward a deeper engagement with culture, especially its musical forms. "Congregational cultural intelligence is a trait that is sorely missing in many churches today," writes Matthew D. Kim. [158] Listening to "Latin Jazz" is one place to start.

"Before this 'Latin Jazz' occurs in our church and in our cities, we need to understand a little of the informing sources of its rhythms. African Americans need to know more about Hispanics, Hispanics need to know more about African Americans. Anglos and others need to know more of both! Understanding our commonalities and differences is prerequisite to reconciliation and celebration writes Villafañe."[159] Through the lens of the Black Christian experience seeking liberation of racial oppression, a "Latin Jazz" approach to migratory missiology, rooted in what Chao Romero calls the "Brown Church" offers a promising intercultural paradigm for Christian witness in the third millennium.

When evangelical churches work collaboratively across the lines of race, we bear witness to the love of God we express in worship; this is not different from love of justice that we embody in our collaborative social action. Open to the Holy Spirit's improvisations, the evangelical movement has a window of witness to lost, hurting and needy world. Led by the Spirit, let's build a better tomorrow for all God's children in our age of Global Cities.

---

[157] Eldin Villafañe, "A 'Latin Jazz' Note: Hispanic and African-American Racial Reconciliation." In *Seek the Peace of the City : Reflections on Urban Ministry*, 53. Grand Rapids, MI: Eerdmans, 1995.

[158] Matthew D. Kim, *Preaching with Culture Intelligence: Understanding the People who Hear our Sermons* (Downers Grove: InterVarsity, 2017), 3.

[159] Eldin Villafañe, "A 'Latin Jazz' Note: Hispanic and African-American Racial Reconciliation," In *Seek the Peace of the City : Reflections on Urban Ministry*, 54. Grand Rapids, MI: Eerdmans, 1995.

Conclusion

In this chapter, we discern the movement of the Holy Spirit in the lives of migrants. Inspired by Peter C. Phan's naming God ("Deus Migrator"), we have sought to strengthen the prophetic pneumatology of Phan's Vietnamese Catholic migratory theology through arguing that the Holy Spirit is the *El Espíritu Migratorio*. Reading Acts as Acts of the Apostles through the Holy Spirit, opens up illuminating sites of revelation through dynamic migratory ministries of the missioners in the early Christian period and today. Like a river, God's migratory spirit flows where it will. Inspired by Robert Chao Romero's genealogy of the tributaries to the river of the "Brown Church," we have sought to chart the flowing river of God's life and love through the migrations of Africans, Anglos and Puerto Ricans. Going before God's migrant people, *El Espíritu Migratorio* gives migrants heart strength to continue to walk on this day, and every day toward brighter, better, and peaceful tomorrow.

Our central claim is *El Espíritu Migratorio* is the merciful power of God is made manifest in the lives of migrants in their journey toward justice, love, and life. Those who oppose merciful migration may be opposing the Spirit of God and all that is good in the world, including every person who is made in God's image. Regardless of race, gender or nationality, God infinitely loves everyone. As ICE (Immigration and Customs Enforcement) continues to separate children from their families, God's Migrating Spirit is moving with them. While we ask, "How much longer, God?" God is asking us "How much longer will Spirit people be silent and inactive?" Let us be bold and courageous as we follow the Spirit, trusting that as we cross over roaring rivers, praying that we and our children don't drown that God is guiding us to leading us "beside still waters..." (Psalm 23:2b)

SECTION TWO

History and Anthropology

CHAPTER SIX

United States Immigration History

Robert Chao Romero

"God blessed them and said to them, 'Be fruitful and increase in number; fill the earth and subdue it'" (Genesis 1:28). As reflected in this passage from the earliest pages of Genesis, God's first command to human beings included the command to "fill the earth," or *migrate*. Since earliest human history, migration has been a fundamental characteristic of what it means to be human, and one might even say that to be human is to migrate. From other passages of Scripture such as Abraham's call to leave his country for the land that God would show him (Gen. 12:1), and the Exodus narrative (Exod. 2–15), we also learn that migration is a fundamental means by which God reveals Himself to humankind. As borne out in many examples from Scripture, *God uses the migration process to extend His grace both to migrants and their host countries.*[160]

In contradistinction to this principle of "migration as grace," we find a second migration-related principle revealed in the pages of Scripture: *Xenophobia, or fear of the foreigner, reflects an individual or nation whose heart has turned from God.* Jesus teaches this principle in Matthew 25 when he states that hospitality towards the "xenos," or stranger, is hospitality towards Jesus Himself (Matt. 25:35), and that rejection of the foreigner is rejection of Jesus Himself (Matt. 25:43). On a

---

[160] For a detailed discussion of the biblical principle of "migration as grace," see, Robert Chao Romero, "Migration as Grace," *International Journal of Urban Transformation*, Volume 1, 10–35, October 2016.

national level, this principle is most clearly articulated in the Exodus narrative in which the ancient Egyptians enslaved the descendants of Jacob out of alleged fears of national security in a potential time of war (Exod. 1:8–14).

It is vital to note that such exclusionary nationalism and xenophobia is not limited to any particular ethnic group, but is a fundamental social characteristic of sinful human nature across space and time. "Goshens," "Pharaohs," and immigrant threat narratives characterize the national histories of most nations throughout the globe. It is also important to note that the discussion of xenophobia is a sensitive project because it often disrupts "official" national histories and founding myths which rely upon romanticized historical accounts. Pointing out such historical inaccuracies often produces angry, knee-jerk reactions for it can upset deep-rooted notions of nationalism. As followers of Christ, however, our identity as children of God must necessarily transcend any commitment to narrow ethnic nationalism and compel us to pursue the beloved community comprised of persons of every national, cultural, and ethnic background.

This essay examines United States immigration history in light of these two biblical themes of migration as grace and xenophobia. Since the initial Puritan migration to the Americas in the 17th century, United States immigration history has been characterized by a tension between the stated ideal of migration as grace—"bring me your huddled masses and all who long to be free"-- and xenophobia.[161] Although the Puritan founders of the United States perceived God's grace in their own migration and settlement in North America, most did not extend this same grace to the Native Americans of the land. From the perspective of Native Americans who experienced physical and cultural genocide at the hands of European immigrants, European colonization was not grace, but a curse. The same is true for the 12.5 million African slaves torn from their families and native lands to serve as chattel and forced labor in the Americas.

---

[161] This famous line from the Statue of Liberty is part of Emma Lazarus' sonnet, "The New Colossus." (1883). https://www.poetryfoundation.org/poems/46550/the-new-colossus.

Moreover, from the earliest wave of German migration to the United States in the 18th century, to the 19th and 20th century migrations of Southern and Eastern Europeans and Asians, to the various Latino migrations to the U.S., unbiblical xenophobia has unfortunately characterized the reception of most immigrant groups in the United States.

Migration As Grace

The principle of "migration as grace" is born out in many examples from Scripture. Time and time again we find biblical examples of God using the migration process to draw people to Himself and to extend to them His unmerited love and favor. One clear Scriptural example of "migration as grace" is found in the call of Abraham found in Genesis 12: 1–3:

> "The Lord had said to Abram, 'Go from your country, your people and your father's household to the land I will show you.
>
> 2 'I will make you into a great nation, and I will bless you;
>
> I will make your name great, and you will be a blessing.
>
> 3 I will bless those who bless you, and whoever curses you I will curse; and all peoples on earth will be blessed through you.'"

In this passage, God commands Abraham to migrate – go from his country, his people, and his father's household. Through Abraham's faithful act of migration, the end result is that all peoples of the earth would be blessed through him. Through Abraham's faithful act of migration, God would ultimately extend His grace and salvation to all the ethnic groups of the world.

Other examples of migration as grace include: the flight of the infant Jesus and the Holy Family to Egypt to be saved from the political wrath of King Herod (Matt. 2:14–15); God's redemption of Joseph's forced migration and enslavement in Egypt to save the lives of thousands of Egyptians from famine (Gen. 50:20); and the scattering of the persecuted Jerusalem church which led to the spread of the Gospel throughout Judea, Samaria, and, eventually, the Roman Empire (Acts 8:1–2).

Xenophobia

In contradistinction to the biblical principle of migration as grace, Jesus teaches that xenophobia—the fear and rejection of foreigners—is indicative of a human heart which does not truly know Him. According to Matthew 25:41, 43–45:

> "Then he will say to those on his left, 'depart from me, you who are cursed, into the eternal fire prepared for the devil and his angels. For...I was a stranger (xenos) and you did not invite me in...They also will answer, 'Lord when did we see you...a stranger(xenos)...and did not help you?':" He will reply, 'Truly I tell you, whatever you did not do for one of the least of these, you did not do for me."

In this passage, Jesus teaches that failure to show hospitality to the "xenos," or stranger, in our midst, is a rejection of Jesus Himself. In fact, the word "xenos" used in this passage, forms the linguistic root of our English word, "xenophobia" Understood in this light, fear of the stranger may be seen as fear of Jesus Himself. Moreover, according to Jesus, xenophobia calls into question whether one's relationship with Him is authentic (Matt. 25:44–46). In the converse, Jesus teaches that when we welcome the stranger, we are actually welcoming Jesus Himself (Matt. 25:35, 40). Hospitality to immigrants, moreover, evidences a sincere relationship with Jesus (Matt. 25:37–40).

In the Old Testament, Egypt exemplifies the grave danger of xenophobia played out on a national level. In Exodus 1, we learn that the Egyptians enslaved the Israelites and "made their lives bitter with hard service in mortar and brick and in every kind of labor" because they viewed them as a potential military threat in a time of war (Exod. 1:9–14). Their xenophobia did not end with the ruthless imposition of forced labor, however, but continued with the genocide of Hebrew male children (Exod. 1:16). Egyptian xenophobia also expressed itself in the geographic segregation of the Israelites in Goshen (Exod. 9:26). The example of Egypt in the Old Testament reveals the dangerous continuum of xenophobia: a dominant ethnic group oppresses another because of a perceived threat to power. The ethnic minority group is subjected to oppressive labor and geographic segregation. Hatred towards the minority group rises to such an extreme level that the majority feels morally justified to commit genocide. The story of Esther and Haman is another biblical example of the dangerous continuum of xenophobia.

Native American genocide, African slavery, lynching and murders of African Americans, Mexicans, Italians, and Asian Americans, Jim Crow segregation, and Japanese internment are fearful examples in U.S. history. The Jewish and Armenian genocides, and the Rwandan massacre, are also dreadful examples in global history of the past century. Playing with racism is toying with dangerous fire. The understanding of xenophobia as a slippery continuum leading ultimately to genocide, should give much pause to all, especially to those of the household of faith: "14 We know that we have passed from death to life because we love one another. Whoever does not love abides in death. 15 All who hate a brother or sister are murderers, and you know that murderers do not have eternal life abiding in them:" (1 John 3:14–15).

Xenophobia: U.S. Immigration History

Unfortunately, most of U.S. immigration history does not square with biblical notions of hospitality and migration as grace. Instead, U.S. immigration law and policy has more often than not mirrored the xenophobia of Pharaoh and Egypt.

As early as 1751, Benjamin Franklin wrote to express his dislike for Germans and other "tawny" European groups from southern and eastern

149

Europe. Franklin specifically singled out German immigrants for their refusal to "assimilate" into the Anglo colony of Pennsylvania. In his essay, "America as a Land of Opportunity," he famously declared:

> [W]hy should the Palatine Boors [Germans] be suffered to swarm into our Settlements, and by herding together establish their Language and Manners to the Exclusion of ours? Why should Pennsylvania, founded by the English, become a Colony of Aliens, who will shortly be so numerous as to Germanize us instead of us Anglifying them, and will never adopt our Language or Customs, any more than they can acquire our Complexion."[162]

As reflected in this quote, Franklin not only looked down upon the Germans for their purported refusal to integrate themselves within English society, but also for their darker complexion. In the same essay, he shuns not only Germans but also most other nations of Europe for their swarthy complexions:

> "And in Europe, the Spaniards, Italians, French, Russians and Swedes, are generally of what we call a swarthy Complexion; as are the Germans also, the Saxons excepted, who with the English, make the principal Body of White People on the Face of the Earth. I could wish their Numbers were increased."[163]

Building upon this prejudice against all non-Anglos, Irish, Italian, and Eastern European Jewish immigrants were met with xenophobia upon arrival in the United States during the nineteenth and early twentieth centuries. Fleeing the Irish Potato Famine, more than 1.75 million Irish immigrated to the United States between the years of 1846–1854. Irish immigrants experienced deep ethnic

---

[162] "Document 1, Benjamin Franklin, 'America as a Land of Opportunity,'?" Kathleen R. Arnold ed., *Anti-Immigration In the United States: A Historical Encyclopedia, Volume 2, S-Z* (Santa Barbara: Greenwood, 2011), 523.

[163] Ibid.

and anti-Catholic prejudice.[164] Irish homes and churches were burned, and "No Irish Need Apply" was a common sight in employment ads. Clustered in the Mid-Atlantic States, Italian immigrants of this era were also the targets of intense xenophobia. They often worked in low wage jobs as garment workers, day laborers, and street vendors, and were looked down upon for their darker complexion and condemned as unhygienic, violent, and unassimilable. Italian Catholicism was also viewed with suspicion, even by American Roman Catholics, because of an alleged superstitious and anti-clerical bent.[165] Although Jewish migration to the United States dates back to the colonial period, Jewish mass migration to North America from Eastern Europe took place between 1880–1914. During these years, more than two million Jewish emigrants arrived in the United States from Eastern Europe. Tragically, the anti-immigrant movement which targeted Italians, Eastern, and Southern Europeans, also attacked Jewish immigrants with anti-semitic prejudice and stereotypes.[166]

Although Southern and Eastern European immigrants were targets of virulent nativism during the late nineteenth and early twentieth centuries, it was Chinese immigrants who first were targeted for official legal exclusion from the United States. Tens of thousands of Chinese immigrants were recruited to the United States during the mid to late nineteenth century to serve as unskilled laborers in railroad construction, agriculture, mining, fishing, and canning.[167] By the 1870's, however, Chinese immigrants were the targets of an official anti-

---

[164] Kanstroom, Daniel, Emily Crowley, Katherine Guarino, and Michael Buckley, "Irish Immigrant Experience (Mid-1800's to Early 1900's)," In *Anti-Immigration in the United States: A Historical Encyclopedia, Volume 1, A-R,* edited by Kathleen R. Arnold, 282-283. Santa Barbara, CA: Greenwood, 2011.

[165] O'Mahen Malcom, Allison, "Italian Immigrant Experience, Early 20th Century." In *Anti-Immigration in the United States: A Historical Encyclopedia, Volume 1, A-R,* edited by Kathleen R. Arnold, 285-286. Santa Barbara, CA: Greenwood, 2011.

[166] Brinkmann, Tobias, "Jewish Immigration to the United States Before 1938." In *Anti-Immigration in the United States: A Historical Encyclopedia, Volume 1, A-R,* edited by Kathleen R. Arnold, 295-298. Santa Barbara, CA: Greenwood, 2011.

[167] Lew-Williams, Beth, "Chinese Immigration." In *Anti-Immigration in the United States: A Historical Encyclopedia, Volume 1, A-R,* edited by Kathleen R. Arnold, 110. Santa Barbara, CA: Greenwood, 2011.

Chinese campaign led by white workers in California.[168] Anti-Chinese attitudes of the 1870's and 80's are reflected in the following prayer from a San Francisco pastor, Isaac Kalloch, (who later went on to become mayor). On a 4th of July commemoration in 1878 he prayed:

> "We believe, O Lord, that the foundations of our government were laid by Thine own hand; that all the steps and stages of our progress have been under Thy watch and ward. We meet together today to celebrate the anniversary of our national birth, and we pray that we may be enabled to carry out the divine principles which inspired our noble sires and others, and we pray that our rules may be righteous; that our people may be peaceable; that capital may respect the rights of labor, and that labor may honor capital; that the Chinese must go… and good men stay. We believe Thou wilt hear our prayer when we pray that we believe to be right."[169]

The anti-Chinese movement culminated in the passage of the Chinese Exclusion Act of 1882.[170] This law banned Chinese immigrant laborers from the United States and was the first law to target an entire ethnic group for exclusion. It also created the framework of "legal" and "illegal" immigration which continues to the present day. Prior to the passage of the Chinese Exclusion Act, immigration to the United States did not require formal or extensive legal processes of documentation. In response to their exclusion, tens of thousands of Chinese immigrants flocked to Mexico and Cuba and created a transnational network of undocumented immigration to the United States. Chinese immigrants "invented" undocumented immigration from Latin America and were the first "undocumented immigrants."[171] This law and its subsequent legislative

---

[168] Ibid., 111.

[169] Alexander Saxton, *The Indispensable Enemy: Labor and the Anti-Chinese Movement in California*. (Berkeley: University of California Press, 1971).

[170] Robert Chao Romero, *The Chinese in Mexico, 1882–1940* (Tucson: The University of Arizona Press, 2010), 24.

[171] Ibid., 29.

extensions effectively banned Chinese immigration to the United States until 1965.

Following the exclusion of Chinese immigrant laborers, U.S. employers turned to immigrants from Japan, Korea, and the Philippines to fill important labor needs in agriculture and other industries.[172] Like their Chinese counterparts, they also eventually became targets of racism and exclusionary immigration policy. Japanese immigrants were labeled a "yellow peril," and, speaking of the general hostility towards Asian immigrants, Madison Grant, founder of the American Eugenics Society wrote, "There is immediate danger that the white stocks may be swamped by Asiatic blood...Unless [the white man] erects and maintains artificial barriers [he will] finally perish."[173] Like their Chinese and Japanese counterparts, Koreans were labeled unassimilable "Orientals" who stole jobs from whites, and South Asian immigrants were condemned as the "Hindu Invasion" and the "Tide of Turbans." Filipinos were called "untamed headhunters" and "jungle folk," and one California judge, D.W. Rohrback, shunned Filipinos as "little brown men about ten years removed from a bolo and breechcloth."[174]

Xenophobia resulted in the creation of an "Asiatic Barred Zone" of immigration in 1917,[175] and, in 1924, Asian immigration to the U.S. was permanently closed off as part of the Johnson-Reed Act. This law, also known as the 1924 Immigration Act, denied admission to all aliens ineligible to become naturalized citizens.[176] Since between 1790–1952, naturalization was available

---

[172] Christopher Capozzola, "Filipinas/os"; Daniel Kanstroom and Oliver Tang, "Japanese Immigration to the United States"; and, Daniel Kanstroom, Diana Chang, and Stephanie M. Garfield, "Korean Immigrant Experience.?" In *Anti-Immigration in the United States: A Historical Encyclopedia, Volume 1, A-R*, edited by Kathleen R. Arnold, 201 289, 306. Santa Barbara, CA: Greenwood, 2011.

[173] Erika Lee, *The Making of Asian America: A History.* (New York: Simon and Schuster 2016), 134.

[174] Ibid.,149, 165, 185.

[175] Ibid., 134.

[176] Ibid., 134–135.

only to those legally defined by the law as "white,"[177] this law effectively barred the immigration of Asians and other non-white immigrant groups.

The Johnson-Reed Act also closed off immigration from Southern and Eastern Europe.[178] In particular, it targeted Jews, Slavs, Russians, and Italians by establishing immigration quotas at two percent of the ethnic population of immigrant groups present in the 1890 census. This policy had the effect of limiting immigration from Eastern and Southern Europe and expanding immigration from Northern and Western Europe. It is significant to note that the 1924 immigration law was based explicitly upon racist notions of eugenics. Eugenics was the pseudo-scientific belief that certain racial and ethnic populations were biologically superior to others, and that selective breeding could produce a master race.[179] According to eugenics, Anglo-Saxons and Nordic peoples were superior to Jews, Slavs, Italians, Asians, and Africans, and therefore, U.S. immigration policy should be structured in such a way as to encourage migration of the former and exclusion of the latter. According to the U.S. Department of State Office of the Historian the goal of the 1924 Act was "to preserve the ideal of American homogeneity."[180] The 1924 immigration law was drafted by Madison Grant and sponsored by House member Johnson who was a member of the American Eugenics Society.[181]

The exclusion of Asians and Southern and Eastern Europeans from the United States created labor shortages, especially in Southwestern states. In order to fill the demand for cheap labor, the United States turned to its neighbor Mexico. It was a perfect historical match because Mexico was experiencing

---

[177] Ian Haney-Lopez, *White By Law: The Legal Construction of Race* (New York: New York University Press, 2006), 1.

[178] Nancy Ordover, "Johnson-Reed Act (The 1924 National Origins Act, or the Immigration Act of 1924)." In *Anti-Immigration in the United States: A Historical Encyclopedia, Volume 1, A-R* edited by Kathleen R. Arnold, 301-302. Santa Barbara, CA: Greenwood, 2011.

[179] Sahar Sadeghi, "Emergency Quota Act of 1921," In *Anti-Immigration in the United States: A Historical Encyclopedia, Volume 1, A-R* edited by Kathleen R. Arnold, 175-176. Santa Barbara, CA: Greenwood, 2011.

[180] U.S. Department of State, "The Immigration Act of 1924 (The Johnson-Reed Act)," https://2001–2009.state.gov/r/pa/ho/time/id/87718.htm.

[181] Ordover, "Johnson-Reed Act," 302.

violent revolution at the same time that the U.S. was in dire need of labor for agriculture, the railroad industry, construction, mining, and factories. Between 1900 and 1930, fleeing the violence and social disruption of the Mexican Revolution, and answering the invitation of U.S. employers, nearly 750,000 Mexicans immigrated to the United States. These immigrants established vibrant communities in the former Mexican states and territories of California, Arizona, New Mexico, and Texas.[182]

With the onset of the Great Depression in 1929, Mexican immigrants-- like their European and Asian predecessors—became scapegoated for the economic woes of the country and were blamed for taking jobs away from "real Americans" Similar to Italians just a few decades before, they were condemned as unassimilable, unhygienic, and culturally inferior. Widespread anti-Mexican sentiment led to massive deportations, and, between 1930 and 1935, 345,839 Mexicans were repatriated or deported back to Mexico. Tragically, Mexican Americans were also not excluded from these deportations. In California, over 80% of the repatriates were U.S. citizens or legal residents of the U.S. Moreover, between 1947 and 1954 the Immigration and Nationalization Service boasted of apprehending more than 1 million unauthorized Mexican immigrants as part of the notorious "Operation Wetback."[183]

A monumental shift in U.S. immigration policy took place with the passage of the Immigration and Nationality Act Amendments of 1965. Signed into law that year by President Lyndon B. Johnson, the Immigration Act of 1965, also known as Hart-Celler, ended the ethnically and racially discriminatory quota

---

[182]Robert Chao Romero and Luis Fernando Fernandez, "Doss v. Bernal: Ending Mexican Apartheid in Orange County," UCLA CSRC Research Report, No. 14, February 2012; Zaragosa Vargas, *Crucible of Struggle: A History of Mexican Americans from Colonial Times to the Present Era* (Oxford: Oxford University Press, 2011), 189, 191–192. George Sánchez, *Becoming Mexican American: Ethnicity, Culture and Identity in Chicano Los Angeles,* 1900–1945 (Oxford: Oxford University Press, 1993), 19.

[183] Vargas, Crucible of Struggle, 220; David Gutierrez, *Walls and Mirrors: Mexican Americans, Mexican Immigrants, and the Politics of Ethnicity* (Berkeley: University of California Press, 1995), 142.

systems which had been established by the Johnson-Reed Act.[184] In his Liberty Island speech given in support of this new legislation, Johnson in fact explicitly declared it was aimed at remedying the previous wrongful exclusion of Southern and Eastern European immigrants.[185] In a sense, the U.S. experienced a partial national repentance over its discriminatory immigration laws. In place of racist quotas based on national origins, the Immigration Act of 1965 created equitable hemispheric migration quotas from the "Old" and "New" world. It also established preferences for professionals, scientists, skilled workers, and family members of U.S. citizens and green card holders.[186] Immediate family members of U.S. citizens such as spouses, unmarried minor children, and parents of U.S. citizens, moreover, were exempted from the new numerical quotas altogether. Family reunification was an important guiding principle of the new law.

Although U.S. immigration policy experienced a dramatic change for the better after 1965, it still failed to adequately consider the expansive labor needs of the growing American economy in the decades to come. The Immigration Act of 1965 capped the issuance of both skilled and unskilled labor visas at a mere 10% of all annual visas—woefully inadequate to meet the country's need for unskilled, inexpensive labor. As a result, over the ensuing four decades, the U.S. economy turned to undocumented labor to supply its voracious appetite for cheap labor in agriculture, construction, the service sector, and many other areas. Between 2000-2015 alone, approximately 850,000 unauthorized immigrants traveled each year to the United States. It is estimated that undocumented workers now contribute more than $420 billion dollars to the annual Gross Domestic Product, and billions more in state and local taxes.[187] In fact, unauthorized immigrants

---

[184] Cheryl Shanks, "Hart-Celler." In *Anti-Immigration in the United States: A Historical Encyclopedia, Volume 1, A-R*, edited by Kathleen R. Arnold, 241-245. Santa Barbara, CA: Greenwood, 2011.

[185] Roger Daniels, *Coming to America: A History of Immigration and Ethnicity in American Life* (New York: Perennial, 2002), 341.

[186] Ibid., 342.

[187] Romero, "Migration as Grace," 28–31.

have been credited with saving social security through their multi-billion dollar contributions in the form of federal payroll taxes.[188]

Despite their vital economic contributions, undocumented Latino immigrants have been frequently scapegoated during times of economic crisis over the past 20 years. Examples include California Proposition 187 (1994), the federal Sensenbrenner Immigration Bill (2005), the Hazleton "Illegal Immigration Relief Act" (2006), Arizona SB-1070 (2010), Alabama House Bill 56 (2011), and 162 other anti-immigrant laws passed by state legislatures in 2010 and 2011.[189]

Although held to be largely unconstitutional and never implemented, Proposition 187, the so-called "Save Our State" initiative, barred undocumented immigrants in California from receiving health care, K-12 public education, and other public social services. It also required police, teachers, public school officials, and public healthcare providers to check the immigration status of individuals and report undocumented immigrants to the federal government for deportation.[190]

The Sensenbrenner Bill, passed by the U.S. House of Representatives in 2005, sought to construct a 700-mile fence along the U.S.-Mexico border, eliminate the Diversity Immigrant Visa Program, categorize all forms of unlawful presence and visa overstays as felonies, and arguably made it a crime for churches to minister to undocumented immigrants. In passing the "Illegal Immigration Relief Act" in 2006, the city of Hazleton, Pennsylvania tried to take the issue of undocumented immigration into its own hands by fining landlords who rented to undocumented immigrants and suspending the business licenses of people who hired them.[191]

---

[188] Ibid., 29.
[189] Ibid., 21.
[190] Ibid., 21-22.
[191] Ibid., 22.

In its explicit terms, Arizona SB-1070 called for the goal of immigrant "attrition through enforcement." SB-1070 requires police to determine the immigration status of someone arrested or detained if they have "reasonable suspicion" that such individuals are undocumented. Civil rights organizations have criticized the law because of the severe danger it poses for racial profiling. Indeed, in July 2017, Maricopa County Sheriff Joe Arpaio was found guilty of criminal contempt by the Federal District Court judge Susan Bolton for his failure to limit racial profiling of Latino drivers in Arizona.[192]

In stark moral condemnation of Arizona SB-1070, Archbishop Desmond Tutu declared forcefully:

> "I am saddened today at the prospect of a young Hispanic immigrant in Arizona going to the grocery store and forgetting to bring her passport and immigration documents with her. I cannot be dispassionate about the fact that the very act of her being in the grocery store will soon be a crime in the state she lives in.
>
> Or that, should a policeman hear her accent and form a "reasonable suspicion" that she is an illegal immigrant, she can – and will – be taken into custody until someone sorts it out, while her children are at home waiting for their dinner…
>
> But a solution that degrades innocent people, or that makes anyone with broken English a suspect, is not a solution. A solution that fails to distinguish between a young child coming over the border in search of his mother and a drug smuggler is not a solution.
>
> I am not speaking from an ivory tower. I lived in the South Africa that has now thankfully faded into history, where a black man or woman could be grabbed off the street and thrown in jail for not having his or her documents on their person."[193]

---

[192] Colin Dwyer, "Ex-Sheriff Joe Arpaio Convicted of Criminal Contempt," NPR, July 31, 2017. Arpaio was subsequently pardoned by President Donald Trump on August 25, 2017.
[193] Desmond Tutu, "Arizona: The Wrong Answer," *Huffington Post,* August 7, 2010. https://www.huffpost.com/entry/arizona-the-wrong-answ_b_557955.

Alabama House Bill 56 and Georgia House Bill 87 are like Arizona SB-1070 on steroids. Though partially invalidated by the 11th Circuit Court of Appeals, Alabama HB-56 barred undocumented immigrants from attending college, criminalized the rental of residential property to undocumented immigrants, and prohibited them from applying for or soliciting work. It also required school officials to submit an annual tally of all suspected undocumented K-12 students to the state department of education. Georgia House Bill 87 signed into law by state governor Nathan Deal in May 2011, authorized police officers to question individuals about their immigration status in certain criminal investigations and threatened to fine undocumented immigrants $250,000, or send them to jail for 15 years, for using fake identifications in search of employment. In 2010, the Georgia Board of Regents also passed rules effectively barring undocumented students from all public universities in the state.[194]

Political Scapegoats: President Donald Trump and the Rise of White Nationalism

These various anti-immigrant laws and policies of the past decade have occurred within the context of political scapegoating. Since the economic downturn of 2008, undocumented immigrant labor has been scapegoated by some members of the white working-class population and opportunistic politicians eager for election.

Such anti-immigrant rhetoric has fueled the rise of white nationalism. Reminiscent of the racial nationalism of the 19th and early twentieth centuries, some white workers have condemned immigrant workers as unfair labor competition and culturally unassimilable; politicians have seized upon this discontent among the electorate, adding that immigrants are also a drain upon state and local economic resources because of their use of social services such as

---

[194] Romero, "Migration as Grace," 24–25.

education and healthcare. Post-9/11, Muslim Americans have also been the targets of virulent racism as part of the so-called "war on terror." Campaigning on this anti-immigrant, restrictionist platform, many politicians have been successfully elected to local, state, and federal office over the past decade. Most notably, reality television personality Donald Trump has successfully ridden the tidal wave of anti-immigrant sentiment to the steps of the White House. In his now notorious words:

> "When Mexico sends its people, they're not sending their best…They're bringing drugs. They're bringing crime. They're rapists. And some, I assume, are good people. I will build a great wall—and nobody builds walls better than me, believe me—and I'll build them very inexpensively. I will build a great, great wall on our southern border, and I will make Mexico pay for that wall. Mark my words."[195]
>
> "'Donald Trump is calling for a total and complete shutdown of Muslims entering the United States…'"[196]

Such xenophobic rhetoric has unfortunately been transformed into policy and led to unconscionable arrests, deportations, and enforcement tactics over the past two years. Families have been separated at the border, children have been placed in cages and forced into foster care, and parents have been deported to Central America without their sons and daughters. As other grievous examples, immigration authorities have arrested and detained a 10-year-old girl with cerebral palsy who had just left the hospital after receiving emergency gall bladder surgery; an undocumented mother who was hospitalized with a brain tumor; an undocumented father who was dropping his child off at school, and another who was driving his pregnant wife to the hospital to give birth; and,

---

[195] Will Heilpern, "Trump campaign: 11 outrageous quotes," *CNN politics*, February 23, 2016. https://www.cnn.com/2015/12/31/politics/gallery/donald-trump-campaign-quotes/index.html.
[196] Ibid.

domestic violence victim who was testifying in court.[197] And equally unconscionable has been the repeal of Deferred Action for Childhood Arrivals (D.A.C.A.) which has served as a life raft for more than 800,000 undocumented young adults and their families.[198]

Conclusion

"A mighty woman with a torch, whose flame is the imprisoned lightning, and her name Mother of Exiles. From her beacon-hand Glows world-wide welcome; her mild eyes command

The air-bridged harbor that twin cities frame. "Keep, ancient lands, your storied pomp!" cries she

With silent lips. "Give me your tired, your poor, your huddled masses yearning to breathe free,

The wretched refuse of your teeming shore.

Send these, the homeless, tempest-tossed to me,

I lift my lamp beside the golden door!"[199]

As reflected in this famous poem from the Statue of Liberty, official United States immigration history is often portrayed as one of welcome,

---

[197]David Sim, "Children Crying at U.S. Border and Sitting in Cages: Trump's Separation Policy in Pictures.?" *Newsweek*, June 20, 2018; Marwa Eltagouri, "A 10-year-old immigrant was rushed to the hospital in an ambulance. She was detained on the way.?" *Washington Post*, October 27, 2017; Chris Sommerfeldt, Erin Kurkin, and Nancy Dillon, "Undocumented woman with brain tumor seized by federal agents at Texas hospital, family fears she will die," *Daily News*, February 24, 2017, http://www.nydailynews.com/news/national/undocumented-woman-brain-tumor-removed-hospital-lawyer-article-1.2979956; Jade Hernandez, "Undocumented dad taken by ICE while dropping kids off at school,?" Eyewitness News, March 3, 2017, http://abc7.com/news/undocumented-dad-taken-by-ice-while-dropping-kids-off-at-school/1782230/; Jonathan Blitzer, "The Woman Arrested by ICE in a Courthouse Speaks Out,?" *The New Yorker*, February 23, 2017, http://www.newyorker.com/news/news-desk/the-woman-arrested-by-ice-in-a-courthouse-speaks-out.
[198]Vanessa Romo, Martina Stewart, Brian Naylor, "Trump Ends DACA, Calls On Congress To Act.?" September 5, 2017. NPR.
[199]Emma Lazarus, "The New Colossus.?" https://www.poetryfoundation.org/poems/46550/the-new-colossus.

especially to the "poor and huddled masses yearning to breathe free" As this essay has demonstrated, however, the U.S. has a three hundred year history of tension between this stated ideal and xenophobia. Contrary to biblical notions of hospitality and "migration as grace," the following pattern has often repeated itself: an immigrant group receives temporary and tentative welcome because of its valuable labor contributions, but when times of economic difficulty arise, these same immigrants become the targets of xenophobia and are condemned as culturally inferior and unfair labor competition. This cycle has unfortunately played itself out many times with immigrants from China, Japan, Korea, the Philippines, Italy, Eastern Europe, Mexico, Latin America, and the Caribbean. Indeed, our current legal categories of "legal" and "illegal" immigrants were developed in the 19th and early 20th century as an explicit means of ending the immigration of those considered racially and ethnically inferior.

As taught by Jesus in Matthew 25, and as reflected in the biblical account of the Exodus, such *xenophobia, or fear of the foreigner, reflects an individual or nation whose heart has turned from God.* As U.S. and global history teach us, exclusionary nationalism and xenophobia is not limited to any particular ethnic group, but is a fundamental social characteristic of sinful human nature across space and time. As ministers of the Gospel in the "Goshens" of the 21st century, may we understand this history and prophetically denounce the xenophobia of "Egypt" and the oppressive immigration policies of "Pharaoh" wherever we see it. May we see and learn from Jesus, who appears to us in the loving disguise of the immigrant among us.[200]

---

[200] This summary statement of Matthew 25 is a paraphrase of Mother Teresa's famous words, "Seeking the face of God in everything, everyone, all the time, and his hand in every happening; This is what it means to be contemplative in the heart of the world. Seeing and adoring the presence of Jesus, especially in the lowly appearance of bread, and in the distressing disguise of the poor.?" Mother Teresa, *In the Heart of the World: Thoughts, Stories, and Prayers.* New World Library, 2010.

CHAPTER SEVEN

Using Anthropology to Better Understand Immigrants

Doug Priest

> The plane landed at Indianapolis International Airport just before midnight June 8, 2010. Out stepped a mother and her three children, strangers in a strange land. Between them, they spoke no more than a dozen words of English. They knew little about the United States and nothing about Indianapolis. Winnie Bulaya and her family had fled their home in the war-ravaged Democratic Republic of Congo in Central Africa several years earlier, resettling as refugees in Nairobi, Kenya. The children's father was killed when he returned to DR Congo… A representative from Catholic Charities' Refugee and Immigrant Services program met the nervous newcomers at the airport and drove them to their new home, a two-bedroom apartment on the west side. Once inside the unfurnished apartment, Bulaya closed the door behind her and didn't open it for three days … The family huddled together, awake at night, then sleeping. Their world was inside out.[201]

Almost twenty years ago I preached a sermon on hospitality[202] titled "Who's Flipping Your Burgers?:" The unusual title led into a discourse regarding the immigrants in our country who work at the lower-level jobs that many of us do not want to do. I challenged the church to seize this opportunity for sharing

---

[201] Portions of an article taken from *The Indianapolis Star*, Dec. 25, 2017.
[202] 1 Pet 4:7–11.

the gospel in the fullest sense rather than seeing immigrants as a problem or an economic threat.

Never in human history has there been so much movement of people throughout the world. Consider these facts from the UN International Report of 2017: "The number of international migrants worldwide has continued to grow rapidly in recent years, reaching 258 million in 2017, up from 220 million in 2010 and 173 million in 2000. Over 60 percent of all international migrants live in Asia (80 million) or Europe (78 million). Northern America hosted the third largest number of international migrants (58 million), followed by Africa (25 million), Latin America and the Caribbean (10 million) and Oceania (8 million)."[203] Globalization is not only about goods being moved from one place to another, capitalization of the world's economy, the spread of democracy, intense political anger, new technologies, and the wealthy getting richer at the expense of the poor. It is also about people in flux and about change.

One of the key features of globalization is the movement of people. As we have seen in the previous chapters, there has been a great influx of immigrants and refugees into the U.S.[204] The study of immigration has become a key subject area in the discipline of cultural anthropology. Anthropology is the study of humankind. When people of different backgrounds contact one another, there is much opportunity for new understanding, and for misunderstanding. Chavez notes that, "anthropologists can offer a great service to whatever society they work in by easing the conflicts that arise as cultures mix, interact, and begin to share space, beliefs, and behaviors."[205] Anthropology helps us to understand others, and in so doing, helps us to better understand ourselves, including our

---

[203] UN International Migration Report 2017: Highlights Key Facts. (New York: United Nations, 2017), 5.

[204] As I write this chapter, today's newspaper had a headline, "U.S. closes door to multitude of refugees.?" The opening paragraph notes: "President Trump had to battle the courts and vocal opposition, but by the end of the year, he was able to slash refugee admissions into the US to historic lows.?" *USA Today*, Jan. 4, 2018.

[205] Leo Chavez, *Shadowed Lives: Undocumented Immigrants in American Society.* (Belmont: Wadsworth, 2013), xii.

prejudices about those who are different—the "other." In our deeply divided and partisan society, we need to master intercultural understanding and communication.

The tools and theories of anthropology help us understand the migration of people from the rural areas to the urban centers, from one country to another, and the accompanying personal and societal changes that occur. We are reminded by Lewellen that "Globalization is at the cutting edge of cultural anthropology… It opens new territory, challenging the bounded world of communities, localities, peasants, tribes, and cultures that has characterized anthropological research in the past."[206]

Most immigrants coming to the U.S. end up in urban centers. Looney suggests that, "International migration is one of the most tangible expressions of globalization that is playing out in an overhaul of local communities worldwide."[207] The field of urban anthropology is rich in providing techniques to exegete the city which provides the context of life for the immigrants. Space, location, movement, interaction, cultural distance, and use of time are all relevant topics to the urban anthropologist, i.e. where does the new immigrant live; with whom does the new immigrant interact; how are the basic necessities acquired?

Some definitions will be helpful. *Internal migration* occurs within a country, often taking place when people from the rural areas move into the city. *International migration* happens when people from one country move (or are moved) to another country. Similarly, there are both *voluntary* and *involuntary* migration, the latter occurring against the migrants' wishes due to factors including weather, natural disaster, war, health, or poverty. The primary difference between a *migrant* and a *settler* is the amount of time one stays in the new country. Another difference is that settlers may never wish to return to their

---

[206] Ted C. Lewellen. *The Anthropology of Globalization.* (Westport: Bergin & Garvey, 2002), vii.

[207] Jared Looney, *Crossroads of the Nations* (Skyforest, CA: Urban Loft Publishers, 2015), 209.

former country, though many may do so for short visits. Settlers may dream of someday returning to their country of birth. Those longings, however, "are offset by the passage of time in the United States, raising a family, and working."[208] *Documented* immigrants are those who can legally reside in their new country. *Undocumented* immigrants are those who entered the country without proper documentation or those whose proper documentation—one that had a time limit—has lapsed.

A globalized economy and a globalized workforce have led to *transnationalism* or *transnational migration*. Immigrants often maintain social relations that keep them in contact with their original homeland. They may cross the border daily for work purposes and they may work in multiple locations. Rynkiewich writes that "Transnationalism refers not to the diaspora[209] community itself, but rather to the constant flow of goods, ideas, and persons that occurs in some diaspora communities."[210] Immigrants are those who come/go to another country to take up permanent residence. Refugees refers to those who are outside of their country of nationality or last habitual residence (i.e. refugee camp). Different from an immigrant, a refugee is either unable or unwilling to go back to that country because of fear of persecution. The fears

---

[208] Chavez, 4.

[209] Wan gives a background of the term 'diaspora' and concludes that the term today implies "a positive and ongoing relationship between migrants' homelands and where they now live and work." Enoch Wan, ed. *Diaspora Missiology: Theory, Methodology, and Practice.* (Portland: Institute of Diaspora Studies, 2011), 97. Looney, 22–23, notes Cohen's nine characteristics for most diaspora communities:
1. Dispersion from an original homeland, often traumatically
2. The expansion from a homeland in search of work, in pursuit of trade or to further colonial ambitions
3. A collective memory and myth about the homeland
4. An idealization of the supposed ancestral home
5. A return movement
6. A strong ethnic group consciousness sustained over a long time
7. A troubled relationship with host societies
8. A sense of solidarity with co-ethnic members in other countries
9. The possibility of distinctive, creative, enriching lives in tolerant host countries.

[210] Michael Rynkiewich, *Soul, Self, and Society.* (Eugene: Cascade Books, 2014), 212.

may be based on grounds of politics, religion, race, or membership in a social group.[211] *Refugee status* is determined by both international and U.S. law.

Some Common Characteristics of Immigrants

Before looking at some anthropological theories and methods for understanding immigrants, a few general comments are in order. No group of immigrants are the same. Similarly, no two immigrants are the same. Though the backgrounds and experiences of immigrants are diverse, there are some commonalities.

Today immigrants arrive in a country that is both suspicious and hostile to these newcomers. They are caricatured as wanting to take "our" jobs, as being possible terrorists, and wanting to soak up benefits such as health insurance and free education. Some are believed to come to the U.S. to have children that will constitutionally become American citizens by birthright. They are stereotyped as being dirty, criminals, and unwilling to adapt to American culture by refusing to speak English. Heyman summarizes: "The present political climate polarizes hosts and immigrants. In this situation immigrant families and children become political 'enemies' of American nationalists, rather than bearers of a shared future."[212] Immigrants are aware of these feelings of hostility that are the result of an exaggerated pejorative narrative.

Chavez, writing about Latino immigrants, notes that they "constantly find themselves the object of a discourse in which they are represented as a threat and danger to the nation."[213]

At the same time many immigrants are welcomed at the airports upon their arrival by charitable groups that assist them in their initial days in finding

---

[211] Bauman, Stephen, Matthew Soerens, and Issam Smeir. *Seeking Refuge: On the Shores of the Global Refugee Crisis.* (Chicago: Moody Publishers, 2016), 100.
[212] Josiah McC. Heyman. *Finding a Moral Heart for U.S. Immigration Policy.* (Arlington: American Anthropological Association, 1998), 67.
[213] Leo Chavez. *The Latino Threat.* (Stanford: Stanford University Press, 2013), 48.

housing, learning the transportation systems, preparing resumes for job interviews, and locating warm clothing during the winter months.

Most immigrants come to the U.S. because they believe there are endless opportunities for personal betterment and social improvement. They believe they will be able to succeed with hard work and sacrifice and will have a better life.

"Many of the immigrants in the United States today were driven by the same dreams and hope for prosperity that attracted the founders of our country to a new land."[214]

Immigrants work hard. They send remittances back home for their families. "With the exception of refugees, most diaspora people are gainfully employed."[215] Sorens and Yang have studied the work habits of immigrants and present the following data.

- The employment rate for adult male undocumented immigrants is an estimated 96 percent, which is significantly higher that U.S. male citizens.[216]

- One-third of immigrants do not have a high school degree, but one-quarter have a college degree or higher.[217]

- Immigrant entrepreneurs have founded thousands of businesses, from engineering companies and cleaning services to restaurants and medical practices, and these businesses often revitalize neighborhoods that were dying off.[218]

- Between 1990 and 2004, over one-third of U.S. scientists who have received Nobel prizes have been foreign born... Yahoo, Google and Sun Microsystems were all founded by immigrants... More than 20 percent of workers in the computers and mathematics industries... are currently foreign born.[219]

---

[214] Soerens, Matthew and Jenny Hwang Yang. *Welcoming the Stranger: Justice, Compassion, and Truth in the Immigration Debate.* (Downers Grove: InterVarsity Press, 2010), 117. Revised edition, July 2018.

[215] Wan, 150.

[216] Sorens and Yang, 42.

[217] Ibid., 126.

[218] Ibid., 125.

[219] Ibid., 127. See also Miguel Ceja, "Chicana College Aspirations and the Role of Parents: Developing Educational Resiliency." *Journal of Hispanic Higher Education.* 3 (2004) 338–62.

- Even if they are not Nobel Prize winners, they are still human and deserve to be treated so, whether documented or undocumented.

Immigrants pass through the normal phases of culture shock when they arrive in a new country—romantic (idealism and optimism), realization (angst and anger), rejection (depression and disillusionment), and readjustment (determination and incorporation). Lewellen reflects that "Immigrants, wherever, often suffer high levels of poverty, maltreatment, instability, insecurity and stress."[220] The younger the immigrant, the easier to accommodate to the new country's culture and language. Older immigrants usually have a more difficult time in this adjustment, and some never master the new language, such as those who choose or are forced to live in ethnic enclaves. Even so, immigrants and refugees have "admirable educational goals for their children. At great cost they invest their savings and emotional capital on their children's future."[221]

Undocumented immigrants live in an almost constant state of fear and tension. They realize that at any moment that could be discovered and deported. Many arrive in this country with migration debts, work erratically and at low-paying jobs, and have to cover high costs for rent, transportation, and perhaps childcare. Chavez's ethnography of undocumented immigrants living in the San Diego area reveals that people describe themselves as being in jail or living in a chicken coop.[222] Because of immigration check points north and east of the city, they cannot move about freely. Their children do not understand why they cannot go to Disneyland like their classmates. Many immigrants come from countries with a strong emphasis on family and community. They carry these tendencies with them and hopefully find a way to espouse them in a country that is much more individualistic, and one with emphasis on the nuclear as opposed to the extended family.

---

[220] Lewellen, 127.
[221] Heyman, 67.
[222] Chavez, 178.

Anthropological Theory and Migration

Theories of Migration

Three general approaches to migration can be enumerated. Lewellen calls these the classic, modern, and emergent approaches.[223] The *classic* approach (assimilation) examined what pulled people away from rural areas into the cities. It also noted what factors pushed people to migrate, such as war and poverty. Once in the new cities the anthropologists studied culture change through accommodation and assimilation into the general culture over time.

In the 1960s the *modern* approach (cost/benefit), influenced by Marxist theories, sought to see immigration through the lens of economics. It looked at the forces that led people to move, such as migrant workers working in the agricultural fields, noting that for a country to have levels of wealth mean that poorer people were required to make the system tenable. Hence, laborers are drawn to the U.S. and end up taking positions such as restaurant and domestic workers. Even today farmers are uneasy with threats to send undocumented immigrants back "home" because they know they will not be able to harvest their fields.

In the *emergent* approach models focus on particular migrations. Migration is now seen as a complex phenomenon, and innovative models and theories are required. The new vocabulary of immigration includes terms like "transnationalism, diaspora, multiculturalism, citizenship acquisition, social movements, and refugees."[224]

Missionary anthropologist Michael Rynkiewich asks what happens when people migrate. He then goes on to list and describe six different models or

---

[223] Lewellen, 131–132.
[224] Lewellen, 132. See also Linda Basch, Nina Glick Shiller, and Cristina Szanton, *Nations Unbound: Transnational Projects, Postcolonial Predicaments, and Deterritorized Nation-States.* (Langhome: Gordon and Breach Publishers, 1994); *Towards a Transnational Perspective on Migration: Race, Class, Ethnicity, and Nationalism Reconsidered*, ed. Nina Glick Schiller, Linda Basch, and Cristina Szanton Blanc. (New York: The New York Academy of Sciences, 1992); Hsu, Madeline. *Dreaming of Gold, Dreaming of Home: Transnationalism and Migration between the United States and South China, 1882–1943.* (Stanford: Stanford University Press, 2000).

theories of migration, all of which can be seen in the various anthropological theories which follow:[225]

- the *disintegration* model where migrants moved to the city only to have life fall apart, and the feeling of anomie set in;
- the *adaptation* or *social construction* model where migrants are not victims but agents in their own right as they determine coping strategies for urban living;
- the *one-way street* model where people are trapped in the city. These immigrants have a family coupled with a low-wage job and they cannot get away;
- the *two-way street* model or *continuous migration* model where people migrate but do not intend to stay and make regular trips to their former country;[226]
- the *multiple identities* model where people construct multiple associations;
- the *culture of hope* model where people are doing as well as they can, given their options.

Territorial Passage Model

Van Gennep analyzed ceremonies and concluded that there were three phases in these rites of passage: separation, transition, and incorporation.[227] Chavez, in his ethnography of immigration in San Diego, used this model to describe territorial passages[228] or boundary crossings. Much of his book focuses on undocumented immigrants, and notes that the border between Mexico and the U.S, is both "a symbolic and physical separation. It is a divide that must be crossed, a barrier that must be surmounted, a moment that must be

---

[225] Rynkiewich, 201–202.

[226] Appadurai makes the point that, "People come here to make their fortunes, but they are no longer content to leave their homelands behind.?" Arjun Appadurai, *Modernity at Large* (Minneapolis: University of Minnesota Press, 1996), 172.

[227] Arnold Van Gennep, *The Rites of Passage*. (Chicago: University of Chicago Press, 1960, translated by Monika Vizedom and Gabrielle Caffee), 11.

[228] Van Gennep's book had a chapter titled "The Territorial Passage.?" Van Gennep, 15–25.

transcended."[229] Once the border is crossed the immigrant passes into the transition phase. Chavez elaborates, borrowing from Turner: "It is the moment that Victor Turner (1974, 231–232) describes as 'betwixt and between,' when an individual is no longer in the old world but has not yet moved into, or been accepted into, the new world. This liminal period is typically a time of ambiguity, apprehensiveness, and fear."[230] We will discuss the third phase in the rites of passage model, incorporation, with the broader topic of assimilation.

Assimilation

Two metaphors were used in the previous century to describe immigrants coming to America. The first was the melting pot. It was believed that immigrants would arrive and over time would blend in with the larger American culture. These people would learn to speak English, they would leave many of their cultural practices behind, would eat the foods that Americans ate, and would follow local sports teams. They would not only accommodate themselves to America, but they would *assimilate* into the culture. This viewpoint was both ethnocentric and paternalistic, and assumed the immigrants were passive and docile.

Then in 1964 Glazer and Moynihan published the critically acclaimed *Beyond the Melting Pot*,[231] a study of different ethnic groups in New York City. Contrary to what had been assumed about immigrants, many of them chose not to fully assimilate into the predominant culture. Instead, they retained many of their customs, lived with other members of their ethnic group, and spoke in their mother tongue.

America was not a melting pot at all. Instead, it was more like a stewpot, the second metaphor. In a stewpot, various vegetables of different colors, textures, and tastes are cooked together, resulting in a stew. The vegetables retain

---

[229] Chavez, 49.
[230] Ibid.
[231] Nathan Glazer and Daniel P. Moynihan, *Beyond the Melting Pot*. (Cambridge, M.I.T. Press), 1964.

their characteristics even though the stew is considered a single dish. Rather than an assimilation model for understanding immigration, the new model was the *multicultural* model. Multi-culturalism was a way of understanding that ethnic groups maintained their distinct identity in the middle of surrounding diversity. In the multicultural model, assimilation occurs, but it is a limited assimilation with which the immigrant is comfortable. This limited assimilation is not static in that it changes over time, particularly from one generation to the next. Wan and Casey make the claim that, "The best way to understand assimilation is to view it as a two-way endeavor where, yes, mainstream culture impacts immigrants, but immigrants also impact mainstream culture."[232]

Globalization requires a new metaphor for immigration. Some have suggested that a mosaic would be more appropriate. However, a mosaic is very similar to a stewpot. Each individual piece of the mosaic retains is character, though when combined with all the other pieces the art is seen in its fullest. In a globalized world, people are very fluid. We are long past the days of bounded groups of people who are characterized by their ethnolinguistic similarities. But there still may be some usefulness to the mosaic metaphor, provided that the material of the mosaic is no longer ceramic, but wax. As the wax melts in the sun, the pieces of the mosaic blend into one another. They no longer fully retain their color or shape. They combine with other pieces of the mosaic. The colors of the pieces can still be discerned with effort, but they are changed. Something new is always being created because the wax continuously melts and hardens.

Human and Social Capital

Immigrants come to the U.S. bringing with them either human capital or social capital (though there is some overlapping). Human capital refers to degree of wealth, level of education, and professional work experience. "Immigrants with high levels of human capital tend to be professionals and live in the middle

---

[232] Enoch Wan and Anthony Casey. *Church Planting among Immigrants in US Urban Centers.* (Portland: Institute of Diaspora Studies, 2016), 48.

class or above in their home countries. They have college degrees at least, and many have masters and doctorates as well. These immigrants migrate as families because they have the means to do so."[233] The children of immigrants with high levels of human capital do well in school and most go on to graduate study. They are likely to marry outside of their ethnic group.

Social capital is the opposite of human capital. These immigrants are in the U.S. primarily for labor. They lack education and professional experience. But they come with a wide network of social contacts. These contacts help them to adjust to their new surroundings. They may be acquaintances or relatives from their prior home. Or they may be referred by others to contacts in the new country. They may live with their relatives, who may also find employment for them.

Those arriving with human capital often live throughout the city or in the suburbs. They are able to choose where to live. In opposition, those arriving with social capital are more apt to live in ethnic enclaves. Immigrants muster social resources by developing ties with an array of domestic groups. Such groups help the immigrants to organize their lives to be able to accomplish their goals.[234]

Social capital changes over time, evolving into social networks. Rynkiewich describes social networks: "Individuals in complex societies are faced with a large range of potential relationships, so the individual selects from among the possibilities those with whom he or she will establish social ties. The result is a network of relationships that is centered on the individual. Thus, no two persons have exactly the same network."[235] Additionally, as immigrants come and go, national borders become less important. Their space becomes deterritorialized. Geography becomes less relevant as the emphasis shifts to social ties, even virtual social networks through social media.

---

[233] Ibid., 53.

[234] In addition to human and social capital, and type of capital is termed "community cultural wealth." See Tara J. Yosso. "Whose Culture has Capital? A Critical Race Theory Discussion of Community Cultural Wealth." *Race, Ethnicity and Education.* 2006 (8:1:69–91).

[235] Rynkiewich, 225.

Levels of Assimilation

When immigrants come to the U.S. one of the key questions they face is to what degree they should assimilate. Immigrants can choose between either the *ethnic* option or the *mainstream* option.[236] In the former, the immigrant relies on his or her social networks. In the latter, the immigrant "enrolls children in the American educational system, learns English, and enters the mainstream economy."[237]

From the point of view of the host culture, immigrants should not be forced into assimilating. Forced assimilation upon immigrants by host countries does damage to the multicultural model of the day of Pentecost. Immigrant cultures should not be devalued, but accepted and respected.

Wan and Casey suggest three models of assimilation.[238] First, there is the *ethnic enclave*, which requires the least amount of assimilation. These enclaves provide all that the new immigrant needs—social ties, linguistic familiarity, employment, and cultural identity. There is pressure on the immigrant to retain their ethnic identity. These enclaves reinforce a strong we/them or insider/outsider mentality. Marriage is usually with another member of the ethnic group. Almost every large city has ethnic enclaves ranging in population from dozens to thousands.

Secondly, some immigrants do not group themselves geographically, but they form social and virtual networks functions as *cultural threads* that bind them together. Chatrooms, internet-based newspapers with a focus on their former country, and other social media forms (including immigrant dating sites) are ways that people keep contact with one another. These immigrants have a high level of human capital, so they do not need to live in an ethnic enclave. For example, when I lived in Singapore there were thousands of Filipina maids spread across the densely populated island. If they did not abuse the privilege, they could talk

[236] Wan and Casey, 53.
[237] Ibid.
[238] Ibid., 55–58.

with one another by telephone. They had personal time on Sundays, and they could often be found in the central part of the city socializing with one another. Some believers had their own Filipino church services on Sunday.

The third model, called the *urban tribe*, requires the most amount of assimilation. Individuals from different groups leave behind aspects of their cultures behind and in doing so form a new distinct identity. "The new group is composed of highly heterogeneous individuals, living as a group in the mainstream urban culture or sub-culture of the city."[239]

Territorial Passage Model Revisited

The three steps of the territorial passage model were separation, transition, and incorporation. The incorporation step is closely related to assimilation. Chavez suggests that there are facets of incorporation, including economic, social, linguistic, cultural, and personal. He notes that these facets "are interwoven as the various threads of a rope: each aspect influences the others."[240] As his ethnography is primarily about undocumented immigrants, his comments on each of these facets may be less relevant than for those immigrants who are documented. For example, when discussing economic incorporation, he points out that it is against the law for employees to hire undocumented immigrants. They can be fined or placed in jail. Hence, there is less incentive for undocumented immigrants to remain in the U.S.

He concludes his ethnography with this poignant statement on personal incorporation. "The territorial passage that undocumented immigrants begin when they leave home does not come to an end; many find full incorporation into the new society difficult to achieve. Until the larger society imagines undocumented immigrants as part of the community, they will continue to live as 'outsiders' inside American society."[241]

---

[239] Ibid., 55.
[240] Chavez, 194.
[241] Ibid., 208.

Cultural Identity

As immigrants come into the U.S. one of their tasks lies in constructing a cultural identity. We have already mentioned levels of assimilation, which are all part of constructing an identity. But cultural identity construction means more than how a group (or a person) sees himself or herself. A group presents an identity, on the one hand, and others outside the group confer an identity, and the two may be entirely different. "Identification with a community, as well as incorporation within a community, is a constantly constructed and contested process."[242] Lewellen makes a similar point concerning personal cultural identity, that is, how an individual perceives himself or herself, and how the person is perceived popularly. He comments that "the first is the most complex because the way a person identifies herself at any given time depends on context; she is at one time a sister or daughter, another time a wife, another time a church member … The second definition, how the individual is popularly seen, is quite different, less complicated. Society lives through its stereotypes, its overtly generalized and monolithic classifications."[243]

Cultural identity is a dynamic process of becoming that never is completed. It always takes place in a context that needs to be interpreted. In a globalized world being a member of a community need not be rooted in a place of geographical nearness. Today community is about "a shared collective cultural consciousness." Immigrants can share community while living at great distance from other members of their immigrant community. "The technical term of this phenomenon is heterolocalism—a connected dispersion."[244] Appadurai makes the same point: "Our very models of culture shape will have to alter, as configurations of people, place and heritage lose all semblance of isomorphism… The landscapes of group identity—the ethnoscapes—around the world are no longer familiar anthropological objects, insofar as groups are no longer tightly

---

[242] Rynkiewich, 211.
[243] Lewellen, 92.
[244] Wan and Casey, 57.

territorialized, spatially bounded, historically unselfconscious, or culturally homogeneous."[245]

Anthropological Tools for Researching Immigrant Communities

The tools of anthropological research help to better understand immigrants. Anthropological research is a discovery process. It differs from other types of research in that it intends to let the community (or family/families) inform and determine the cultural categories. The anthropologist/observer does not enter a community to prove a preconceived thesis. Information comes from the members of the community from face-to-face interactions rather than from pre-scripted questionnaires. The culture is not determined inside the confines of a sterile laboratory but rather in everyday life as people interact with one another. The immigrant's culture should be viewed as "a system of knowledge shared by members of a group. Discovery ethnography is the process of uncovering, recording, and describing that knowledge."[246] The culture is inferred from observation of behavior and the artifacts that the culture has produced, which includes their worldview and ideas.

Studying a culture is often termed cultural exegesis, which usually goes along with or is preceded by bibliographic and demographic research on the immigrant community. There are two tasks involved in cultural exegesis, according to Leong: "1) *descriptive examination* of the culture, and 2) *prescriptive evaluation* of the culture. To 'read' and interpret the culture as a text is to first examine its *content*—traditions, experiences, values—and then to evaluate this examination ... according to its *context*—social, historical, religious, and so on."[247]

---

[245] Appadurai, 46–48.
[246] David McCurdy, James Spradley, and Dianna Shandy. *The Cultural Experience: Ethnography in Complex Society.* (Long Grove: Waveland Press, 2005), viii.
[247] David P. Leong. *Street Signs: Toward a Missional Theology of Urban Cultural Engagement.* (Eugene: Pickwick Publications, 2012), 111.

Demographic Research

U.S. census data is necessary to physically locate the immigrants in their state, county, and city. Government publications provide data at the national, state, and city level. However, the data at the city level is not strong on the geographic location and boundaries of immigrants. It is easiest to research immigrants who have joined together in ethnic enclaves. Wan and Casey report that "Immigrants and refugees often congregate in apartment complexes in the city, many of which are part of a government housing program designed to help internationals transition into the U.S. ... A listing of apartments housing immigrants may be obtained through a visit to the local immigrant social services facility."[248] After the community or communities have been determined, the researcher attempts to locate likely sites where the immigrants gather and frequent—restaurants, ethnic grocery stores, employment locations, parks, places of worship, libraries. These locations in the community should be noted and described on a city map which helps to delimit the geographic disbursement of the immigrants.

Participant Observation

For well over a century the key research method used by anthropologists has been participant observation. The researcher enters a community and takes up residence there, or perhaps more appropriate today, thereby. The researcher spends much of his or her time observing what the members of the immigrant culture do. Perhaps a new language must be learned to be able to communicate with the people. Observations are noted and recorded to be studied as a later time. As the researcher become accepted into the community, he or she begins to participate in the activities that are taking place. Wan and Casey suggest that there are three levels of participant observation. *Non-participant observation* is where the observer does not participate in the activities, selling drugs, for example. *Partial participation* means the researcher can

---

[248] Wan and Casey, 72.

participate to a limited degree, but not playing a central role. An example of partial participation would be attending a wedding as a guest, but not having a central role in the ceremony. *Full participation* is "when the researcher has an essential and integral part of cultural process."[249] To illustrate full participation, when our first daughter was born while we lived in a Maasai village in Kenya, we participated in a traditional Maasai naming ceremony for her. We were full, not partial, participants in this ritual.

Interviewing

Participant observation has its limits as a research method, so it is usually enhanced with ethnographic interviewing. In studying an immigrant community those with inside information should be sought out to share this information with the researcher. Rapport with these individuals should be achieved as they can also provide access to others in the community. Ethnographic surveys with interviewees can be undertaken, and like any general survey, should include a variety of people in the community and from a variety of ages. A benefit of interviewing immigrants is that the researcher's desire is to understand data and observations from *their* point of view. Returning to Lewellen: "Postmodernism demands that the subaltern be given a voice, that we try to understand the world through the eyes of our subjects. It points out the arbitrariness of our classification systems and forces us to recognize the degree to which categories like tribe or peasant suggest firm boundaries around groups that are fluid and malleable."[250] The interviewer enters the immigrants' *frame of reference*, rather than expecting the immigrant to enter the researcher's frame of reference.

Ethnosemantics

As culture also includes what immigrants think, it is important to be able to access that data. While some thinking results in activities which can be

---

[249] Ibid., 75.
[250] Lewellen, 46.

observed, there is much which cannot be observed. One research method in interviewing has been termed *ethnosemantics* (or ethnoscience, componential analysis, or cognitive anthropology). The technique is "built on the idea that culture is learned, shared knowledge, much of which is coded in language."[251] The shared knowledge is "stored as a system of categories in the human brain. A category is a group of things that people classify together and treat as if they were the same."[252] The interviewer records the actual words used which are used when immigrants talk to one another, deemed folk terms.[253] From these folk terms, McCurdy, Spradley, and Shandy go on to describe taxonomies, domain analysis, and cultural themes coming from those being interviewed, or even a single interviewee who represents the culture.

Semiotics

Another research method is called *semiotics*. Geertz writes, "The concept of culture I espouse … is essentially a semiotic one," which he calls "thick description."[254] Leong used this method in his study of Seattle's Rainier Valley. He explains, "Semiotics is a diverse, interdisciplinary field that studies how signs and symbols create meaning in contexts ranging from linguistics and anthropology to biology and computer science. Its fundamental inquiry has to do with the nature of the sign, and its function in the realm of meaning, with all the dimensions of complexity therein."[255] Semiotics would see immigrant culture "as a vast network, whereby both verbal and nonverbal messages are circulated along elaborate, interconnected pathways, which, together, create systems of meaning."[256] Describing a culture using a semiotic approach points to the four areas of location, definition, interpretation, and categorization. Leong elaborates: "These four areas—1) the location of cultural texts; 2) the definition of their

---

[251] McCurdy, Spradley, and Shandy, x.
[252] Ibid., 35–36.
[253] Ibid., 28.
[254] Clifford Geertz. *The Interpretation of Cultures.* (New York: Basic Books, 2000), 5–6.
[255] Leong, 170.
[256] Robert J. Schreiter. *Constructing Local Theologies.* (Maryknoll: Orbis Books, 1985), 49.

dual-natured signs, 3) the interpretation of their messages, and 4) the categorization of their meaning into domains—encompass a systematic analytical method of semiotic description of culture."[257]

For immigrants who do not live in an ethnic enclave, but rather have dispersed throughout the community, state, and nation, different research methods will be required. While participant observation and interviewing can be done at the individual or family level, one does not have the benefit of a geographic community in which to conduct research. Immigrants not residing in the ethnic enclave are transient. The cultural threads must be discerned and followed, which can involve virtual research.

Conclusion

The question remains—why would anthropologists, especially those who would be reading a book such as this one, want to study immigrants? Because we are human, and because those we research are human, bonds are developed. Friendships are created. Human empathy comes into play. We make moral connections with immigrants. Our research is not a "disinterested search for knowledge."[258] are involved.

While the researcher may come to the study with personal goals, it is imperative that the goals of the immigrant community also be considered. What are their problems and have can the research have a role in addressing those problems? Anthropologists of the past approached a community with the naïve idea of "not doing any harm." But anthropologists brought change to a community just as did travelers, tourists, missionaries and traders, and today's globalization. Some of the changes proved to be harmful. Anthropologists now desire not simply to do no harm, but to make a positive contribution to the community.

---

[257] Leong, 174.
[258] Heyman, 2.

Advocacy anthropology is where the researcher desires to stand up for those who have been studied, to make their voices heard, to represent them to the local authorities and majority culture. Regarding immigrants, this is a part of our mission and ministry.

SECTON THREE

Worship

CHAPTER EIGHT

The Significance of Food and Meal-Sharing in Migrant Churches: A Biblical, Cultural, Eucharistic, and Practical Theological Approach

HyeRan Kim-Cragg

In June 2017, I was on a train going to the city/region of Wuppertal that includes the town of Barmen where the German Protestant Christians made a theological declaration against the Nazi government in 1934. On the train, I met a retired German couple who live in Dusseldorf, one hour from Wuppertal via train. We began to talk about migration once I learned that both Wuppertal and Dusseldorf had recently received many refugees. I asked, "what is it like to have so many refugees in your city?:" They said, "One thing that has been changed is German diet. We used to eat meat mainly and few vegetables. Now we have so many other kinds of food that come from the Mediterranean diet thanks to new immigrants and refugees. We think this is good" I agreed with them because I also noticed during my time teaching at Wuppertal that salad bars were prominent and various kinds of vegetables and olives, as well as hummus, were regularly on offer, a change from previous experiences I had had with German food.

The scale and the scope of migration has drastically changed in the last century. Canadian historian Jennifer Welsh shows how the Second World War was a high-water mark in the global history of migration, with huge numbers of people crossing multiple national borders.[259] The data in 2015 shows, however, that we have now exceeded the Second World War levels with the total number of displaced people across the globe in that year was 65 million. These are the highest levels human history has seen thus far.[260] There is an urgent need for theologians to "engage with this developing migratory context in depth and with nuance,"[261] if we Christians and the Church are going to be responsive to the world in which we participate. That is why the topic of "Mission, Migration, and Ministry," which this book presents, is critical for our church and church leadership as well as for theological education.

My recent experience in Germany affirms that when migrants travel their food also travels. While lifting up for a particular significance of meal-sharing in migrant churches, first, we will argue for the importance of food in human society in general, followed by how the early Christian community understood food including the debate about which food should or should not be eaten. Secondly, we will examine the practice of post-worship meal-sharing in migrant churches and will feature Korean diaspora faith communities in this discussion to highlight how this practice may be regarded as a gift of migrant churches to the established Christian churches in North America and Europe. This paper will also explore the division between the practice of the Eucharist during the Sunday liturgy and the practice of meal-sharing after worship as a result of liturgy detached from everyday life. To mend this division, finally, we look at table fellowship as the central element of worship, expounding the meanings of Eucharist as *koinonia* and solidarity.

---

[259] Jennifer Welsh, *The Return of History: Conflict, Migration, and Geopolitics in the Twenty-First Century* (Toronto: House of Anansi Press, 2016), 121.

[260] http://reliefweb.int/report/world/unhcr-global-trends-forced-displacement-2015, accessed on December 29, 2017.

[261] Susanna Snyder, *Church in an Age of Global Migration: A Moving Body,* Susanna Snyder, Joshua Ralston, and Agnes M. Brazal, eds. (New York: Palgrave Macmillan, 2016), Introduction, 3.

Food and Faith: A Delicate Relationship in Christianity

Eating is the most fundamental social practice. What people eat or do not eat shapes their life. While eating itself is essential to life, eating is more than simply survival. Eating contributes to the development of one's physical, emotional, intellectual, and spiritual well-being. Eating and not eating, including fasting, is also one of the most distinctive features of religious practice. "Practices related to food, undertaken over time and in the company of wise and seasoned practitioners, have the power to form and even to transform persons and communities—a power acknowledged not only within Christianity but also in other religious traditions," practical theologian Dorothy Bass contends.[262] Theologically speaking, Mexican Catholic Dominican scholar, Angel Méndez-Montoya, puts it this way, "Food matters so much that God became food, our daily bread."[263] A Reformed liturgical theologian from the USA, Ruth Duck, similarly contends that meal sharing was the center of Jesus's earthly ministry as he fed the thousands, welcomed outcasts into his table, and celebrated the Passover meal as a last act with his disciples.[264]

But food sometimes divides communities. The early churches' struggle around food offered to idols is a case in point. Some believed that it was not a problem to eat food that was dedicated to idols if they did not believe in the idols. Others were bothered by this practice and considered it blasphemy (1 Corinthians 8:1–12). To this, the Apostle Paul advises that food should not be a community dividing issue. However, he says, the issue of who eats and what they eat should be handled with care and conscience. He was clear that the personal choice of eating certain food or not should not harm community or wound others.

---

[262] Dorothy Bass, "Eating," in *The Willey-Blackwell Companion to Practical Theology,* Bonnie Miller-McLemore, ed. (Chichester: Blackwell, 2012), 57.

[263] Angel Méndez-Montoya, *The Theology of Food: Eating and the Eucharist* (Sussex: Wiley-Blackwell, 2012), 73.

[264] Ruth Duck, *Worship for the Whole People of God: Vital Worship for the 21st Century* (Louisville: Westminster John Knox, 2013), 68.

Of course, there were strict rules in Judaism at that time about what could be eaten and what could not. Food was used to indicate the separation of the people of God from others in the same way circumcision was. Choosing not to eat certain kinds of food was an important value for Jewish religious understanding and still is today. This intentional act of setting oneself apart is central to the act of worship. Sacrifice, coming from the Latin word 'sacrificare,' understood as offering and worship literally means "setting apart for special use or purpose" or "making sacred."[265] However, setting apart or separation became a problem when it excluded people. Peter had to deal with this issue specifically as it related to food. He was confronted with it in a dream where God told him that everything God made is clean, thus may be eaten (Acts 10: 9–16). Peter came to understand that "profane and unclean are human terms that establish between persons seeking God."[266] This epiphany moment of Peter's conversion breaking the food barrier between Jews and Gentiles was a life changing moment in his ministry where he boldly preached, "God has no partiality" (Acts 10:34), opening up to proclaiming the Gospel of Jesus Christ to gentiles. This is pivotal because up until then, those Jewish Christians who were set out to gentile mission thought that gentiles could become Christian but only after they became Jews; they must become first assimilated into Judaism, culturally speaking, following Jewish rules, customs, and practices. This assimilation included circumcision for men. Peter's report to the Jerusalem Council on this matter is decisive. Acts reports that Peter's argument was so convincing that the circumcised believers who criticized him had to be silenced. His argument was theologically warranted: "If then God gave them the same gift that he gave us when we believed in the Lord Jesus Christ, who was I that I could hinder God?" (Acts 11:17)

---

[265] Mary Ann Beavis and HyeRan Kim-Cragg, *What Does the Bible Say? A Critical Conversation with Popular Culture in a Biblically Illiterate World* (Eugene: Cascade, 2017), 144.
[266] Kathy Black, *Culturally-Conscious Worship* (St. Louis: Chalice, 2000), 40.

The witnesses of Paul and Peter are important for worshipping practices of migrant churches and those who encounter new migrants today. It could be an effective analogy, comparing Jewish Christians in the early Church with European white Christians in most mainline churches today, while comparing gentile Christians with new migrants, as far as the assimilation and the entitlement of certain practices and certain worship matters are concerned. Russell Yee, a third-generation Chinese American liturgical theologian, invites us to imagine what would happen if the same Peter in Acts 11 were sent today as a missionary to share the Good News about Jesus in an Asian North American migrant home. Yee writes, Peter "would come in; take his shoes off; perhaps be served tea…; eat with thanksgiving the udon noodles, pho, roast duck, kim chee, rice porridge, lumpia, or whatever else was served him; and embrace that setting as a fully worthy place for God to give the gift of saving faith in Jesus."[267]

The context of the early Christian community in Greek-Roman times was multicultural, multiethnic and multireligious. It was no stranger to the phenomenon of migration. The very debate surrounding food in Paul's letter to Corinth and the story of Peter in Acts demonstrates the challenge of dealing with diversity of cultures and religious practices, including Jewish and newly converted gentile Christians. People were wrestling with differences, adjusting to new customs, and inevitably running into conflict. New Testament scholar Burton Mack describes this early Christian's struggle as "clashing cultures" where "peoples of all ethnic extractions [were] living together in cities without a common culture…Beneath the surface, serious cultural conflicts swirled around such issues as…the cultural and cultic significance of foods and family meals; the public role of women, proper attire… Difference in codes of purity, propriety, ranking, honor, and shame created friction for people of diverse cultural and

---

[267] Russell Yee, *Worship on the Way: Exploring Asian North American Christian Experience* (Valley Forge: Judson, 2012), 31.

ethnic backgrounds."[268] It is comforting to know this early church community had a similar challenge to ours today. It seems that the society in which the first Christians lived was not much different from the society of Christians in the 21st century as far as the migration is concerned. Indeed, the early Christian communities in the first few centuries were filled with multiple migrations.[269] How can we learn from our ancestors of faith regarding the importance of food in the context of migration?

As mentioned earlier when migrants come to a new place, they bring their own religious, ethnic, and cultural customs with them. There is an African saying "When the people move the church moves."[270] Christianity as a religion carries all of these as spiritual matters and cultural practices in worship. They include "language, music, time, schedule, posture, gesture, movement, deportment, gender, generation, architecture, decoration, furniture, technology, dress, and leadership."[271] These are worship matters as much as cultural matters in migrant churches. The line between liturgy and culture is blurred in migrant churches, although a dominant liturgical theology is shaped by distilled thinking about liturgy and culture.[272] The reality of migration challenges this distilled thinking because when "worship does not have its grounding in people's lives and cultural expressions, it will remain foreign, imposed and irrelevant."[273] The challenge of distilled thinking faces the challenge of these customs, beliefs, and practices that are mixed with and embedded in worship. Some of them are

---

[268] Burton Mack, *Who Wrote the New Testament?: The Making of the Christian Myth* (San Francisco: Harper Collins, 1995), 26–27.

[269] Peter Phan, "Migration in the Patristic Era." In *A Promised Land, a Perilous Journey: Theological Perspectives on Migration,* Daniel G. Goody and Gioacchino Campese, eds. (Notre Dame: University of Notre Dame Press, 2008), 35–61.

[270] Beatrice Okyere-Manu, "The Ethical Implications of Migration on Liturgy: An African Postcolonial Perspective." In *Liturgy in Postcolonial Perspectives: Only One Is Holy,* Cláudio Carvalhaes, ed. (New York: Palgrave Macmillan, 2015), 71.

[271] Yee, *Worship on the Way*, 7.

[272] HyeRan Kim-Cragg and Stephen Burns, "Liturgy in Migration and Migrants in Liturgy." In *Church in an Age of Global Migration: A Moving Body,* Susanna Snyder, Joshua Ralston, and Agnes M Brazal, eds. (Houndmills, Basingstoke: Palgrave, 2016), 115.

[273] Pedrito Maynard-Reid, *Diverse Worship: African-American, Caribbean, and Hispanic Perspectives* (Downers Grove: Inter Varsity Press, 2000), 19.

explicit, while others are not. Culture includes outward rituals and obvious customs as much as it includes subtle movements and non-verbal behaviors that are neither obvious nor visible. Navigating these obvious, hidden, and blurred cultural practices that are blurred in Christian liturgy is key to understanding worship in migrant churches.

A well-grounded liturgy as a way of life that reflects and shapes daily practices is closely related to culture when culture is understood as "shared ways of acting that are related to ethnic identity."[274] Of course, we must be aware of the danger of essentializing culture as if it can be described as unified or homogenous. For that matter, it is also extremely dangerous to attempt to sum up any ethnic migrant worship culture as if it can be described as one uniformed reality. Asia, as an example of an ethnic and geographical category, is a continent that is most religiously and culturally pluralistic. Catholic liturgical theologian Jonathan Tan who hails from Singapore, previously lived in Australia, and now resides in USA, criticizes the ahistorical essentialism of early theologies of Asian liturgical inculturation which emphasized the ideals of cohesive group identity. Seeking harmony and unity for liturgical inculturation ends up dismissing differences and contributing to exclusions of groups that cannot fit into a neat "Asian" box. Tan identifies a specific group that is often excluded from discussions of Asian-ness, the group known as the 1.5 generation and east-Asian immigrants to the US. This group is diverse; they are made up of people who came to the US as children or who were born in the US to first and second generation Asian immigrants, Asian American adoptees of white parents, and bi/multiracial Asian Americans.[275] The term "Asian American" or "Asian" has been contested by many scholars and theologians when such term mainly points

---

[274] Yee, *Worship on the Way*, xvii.
[275] Jonathan Y. Tan, "Asian American Catholics and Contemporary Liturgical Migration: From Tradition-Maintenance to Traditioning," in *Liturgy in Migration: From the Upper Room to Cyberspace,* edited by Teresa Berger (Collegeville: Liturgical Press, 2012), 243–44.

to uniformity or sameness.[276] While it is a helpful term, in terms of distinguishing themselves from European descent migrants and African or South American descent migrants, it may fail to disclose vast differences among people under the roof of this term Asian or Asian-American. For in some cases, "we [Asian Americans] are perhaps even more different, and more diverse among ourselves," as Lisa Lowe who studied Asian migrants in the USA noted.[277] Such is the dilemma of diversity which the current context of immigration presents. While challenging, ethnic pluralism portrayed in biblical traditions is "a divine blessing."[278]

Meal-Sharing Practice in the Migrant Churches: Challenges and Promises to Eucharist

Liturgical theologian Kathy Black derives four essential practices of worship based on and the passage in Acts that describes the early Christians as having "all things in common" (Acts 2:44). The first practice, according to Acts, is studying biblical texts together. It includes discerning present-day apostles and prophets to impart wisdom to the next generation. Second is fellowship. It involves activities of sharing resources and building up the community. Third is breaking bread together. This included the Eucharist on Sunday and sharing meals at the church or various homes on other days. Finally, praising (singing and praying) was the core practice of Jewish and Christian worship in the early community.[279] Black identifies these ancient practices in order to draw attention

---

[276] Namsoon Kang, "Who/What is Asian? A Postcolonial Theological Reading of Orientalism and Neo-Orientalism." In *Postcolonial Theologies, Divinity, and Empire*, Catherine Keller, Michael Nausner and Mayra Rivera, eds. (St. Louis: Chalice, 2004), 101 (100–17). HyeRan Kim-Cragg, "Between and Beyond Asian-ness: A Voice of a Postcolonial Hybrid Korean-Canadian in the Diaspora." In *What Young Asian Theologians Are Thinking*: the CSCA Christianity in Southeast Asia Series No 7, edited by Leow Theng Huat (Singapore, Trinity Theological College, 2014), 90–102.

[277] Lisa Lowe, "Heterogeneity, Hybridity, and Multiplicity: Making Asian American Differences," *Diaspora* 1 (1991): 27 (22–44).

[278] Bernard Anderson, *From Creation to New Creation* (Minneapolis: Fortress, 1994), 177.

[279] Black, *Culturally Conscious Worship*, 39.

to culturally conscious contemporary worship services that take cultural difference seriously in the 21st century. Although she did not explicitly name migration as a driving force in these pluralistic contexts, we contend a need for culturally conscious worship due to migration. Attention to a particular context and a particular experience in the changing religiously and culturally pluralistic contexts is necessary in an age of global migration. Some may argue that Black's approach, identifying four essential practices of worship, sounds too much like a prescription of a universal norm dressed up like a transcultural liturgy, "the same substance for everyone everywhere, beyond cultural."[280] However, what is shaping liturgy today is not a prescription but the lived experience of changing pluralistic migrant realities.

Among the four practices that Black suggests as central to Christian worship, our focus is the third practice of breaking bread together.[281] However, we find that there is a strong relationship of breaking bread to the second practice of fellowship. For the migrant churches, these two practices often go together. While we discuss the issues of breaking bread together around Eucharist, our discussion is not so much the Eucharist of the Sunday liturgy as the experience of meal sharing outside of Sunday morning worship practice. In fact, early Christian worship included the meal along with the service, holding a synagogue-type worship early Sunday morning (before work) and a meal Sunday evening (after work).[282] Catholic liturgical theologian Edward Foley shows how this eating tradition in Roman-era Judaism was adopted by the early Christian church.[283] Today however, having both formal and informal practices of meal-

---

[280] The Nairobi Statement on Worship and Culture, 1.3. found at https://worship.calvin.edu/resources/resource-library/nairobi-statement-on-worship-and-culture-full-text.

[281] Gordon Lathrop, *Central Things: Worship in Word and Sacrament* (Minneapolis: Fortress, 2006). Connecting Scripture with Sacrament, he names word, prayer, bath, and table as essentials to worship.

[282] Ruth Duck, *Worship for the Whole People of God* (Louisville: Westminster/John Knox, 2013), 68.

[283] Edward Foley, *From Age to Age: How Christians Have Celebrated the Eucharist* (Collegeville: Liturgical Press, 2008), 29.

sharing in and outside Sunday liturgy offers gifts and challenges, promises and problems to white European mainline churches and ethnic minority migrant churches.

One of the distinguishing features of most, if not all, Korean and Korean immigrant churches in North America is meal sharing after worship every Sunday. While this practice is not exclusive to Korean Church culture in the migrant church contexts, a particularly strong connection is made between ethnicity and food sharing as a Christian practice.

Sophia Park, focusing on the first generation of Korean American immigrant Christians, and their children argues that food for Koreans is significant in shaping their psychological, emotional, social, and cultural self. Sharing Korean meals as a church community helps the members to heal from to racism in white dominant society. Korean food as a cultural connector reminds them of who they are in their liminal bicultural realities. Korean food is also a comfort food that may contribute to their psychological healing in a foreign land.[284] Food helps them to remember who they are, to connect with each other in fellowship, and finally to make them realize whose they are, God's claim upon them as a beloved people.

Here a theological doctrine of "justification by grace" may be helpful to further articulate this claim that God had upon marginalized migrants. Justification by grace is partly about one's status before God. The Apostle Paul first framed this doctrine in relation to the marginalization of Gentile converts to Christianity. As discussed earlier, they had not adopted the practice of adherence to the Jewish law, leaders in the early church taught that Jewish Christians could not eat with them. When the church in Galatian celebrated a communal meal, Gentile Christians had to eat separately. They were treated lesser than Jewish Christians because of food. Paul argued against this on the basis of the principle that in Christ, all members are equal (Gal. 2:16–17). This principle is partly

---

[284] Sophia Park, "Come and Eat: Sharing Food as a New Cultural Space that Heals," *Sacred Spaces: The e-Journal of the American Association of Pastoral Counselors* Vol. 3 (2011): 71, 75, 76.

composed of a doctrine of justification by grace. Paul's argument is that the judgment of others is of no ultimate consequence in relation to the judgment that God rendered on us and all others in Jesus Christ. Knowing that we are justified before God through Jesus Christ grants to one a sense of dignity and purpose that towers above the judgments of others. Korean American theologian Sang Hyun Lee writes, for Korean and Asian Americans, "justification means acceptance, belonging, recognition, and inclusion."[285]

Equipped with justification by grace, Korean Christian migrants develops ways to support each other. A church community is one such place where support of acceptance, belonging, recognition, and inclusion happens. Meal-sharing as a concrete, physical, and communal practice is arguably the most important act that they foster their own agency. In the Korean language, "Have you eaten?" is a phrase that expresses a care and a concern of one another's well-beings.[286] When one is asking this question to another, she or he is not only concerned about whether that person's stomach is empty or not. It is a question directed to the well-being of that person. In other words, the phrase, "Have you eaten?" includes meanings such as "Are you well?" "Are you in peace?" Dong-Sun Kim, who studied Eucharist in Korean cultural contexts, contends that Koreans regard family more in terms of food sharing than in terms of bloodlines.[287] One term referred to family in Korean language is "the mouth that needs to be fed" His scholarship deepens our understanding of this simple cultural question that emphasizes the importance of food and meal-sharing.

The Korean linguistic culture surrounding food finds a kindred spirit in Judeo-Christian traditions. Gillian Feely-Harnik who studied early Christianity and Judaism contends that food is the most important language in which Jews

---

[285] Sang Hyun Lee, *From a Liminal Place: An Asian American Theology* (Minneapolis: Fortress, 2010), 101.
[286] HyeRan Kim-Cragg, "Through Senses and Sharing: How Liturgy Meets Food," *Liturgy* 32:2, 38 (34–41).
[287] Dong-sun Kim, *The Bread for Today and the Bread for Tomorrow: The Ethical Significance of the Lord's Supper in the Korean Context* (New York: Peter Lang, 2001), 99.

expressed relations among people and between human beings and God.[288] It is no wonder why the ministry of Jesus was heavily centered around food! He ate and drank with people as a way of showing God's love beyond social boundaries and human made barriers.

To claim that our sense of peace is determined by access to food is not to contend that one's own well-being is only subject to a physical and biological conditions. Instead, it stresses that embodied physical needs is integral to the person and connected to the spiritual and the communal dimension of one's life. When one is hungry, it is not just a personal and physical matter; but it also becomes a spiritual, theological, and social matter, to which we must attend.

Yet, it is puzzling to note that the practice of Eucharist in Sunday worship in Korean protestant migrant churches is not significant, given its highly elevated and common practice of meal sharing. One Korean church historian explores this paradox. According to Kyungbae Min, "[The Rev.] Underwood landed in Inchon in April 1885, but he could not imagine celebrating the eucharist with Korean believers...It was on 27 April 1889 that the first Korean could participate in the eucharist not in Korea but in China, four years after the gospel had been proclaimed in Korea. Long afterwards, the first official eucharist could be celebrated in Pyungyang on 8 January 1894, eight years after the Korean Bible had been published."[289] Rather than on the Eucharist, the emphasis on preaching was so strong that worship attendance was identified with and actually translated as "listening to a sermon" Such European and American missionary's influence has permeated over the centuries in Korea. The balance between Word and Sacrament is still a challenge for most Reformed churches in Korea and Korean migrant churches in North America. Kathy Black has learned that migrant churches are more apt to follow worship practices of the Eucharist as passed down by the missionaries in their countries of origin. For example,

---

[288] Gilliam Feely-Harnik, *The Lord's table: The meaning of food in the early Judaism and Christianity* (Washington DC.: Smithsonian Books, 1994), 19.

[289] Kyungbae Min, "Church Patterns in Early Stage?" *Christian Thought* (March 1965): 85, cited in Kim, *The Bread for Today,* 147.

Vietnamese, Cambodian, Hmong and Lao migrant congregations in the USA follow the Eucharistic practice of the Christian Missionary Alliance that missionized many South Asian people.[290] Thus, a work of developing a liturgy for migrants involves decolonizing work, free from the century old missionary thinking and practice.[291] It calls for a critical examination of how certain missionaries' teaching and their ways of worshipping are transplanted into local cultures and considered as superior to the local practices.

However, not every missionary work was dismissive of the local culture. A historical example provided by Yee is salient in this regard. Pope Alexander VII offered an instruction to those who were ready to go to Asia including China for their missionary work: "Do not in any way attempt, and do not on any pretext persuade these people to change their rites, habits, and customs, unless they are openly opposed to religion and good morals. For what could be more absurd than to bring France, Spain, Italy, or any other European country over to China? It is not your country but the faith you must bring, that faith which does not reject or belittle the rites or customs of any nation as long as these rites are not evil, but rather desires that they be preserved in their integrity and fostered.... [The] customs of their country and especially their country itself should be esteemed, loved, and respected above anything else in the world... Admire and praise whatever merits praise."[292] His Pope given to the missionaries is remarkable. A sense of the appreciation of the local culture with deep respect is profound. This instruction given in 1659 is relevant 450 years later in the age of global migration. The lesson from this instruction must be remembered to practice today.

---

[290] Kathy Black, *Worship Across Cultures: A Handbook* (Nashville: Abingdon, 1998), 12.
[291] Kim-Cragg and Burns, "Liturgy in Migration and Migrants in Liturgy," 117.
[292] J. Neuner, SJ and J. Dupuis, SJ, eds., *The Christian Faith in the Doctrinal Documents of the Catholic Church* (New York: Alba House, 1982), 309–10, cited in Yee, *Worship on the Way,* 72–73.

Eucharist as Koinonia and Solidarity: Connecting Liturgy with Life in Migrant Churches

To share meals after Sunday worship as a migrant community is an essential practice that connects to daily life. The Eucharist alone does not allow immigrants to experience the communion with God and one another for which they hunger. It is always a challenge for any liturgical theologian or committed Christian worship leader to create worship experiences for their congregation that integrate a way of life and a range of experiences that carry on through the week. Yet our understanding of liturgy as the work of the people seems to demand daily practice that shapes lives over the course of the week and even influences patterns of secular society. Such a view has been suggested by liturgical theologians who are influenced by political theology.[293] It is imperative that what we do in worship should matter to the world. Lutheran ethicist Cynthia Moe-Lobeda addresses this issue by asking, "How will the church receive and celebrate the meal in a manner that opens our eyes to see what is, what could be, and the power and presence of God 'compassioning' the world so that we may participate in God's work 'to change and renew the world?'"[294] To her, connecting liturgy, especially Eucharist, with daily life for shaping society has to do with deepening the meaning of the meal-sharing practice of the Christian churches as *koinonia*. The Apostle Paul uses this term referring to the eucharist, as he expanded its Hellenistic meaning of *koinonia* referred to "financial partnership," or "partnership in work, friendship with a willingness to share material possessions" Paul says, "I speak as to sensible people; judge for yourselves what I say. The cup of blessing that we bless, is it not a sharing in the

---

[293] Liturgical theologian Bruce Morrill in conversation with political theologian Johann Baptist Metz wrote a compelling book on Eucharistic prayer, *Anamnesis as Dangerous Memory: Political and Liturgical Theology in Dialogue* (Collegeville: Liturgical Press, 2000). Cynthia Moe-Lobeda examines baptism as political theology in *Public Church: For the Life of the World* (Minneapolis: Fortress, 2000).

[294] Cynthia D. Moe-Lobeda, "Liturgy Shaping Society." In *Ordo: Bath, Word, Prayer, and Table: A Liturgical Primer in honor of Gordon W. Lathrop,* edited by Dirk G. Lange and Dwight W. Vogel (Akron: OSL, 2005), 171. Emphasis is original.

blood of Christ? The bread that we break, is it not a sharing in the body of Christ?" (1 Cor. 10:15–16).

Koinonia points to the sharing of food and other material things among those in need. In *The Blessed Sacrament of the Holy and True Body and Blood of Christ, and the Brotherhoods,* Martin Luther writes, "Christ has given his body for this purpose, that the one thing signified by the sacrament—the fellowship, the change wrought by love—may be put into practice... The sacrament has no blessing and significant unless love grows daily and so changes a person that he is made one with the others... Thus, by means of this sacrament, all self-seeking love is rooted out and gives place to that which seeks the common good of all."[295] In this Luther's Eucharistic theology, Eucharist is not simply the commemoration of the past but a re-orientation and transformation of the present that seeks the common good of all.

Luther's Eucharistic theology helps us understand how meal-sharing has a political and structural aspect with implications for societies affected by migration today. It is a matter of justice when food is not shared, and people go hungry. That is why the post-service meal-sharing in Korean and other migrant churches is important, and why it strengthens the meaning of the Eucharist. When a migrant has suffered from racism, sharing familiar food with others in community can be a source of healing, as raised earlier. This culturally embedded faith-based practice of sharing food allows migrants to create an alternative world, by challenging the current unjust society that discriminates against migrants. It helps re-reveal the meaning of Eucharist as a communion, a leveling and unifying force. It also invites those of us who are in a dominant position in society to reflect on meal-sharing as form of solidarity. Solidarity includes owning the problem of poverty and inequity to create an alternative way of life where settlers and migrants co-dwell with respect and in peace. That is the meaning *koinonia* presented in the New Testament.

---

[295] Cited in Moe-Lobeda, "Liturgy Shaping Society," 173–74.

The very notion of *koinonia* as solidarity and responsibility points to systematic dimensions. Chinese migrant Christians translate *koinonia* as *Tuen-kai*. *Tuen,* means solidarity and *kai* means responsibility in Cantonese. The late David Ng, a second generation Chinese American theologian and Christian educator, further commented on this translated understanding of *koinonia*: "These terms carry no sentimental sense of camaraderie and unity of likeminded agreeable folks who choose and create their own 'fellowship' as is often the case in North American churches."[296] Rather, the sacramental community of *koinonia*, the people who seek to share the meal at the Table, include the victims who suffer from injustices, as much as the ones who are beneficiary of the unjust distribution of what is needed for life with dignity. That is why the Eucharist can be a practice of solidarity between victims and beneficiaries. That is also why the Eucharist can be also a practice of responsibility of those who benefit from this unjust system.

When this practice ripens to be a full sharing, the Eucharist becomes "communion (*koinonia*) in the fullest sense of the word—profound solidarity—and where communion is eucharist (thanksgiving) in all its plentitude."[297] According to The Didache, one of the oldest documents of the early church, the key to understand the Eucharist is to understand the importance of "the meal-sharing tradition that Jesus practiced" rather than simply remembering and repeating "one account of the meal" This tradition is a breaking tradition, Dirk Lange writes, as Jesus was breaking every ritual norm and social practice that benefited the status quo, through eating and drinking.[298] This very ordinary act of eating and drinking is "interrupted" in the intentional act of discerning the sparks of the grace of God.

---

[296] David Ng, "A Path of Concentric Circles: Toward an Autobiographical Theology of Community." In *Journeys at the Margin: Toward an Autobiographical Theology in American-Asian Perspective*, Peter Phan and Jung Young Lee, eds. (Collegeville: Liturgical Press, 1999), 102.

[297] Moe-Lobeda, "Liturgy Shaping Society," 179.

[298] Dirk G. Lange, "Eating, Drinking, Sending: Reflections on the Juxtaposition of Law and Event in the Eucharist." In *Ordo: Bath, Word, Prayer, Table: A Liturgical Primer in honor of Gordon W. Lathrop,* Dirk G. Lange and Dwight W. Vogel, eds. (Akron: OSL, 2005), 89.

What Next? Identifying Further Work

This study mainly focused on Asian North American migrant Christian experiences of meal sharing, Korean immigrant experiences in particular. While food and meal sharing is ubiquitous across different ethnic groups, meal sharing in Asian ethnic migrant churches has proven to be most essential, something common despite vast differences among Asian migrant communities. We have argued that food, which signifies the material condition of migrant life connects to the practice of the Eucharist and meal-sharing after Sunday liturgy. These can be essential practices of Christian faith for connecting people's daily life in the context of migration and in creating a just society.

Finally, it would be fruitful to identify further work on worship in migrant churches. While we have suggested meal-sharing as an essential practice to worship in migrant churches, it does not mean that other acts of worship are insignificant in migrant churches. For example, prayer is important. Early morning prayer is a distinctive practice developed in Korea but continued in Korean migrant churches.[299] Such emphasis on prayer shows piety and dedicated life to God. The other prayer that is common in Korean worship practice is toungsung kido (literally, "praying together out loud") which shows passion including laments toward God.[300] Praying out loud is also found in Taiwan and China.[301] This kind of fervent prayer is also practiced in African, Afro-American, and Caribbean migrant churches. Thus, it can serve as a potential further study for bridging race relations between Korean American and African Americans, given their hostile relationships.[302] Singing and dancing could be most distinctive

---

[299] Duck, *Worship for the Whole People of God*, 42.

[300] Su Yon Pak, Unzu Lee, Jung Ha Kim, and Myungsil Cho, *Singing the Lord's Song in a New Land: Korean Practices of Faith* (Louisville: Westminster/John Knox, 2005), 36.

[301] Duck, *Worship for the Whole People of God*, in conversation with another liturgical scholar, I-to Loh, 295, footnote #32.

[302] Pak, et al., *Singing the Lord's Song in a New Land*, 43.

and essential in African and Caribbean migrant churches,[303] while spontaneous praying inspired by the role of the Holy Spirit may be an important feature that characterizes Latina/o migrant churches.[304] Much is to be learned from their approach to worship where food is prepared, and room is decorated for all people across different ages, a familia, creating a reverent intimate and welcoming space of worship.[305]

---

[303] Kay Kaufman Shelemay, "Sounding the Challenges of Forced Migration: Musical Lessons from the Ethiopian Orthodox Christian Diaspora." In *Liturgy in Migration: From the Upper Room to Cyberspace,* Teresa Berger, ed. (Collegeville: Liturgical Press, 2012), 229–42.

[304] Néstor Medina, "Being Church as Latina/n Pentecostals." In *Church in an Age of Global Migration: A Moving Body,* Susanna Snyder, Joshua Ralston, and Agnes M. Brazal, eds. (New York: Palgrave Macmillan, 2015), 65–80.

[305] Justo Gonzalez, *Alabalde! Hispanic Christian Worship* (Nashville: Abingdon, 1996), 19–24.

CHAPTER NINE

Worship in Latino Protestant Immigrant Churches[306]

Ricardo L. Franco

In spite of the variety of immigrant stories and experiences present in Latino communities there are certain distinctive theological approaches and spiritual practices shared by the group at large. These common particularities are often overlooked by the literature in the field and constitute the main contribution of this chapter. Central to the Latino understanding of worship is the theological notion of "conversion" and the place of the immigrant experience in the spiritual journey before and after one's conversion experience. Because of the mobility of these communities Latino spirituality is often construe as a *via theological* rather than as a *locus* of theological reflection. For these reasons practices and rituals are much more informal, spontaneous, and less tied to places of worship or liturgical scripts. The Bible is considered a road map and it functions as a reservoir of symbols, metaphors, and stories which provides the raw material for the process of meaning making and the re-enactment of life scripts in the spiritual journey of the community. Finally, several wide-spread misrepresentations of Latino worship experience such as the "salsa flavor" of music or the "fiesta" type of liturgy are contested through a serious, empirical analysis of what actually takes place in Latino immigrant congregations.

---

[306] There are ongoing arguments about the use of terms like "Latina?" or "Latinx?" as designations expressing gender neutrality. In this article the term Latino is used as a gender-neutral descriptor.

This chapter is based on data collected in four Latino Protestant Pentecostal congregations in New England between 2014 and 2017 through the Latino Protestant Congregations Project.[307] The first part presents a brief statistical summary of the main Latino communities in the United States. The second part is a succinct socio-religious analysis made in terms of national origin, historical, political, and economic factors—including the impact of U.S. intervention in those countries—as well as the subsequent patterns of immigration. The analysis includes the theological priorities of these different communities and how they are informed by particular readings of the Scriptures. The third part examines the worshiping practices of the four congregations and uses the narrative of the road to Emmaus in Luke 24:13–35 as a general outline. The conclusion summarizes the main points of the chapter.

Latinos in the United States: A Brief Statistical Summary

Latinos are the largest ethno-racial minority group in the United States. With a population of more than 56 million or 17% of U.S total population, Latinos trace their roots to any of the twenty-one countries of Latin America or the main three islands in the Caribbean (Puerto Rico, Cuba, and the Dominican Republic). Between 1960 and 2015 the Latino population has increased from 6.3 to 56.5 million and although the growth of foreign born Latinos has declined slightly since 2007, the increase for the past 50 years has been mainly due to immigration.[308] In addition to the variety of countries of origin, the long historical presence of Spanish speaking peoples in this country for more than four centuries implies that the designation of "Latino" functions only as a socially constructed umbrella term under which members of multiple ethno-

---

[307]For more information about the LPC Project please see Mujlder, Mark T., Aida I. Ramos and Gerardo Marti. *Latino Protestants in America: Growing and Diverse.* Lanham, MD: Rowman & Littlefield, 2017.
[308]Pew Research Center, Hispanic Trends "Facts of U.S. Latinos, 2015: Statistical Portraits of Hispanics in the United States," September 18, 2017, accessed December 6, 2017, http://www.pewhispanic.org/2017/09/18/facts-on-u-s-latinos/.

racial, cross-generational, and national-origin groups are clustered. In terms of religious affiliation, the PEW Research Center reported in 2014 that 77% of Latinos in their sample self-identified as Christian, 20% as unaffiliated, and 2% as practitioners of non-Christian faiths.[309] Of the nation's estimated 34.5 million of Latino adults in 2014, research showed that 55% of them (roughly 20 million) were Catholics, and 22% were Protestants.

Varieties of Migratory and Religious Experience

The configuration of the Latino population in relation to their countries of origin is essential to understanding the variety of worshiping practices, theological preferences, and missional priorities among these communities. Three of every four Latinos in the United States have their background in Mexico or Puerto Rico. These two communities have a long history of migration to the U.S., each with its own historical, political, economic, geographical, and religious particularities. The next five largest groups, with more than one million people each, are Salvadoran, Cuban, Dominican, Guatemalan, and Colombian. Together they account for 15% of the Latino population. This last wave of immigrants, known as "the other Latinos/as" began to arrive in the late 1960s and early 1970s. It is important to recognize that even among homogeneous groups there is a difference between the religious narratives articulated by academicians and professionals who, experience immigration as an intellectual or work-related enterprise, and the vast majority of Latino immigrants, for whom coming to the U.S. is a matter of survival. At the same time, it needs to be clarified that the second and third generations of Latino immigrants do not necessarily resonate with the migratory experiences of their parents. The following discussion is offered as a heuristic model to better understand the multiplicity of religious meanings and metaphorical interpretations, as well as the experience-informed

---

[309]Pew Research Center, Religious Landscape Study, "Latinos: Religious Composition of Latinos," 2014, accessed December 6, 2017, http://www.pewforum.org/religious-landscape-study/racial-and-ethnic-composition/latino/.

worship practices of the various Latino immigrant communities in the United States.

The Mexican Experience: Mestizo Identity at the Borders

Since the arrival of Hernán Cortez in 1519 and the subsequent Spaniard control of their land for more than three centuries, the people of Mexican ancestry have always grappled with the religions and racial complexities associated with foreign occupation. After the U.S.-Mexican war and the enactment of the *Treaty of Guadalupe-Hidalgo* in 1848, the present states of Arizona, California, Nevada, Utah as well as parts of Colorado, New Mexico, and Wyoming were seized from Mexico by the United States. As a result, border lines were redrawn, and racialized notions of citizenship and public narratives of national security were created to justify the continuous systemic oppression of Mexican communities. These political and economic strategies, however, did not prevent the uninterrupted, massive waves of Mexican immigration throughout the twentieth century. For people of Mexican ancestry, both Catholics and Protestants alike, their dominant religious narrative has been constructed, for more than four centuries of theological reflection, around the experience of mestizaje and the multifaceted category of borderlands. Through this interpretation Mexican Americans re-enact in their own religious experience of migration the same Galilean journey that Jesus the mestizo of Nazareth undertook across the religious, institutional, racial, and economic borders of his time.[310]

The Puerto Rican Experience: The Construction of Diasporic Identity

The habitants of the beautiful island of *Borinquen* share a similar history. First, four centuries of colonization by Spain beginning in 1493. Then the island was taken as the war's booty in the 1898 Spanish-American war. Puerto Ricans

---

[310] For more on Mexican religious experience see the selected bibliography.

were unilaterally granted American citizenship through the Jones Act of 1917 although they never have had voting representation in congress. Throughout the second half of the twentieth century Puerto Rican natural resources, workforce, and human bodies were exploited by U.S. capitalistic policies of industrialization and neo-liberal marketing strategies. After WWII, hundreds of thousands of Puerto Ricans migrated to the U.S. although this resettlement cannot be considered technically foreign immigration since Puerto Ricans hold U.S. citizenship. For the Puerto Rican community, constructing a religious framework to place their experience of ambivalent national identity and the complicated historic labyrinth of colonialism has implied the appropriation of the narrative of *diaspora*. The biblical accounts of the "people on the move" rich on themes of departure, arrival, and return has proved to be the appropriate matrix for a post and neo-colonial construction of a diasporic existence that is marked by the experiences of location, dislocation, and bi-location in terms of identity, language, culture, and religion.

The Cuban Experience: A New Exilic Identity

The exile of Father Felix Varela in 1823 and Jose Martí in 1890 to New York City foreshadowed the trajectory of hundreds of thousands of Cubans that would follow during the second half of the twentieth century. Cuba was under the colonial power of Spain from 1492 to 1898, when the U.S. took economic control of the island for sixty years. With the rise to power of Fidel Castro, in 1959, the first wave of upper-class Cuban exiles—around 215,000—arrived in the cities of Miami, New York, and New Orleans. A second wave of nearly half million middle class Cubans emigrated during the 1960s and 1970s. Today, the Cuban community is the fourth largest Latino group in the U.S. with a population of more than two million.[311] In the Cuban American community, the

---

[311]Antonio Flores, Pew Research Center, "How the U.S. Hispanic Population is Changing," September 18, 2017, accessed December 7, 2017, http://www.pewresearch.org/fact-tank/2017/09/18/how-the-u-s-hispanic-population-is-changing/.

Babylonian and Persian periods of exile provide a biblical and theological referent to interpret their experience of immigration. The political trajectory of the island and the stories of thousands of Cuban families are metaphorically overlapped with these texts. Through a strategic reading, Cuban Americans attempt to make sense of the reality of displacement while creating an idealized image of Cuba which has never existed. Several theologians refer to the determination of this community to re-define an exilic Cuban identity embedded on the American narrative of success and laden with overtones of a religious crusade against the Cuban regime.[312]

The Dominican Experience: A Transnational Religious Identity

When Columbus arrived in the Caribbean island of *Quisqueya* in 1492, he re-named it *La Española;* thus, signaling three and half centuries of Spaniard Catholic domination of the *Taíno* people. Protestantism was introduced during the first American occupation (1916–1924). It was during that same period of time that the first Dominicans emigrated to the U.S. and settled in Manhattan and the Bronx. There was minimal emigration during the three decades of Trujillo's dictatorship (1930–1961). However, after the second American military occupation and the rise of Joaquin Balaguer to power in 1965, many political dissidents were granted visas to come to the U.S. The second massive migratory wave occurred during the 1980's economic agricultural collapse. This crisis pushed many Dominicans to search for better living conditions and job opportunities in the manufacture, agriculture, and service sectors of the U.S. economy. Since the majority of Dominicans came to the U.S. with visas and obtained permanent residency and citizenship through family members who were already established in this country, many have since followed a particular type of "circular migration," in which they make repeated trips back and forth to the

---

[312] See for instance, Margarita M.W. Suárez, "Cubanas/os," in *Handbook of Latina/o Theologies*, ed., Edwin Aponte and Miguel A. De La Torre (Saint Loius, MO: Chalice Press, 2006), 152–159. Miguel A. De La Torre, "The Cuban American Religious Experience," in *Introduction to the U.S. Latina and Latino Religious Experience*, ed., Hector Avalos (Boston, MA: Brill Academic Publishers, 2004), 66–85.

island and develop a sort of dual settlement between the two countries. In addition to circular migration, there are also denominational historic connections between religious groups in the island and the U.S. These factors have repercussions on how Dominicans embody religion and identity. Whereas most immigrants from Central and South America describe the religious dimension of their migratory experience in terms of crisis, disruption of family ties, risk, and danger, for many Dominicans, emigrating to the U.S. represent a continuation in their spiritual journey along the lines of transnational denominational affiliation after re-encountering with forerunner family members.

The Central American Experience: Re-interpreting Evangelical Protestant Identity

El Salvador and Guatemala are the two main sending countries of Central American immigrants to the U.S. The history of U.S. military intervention in the region after the Spanish-American war and the socio-political trajectories in these two countries during the 1980s–1990s are the necessary background to understand the impressive growth in immigration from these nations and its impact on Latino Protestantism in the United States. Civil wars raged from the early 1980s after the assassination of Catholic bishop Oscar Romero in El Salvador (1980), and the bloody military regime of Rios-Mont in Guatemala (1982–1983) until the signing of peace accords in both countries at the beginning of the 1990s. During these two decades, the violence left hundreds of thousands of indigenous peasants massacred, villages desolated, countless displaced communities, and thousands of survivors fleeing across the borders. According to the 1990's U.S. Census, the combined population from these two groups in 1980 was about 150,000.[313] Today, the share of foreign-born Guatemalans and Salvadorans in the U.S. adds to more than 3.5 million.

---

[313]U.S. Census Bureau, "Table 3 Region and Country or Area of Birth of the Foreign-Born Population: 1960 to 1990," March 9, 1999, accessed December 7, 2017, https://www.census.gov/population/www/documentation/twps0029/tab03.html.

Latin-American Catholic and Protestant liberation theology played a major role in the unfolding of the events in the region during the late 1960s and early 1970s. However, it was the influence of the *evangelical* brand of U.S. Protestantism, brought by scores of missionaries through massive crusades and social programs in the 1970s and 1980s, what eventually shaped the religious imagination of these communities. Protestant conservative evangelicalism, with its emphasis on personal salvation, proselytism, and an apolitical stance towards social realities is the hallmark in many U.S. Latino Protestant congregations of Central American immigrants. Consequently, these communities have developed an indigenous Pentecostal interpretative standpoint in line with conservative biblical and theological motives that help them create religious meaning out of their migratory experiences and derivatively deploy contextualized worshiping practices. Characteristics on this approach are (1) a Latino appropriation of a divinely assigned redemptive destiny, (2) an emphasis on piety in its personal rather than social dimensions, and (3) an apolitical and allegorical approach to biblical interpretation.

The South American Experience: Re-Interpreting Mainline Protestant Identity

The immigrant population from South American countries represents a small percentage in the total share of Latinos in the nation. The total number of South Americans is about 3.4 million or 6% of the Latino population in the U.S. Three countries Colombia, Ecuador, and Peru account for two thirds of all South American immigrants in the country.[314] The growth in South American-originated immigration has not escaladed as that of other Latin-American countries. However, the number has quadrupled since 1990. This increase is related to various socio-political factors. The military coups in Argentina, Chile, and Bolivia in the 1970s, the narco-guerilla conflicts in Colombia and Peru in the 1980s, and the Venezuela's crisis in the 2000s–2010s combined to produce the

---

[314]Pew Research Center, Hispanic Trends "Facts of U.S. Latinos, 2015."

influx of thousands of families entering the country driven by dreams of social improvement through education, work, and entrepreneurship.

Although historically South American countries have been mostly Catholic, research conducted in 2013 showed a steady rise in the membership of Protestant churches beginning in the 1970's.[315] Consequently, many South Americans who came during that period had already switched from the Catholic to the Protestant tradition. Argentineans, Colombians, Peruvians, and Venezuelans are the groups with the highest percentage of undergraduate and graduate degrees and have the top median household income among all Latino immigrants in the U.S.[316] If, as Mulder and Ramos suggest, "Latino mainline Protestants are socioeconomically advantaged over their Catholic counterparts,"[317] a case could be made to explain why many South Americans attend mainline Protestant congregations affiliated with Presbyterian, Baptist, or Methodist denominations.[318] Within that tradition, South Americans favor a well-articulated theological reflection about their experience as immigrants and more formal liturgical expressions; although they still retain the spontaneity and passionate imprint of the Pentecostal ethos. Latino Christianity within mainline traditions is not, by any means, limited to the South American experience. Moreover, there is a wide array of theological perspectives and practices of social engagement inside Latino mainline denominations; however, South Americans tend to lean towards the religious culture of this historical brand of U.S. Protestantism.

---

[315] Pew Research Center, Religion and Public Life, "Religion in Latin America: Widespread Change in a Historically Catholic Region," November 13, 2014, accessed December 9, 2017,http://www.pewforum.org/2014/11/13/religion-in-latin-america/.

[316] Antonio Flores, Pew Research Center, "How the U.S. Hispanic Population is Changing," For more on Mexican religious experience see the selected bibliography.

[317] Mark T. Mulder, Aida I. Ramos, and Gerardo Martí, *Latino Protestants in America: Growing and Diverse* (Lanham, MD: Rowman & Littlefield, 2017), 52.

[318] Alberto Hernández, "Historic Mainline Protestants," in *Handbook of Latina/o Theologies*, ed., Edwin David Aponte and Miguel A. De La Torre (Saint Louis, MO: Chalice Press, 2006), 189–190.

Worship in the Latino Context

A classical definition of Christian worship is "the submission of all our nature to God, the quickening of conscience by [God's] holiness, the nourishment of mind with [God's] truth, the purifying of imagination by [God's] beauty, the opening of the heart by [Gods'] love, and the surrender of will to [God's] purpose."[319] Nevertheless, what is missing on this highly doctrinal and theological definition of worship is the fact that the context and the experience of the worshipping person are completely ignored. This sterilized, a-historical, and disembodied notion of worship cannot account for the complex texture of experiences, practices, and theological articulations that take place in Latino Protestant congregations. Any consideration of worship as a human enterprise in the search for religious meaning must be attentive to the socio-cultural location of the worshiper; the worshiper's own notions of personhood, identity, and agency as well as her multilayered set of ways of knowing divine revelation. In other words, the category of worship is always underpinned by ontological, epistemological, and ethical autobiographic dimensions. Furthermore, missionary efforts or practices of ministry among Latino communities which overlook the contextual-incarnational grounding of Christian worship so often tend to reproduce dominant epistemologies and to perpetuate socio-political structures of power and religious systems of control.

This approximation to worship as a continuous interface of autobiography, social context, and religious experience cannot be reduced to a weekly event, an elaborated liturgy, or a doctrinal affirmation of the nature of any specific ritual. In Latino religious understanding and practice, worship involves the totality of one's being, and nothing stands beyond its scope. The binary type of thinking about sacred and secular realms of experience is challenged because Latinos consider life as an incarnated liturgy in which one re-enacts within the quotidian biblical narratives by following the lead of Spirit through sensory

---

[319] William Temple (1881–1944) in *The Oxford Book of Prayer*, ed. George Appleton (New York: Oxford University Press, 1986), 3.

embodiment of divine revelation. For instance, practices of prayer do not belong exclusively to the temple but are embedded in the routines and struggles of daily life. Most Latino places of worship do not have a "fellowship hall" because after the bible study or prayer meeting there is always fellowship in the homes. The importance of rituals such as the Eucharist/Lord's Supper does not rest on the strict observance of certain script or liturgy at a particular place and time, but instead on the fact that sharing bread has, in Latino culture, an enhanced meaning in which sacred and quotidian realities are weaved together.[320] In sum, right worship is not based on correct believing, but rather on the re-enactment of the disciples' experience on the road to Emmaus where "their eyes were open and their hearts were burning" (Luke 24:31–32).

In order to describe Latino worship within the context of Protestant congregations of first-generation immigrants the following outline, based on the narrative of Emmaus in Luke 24:13–35, is proposed: (1) sojourning, (2) encountering (3) recognizing, (4) and returning.[321] Although each one of these headings corresponds to particular sections of the text as the narrative unfolds, the actual experience of these communities has not clear-cut divisions. Instead of a linear progression, the spiritual journey of Latino worshiping communities resembles more a spiral in which each experience points toward internal processes of insight and transformation.

Sojourning: Worship and the Crisis of Relocation

What are you discussing with each other while you walk along? (Luke 24:17)

To sojourn means to travel in order to dwell for a limited period of time in a certain place. Throughout the entire narrative of Emmaus there is sense of movement, of being "on the road," walking and changing geographical locations. This idea of temporality is complemented by the fact that the disciples referred

---

[320] See, Roberto S. Goizueta, *Caminemos con Jesus: Toward a Hispanic/Latino Theology of Accompaniment* (Maryknoll, NY: Orbis, 1995), 68.
[321] Efrain Agosto, "The Way of Justice: A Latino Protestant Reading of Luke 24:13–35," in *The Word of God and Latino Catholics: The Teachings of the Road to Emmaus,*ed., Jean-Pierre Ruiz and Mario J. Paredes (n.p: American Bible Society, n.d.), 107–120.

to Jesus as a "stranger" in Jerusalem. The Greek word *paroikeo* is used in biblical literature mostly to describe visitors, foreigners, sojourners, and people who live in a place without holding citizenship. When Cleopas called Jesus a foreigner, he did not imply that Jesus was an immigrant or a citizen from another country other than Israel. However, Jesus was considered an outsider in Jerusalem because of his Galilean descent.[322] The passage thus provides an adequate entry point to explore the function of geographical change and social displacement and dislocation in the construction of Latino religion.

Migration is an event that displaces one's cultural, familial, and religious axes forever. This experience encompasses the migratory journey (geographical dislocation), the settling in a new socio-cultural setting (social dislocation), and the process of learning how to navigate simultaneously multicultural and multilingual worlds in family, workplace, neighborhood, and sometimes even church environments (socio-cultural relocation). When social and religious membership is decoupled from the place of residence, the initial response is a cultural shock. Whether they crossed the U.S.-Mexican border without documents or flew from Santo Domingo to New York or from Bogota to Miami, Latino immigrants report that after arriving in this country a process of crisis unfolds. For some, it is a crisis that endangers the stability of the marriage. For many others, the crisis implies the separation from spouse or the preoccupation because the children who stay in Central America could get killed or involved in drugs or gang related activities. Like the disciples on the road to Emmaus, they often feel sad, astounded, and desperate.

A constant feeling during the period of crisis is fear. Beginning with the perils of crossing the treacherous natural barriers of the U.S.-Mexican border or the dread of being captured by the *Border Patrol*, immigrants frequently remember the prayers they offer to God in the midst of fear and uncertainty. One person recounts going across the border in the mid-1990s. In the second attempt that

---

[322] See Virgilio Elizondo, *Galilean Journey: The Mexican-American Promise* (Maryknoll, NY: Orbis, 1983).

lasted eleven days, and fearing being detained again, he made a promise to God: "God if you allow me to come to the United States, I will serve you" This sense of fear does not disappear once one is "on the other side" What changes is the source that produces fear, because once in North American soil, life becomes plagued with a new set of unknown challenges. In additions to the cultural barriers of language and customs, shared by all immigrants, those who are undocumented have to add the emotional toll of stigmatization and "illegality" and the continuous fear of deportation. A female informant relates the challenges she has encountered, "it is difficult to be here without the family. For instance, driving [without a driving license] because one knows that wherever one goes they could stop you, so you are always taking that risk and always asking God [not to be stopped]."

Another common source of frustration is the realization that many of the expectations and notions of the *American Dream* are simply false. Instead, newcomers discover the complexities and impersonality entrenched in North American institutions. Many immigrants come to this country through family members who are U.S. residents or citizens. Others come with student visas, and after graduation are able to get work related sponsors to gain permanent residency or citizenship. But in spite of their more secure legal situation, they repeatedly report having endured a crisis of faith and values. Being uprooted from the security of their families and church communities, to be immersed on the humanistic academic environment of colleges and universities, shakes their previous frames of reference to the core. Consequently, worship in the Latino immigrant community is born out of the matrix of displacement and dislocation. The challenge to relocate life under new conditions enables these worshipers to hone new sets of spiritual resources and multicultural ways of knowing the divine in their worshiping practices. Being a people on the move, Latino immigrants learn to *Caminar con Jesus,* their worship experience is by definition more that of a path or a way than a place or location.

Encountering: Worship and Conversion Experiences

Were not our hearts burning within us while he was talking to us on the road...?
(Luke 24:32)

Cleopas and his companion, who may be a woman, encountered Jesus on the road, although they did not recognize him until they were all eating together later that day. They could not name or articulate exactly what happened on the road while Jesus was walking with them and explaining the scriptures. Only one thing was clear; their hearts, which according to Jesus were "slow to believe," began blazing as they listened to well-known passages of the scriptures being interpreted in an unfamiliar way by an unknown walker. It is important to remember that for these disciples of Jesus, the writings of Moses and the Prophets represented their collective history as a community, their religious traditions, and their hopes for the present. Therefore, this encounter with a stranger on the road meant a reassessment of their personal and communal stories in light of God's story as revealed in the person of Jesus.

In Latino communities, people point to crucial moments in their spiritual journeys as immigrants when they have a "conversion" experience. The language used to describe this pivotal moment is varied: "to give one's life to Christ", "to accept or to receive Jesus as a personal Savior and Lord", "to come to know the Lord", or to "surrender one's life to Christ" Those who are raised in Protestant homes but stop attending church during their youth or after arriving to the United States, refer to "reconciling with the Lord", "re-encountering God", or having "a personal encounter with Christ" In most instances the encounter is marked by an extraordinary episode accompanied by sensorial phenomena such as feeling fire in the body, crying, laughing, seeing visions, or hearing an internal voice. But, regardless of the intensity of the supernatural event, what is stressed about the experience is a deep awareness of God's protection, direction, and ultimately God's purpose in using their migratory journey as a means of spiritual revelation.

218

Sometimes this life-changing event entails a revelatory insight into one's entire life journey. One church attendant spoke of "seeing all [her] life reeling as a movie." She continued: "I felt as if [God] spoke to my ear and I felt that God told me, daughter it was not because you deserved to pass through all this [suffering] that I made you go through, but it was necessary that you went through this so that you knew me." Through these encounters Latino worshipers articulate personal and communal interpretations of the meaning and importance of suffering in their spiritual journeys. The incidence of these experiences in worship cannot be overemphasized. It always implies a rupture with other religious practices and beliefs. In spite of the preponderance of a subjective emotional and fleshed awareness as authentication, conversion is always tied to an intellectual acceptance of the biblical worldview against other religious philosophical systems. There is not entering into the life of faith except through the doorway of conversion. Conversion is not about family, religious tradition, or church membership because personal communion with God cannot be inherited or secured through religious rites. The radical exegetical deconstruction that occurred to the disciples in the road to Emmaus corresponds, in the Latino *Caminar con Jesus,* to a spiritual inflexion of the person's story and experiences of migration through the lens of faith.

Recognizing: The Function of the Bible in Worship

Then their eyes were opened and they recognized him…then he opened their minds to understand the scriptures. (Luke 24:31, 45)

The plot of this narrative reaches a climax at the moment when the disciples recognize Jesus in the "breaking of the bread." The symbolic and liturgical nuances of this expression are significant in Latino religious settings as will be shown in the next section. The author also juxtaposes the opening of the disciples' eyes and minds (Luke 24:31, 45) with the opening of the Scriptures (Luke 24:32). Latino biblical scholars and theologians, Catholic and Protestant alike, underscore the importance of the Scriptures in the life of faith and worshiping practices of Latino communities.[323] In a sense, the dramatic experience of encountering Jesus on the road is rendered as the particular event of conversion in the Latino Protestant context. Moreover, once the visceral impact of that experience has passed —once "Jesus has vanished from the sight" —the person needs to learn how to recognize Jesus continually in the Scriptures and in the fellowship of the community. As the bible is read, interpreted, memorized, quoted, and used in prayer and singing from the pulpit or in small bible study groups, it becomes a living well of images, metaphors, and narratives breeding religious meaning, fostering spiritual growth, and healing, and advancing the mission of the Latino worshiping community. For Latino *caminantes*, the bible becomes the road map.

The use of the bible in Latino Protestant congregations is conspicuous. Members in these communities not just assent intellectually to certain biblical doctrines; but also, they develop a close, intimate relation with the texts. A person interviewed put it in these words, "I had a hunger for the word of God…it came to a point that I felt I was pregnant with the word of God" Moreover, the communication of the "word" of God is not limited to biblical verses and narratives, although the bible functions as a frame of reference for any spiritual message. Another person said, "I know when God is talking to me. I have that code which God gives you." When asked about the meaning of that "code", participants across the board retold how they heard the voice of God in their hearts, through visions, experiences of ecstasies, prophetic dreams, prophecies, and inspirations while preaching. But no one could explain with certainty what that "code" was except that in all instances, the array of experiences is infused with the symbolic world of the Scriptures. For these church members, the bible provides a spiritual language, a reservoir of images, promises, and commands they store in their minds and hearts and which surfaces

---

[323] See Ruiz and Paredes, *The Word of God and Latino Catholics.*

consciously and unconsciously in their daily worship disciplines such as prayer, witnessing, or helping others.

In addition to the private use of biblical imagination, the scriptures also have a communitarian function. Biblical paradigms and narratives inform the group self-understandings and practices at the following levels:

(a) **Liturgical scripts:** In many worshiping services and prayer meeting it is possible to identify an overarching biblical narrative or script which informs the rituals. Scripts vary from congregation to congregation. In a particular New England group, the script observed repeatedly followed along these lines: (1) God's presence and power is invoked so that the Holy Spirit takes control and other spiritual forces become inoperative. (2) People feel God's presence during worship. (3) After the sermon, people come to the platform in need of healing, encouragement, deliverance, forgiveness. (4) With faith, the embodied worship performance and prayer the congregation reaches, touches, and moves God. (5) They receive a miracle, a blessing, and spiritual transformation. Around this liturgical script, worship leaders and pastors interchange biblical metaphors and narratives every week such as the Israelites being delivered from Egypt or the woman being healed by touching Jesus' garments. Through this spiritual strategy, worship participants re-enact different biblical motifs, by entering into that symbolic world and attaining the spiritual resources they need for daily life.

(b) **Templates of migratory journeys:** When Latino immigrants are asked to interpret the spiritual dimension of their migratory experience; some of them make reference to biblical narratives. A South American man responded, "When God called me, God placed this feeling to come to serve [God] in this country. I did not have any specifics, and now fourteen years have passed and that makes me think of Abraham and all those years he waited" The journey of Abraham is referred frequently in the context of religious meaning of immigration. The use of biblical stories also appears in worship songs. A Guatemalan musician and worship director explained her interpretation of the lyrics of a worship song based in Psalms 126, *when Jehovah makes the captivity come* *back, we will be like those who dream. I will rejoice in Jehovah because he has taken all my pain and has made me free.* "…that worship song in so beautiful because…it is something inexplicable. You do not have words to explain because all that we have gone through and so many things. The Lords has been glorified greatly in us in all [things] as we are immigrants," she adds.

(c) **Visions of congregational identity and mission:** In each one of the congregations studied, the senior pastor had a spiritual experience that determined and informed the direction and identity of the ministry. These experiences–dream, vision, internal voice, miracle- have a common substrate in the symbolism of the bible and constitute the central metaphor for the community of faith. In one of the interviews a pastor from the *Congregations Leon de Judá* explained the image of the Lion of Judah by saying: "We are being motivated, literally by a fresh prophetic vision which came to the pastor. [The vision] is ours; unique, we can say, of this church. That God reveals himself to the pastor as the Lion of Judah presiding above the skyscrapers of Boston" Interestingly, in this congregation, the Lion of Judah metaphor is combined with the narrative of Joshua crossing the Jordan River (Joshua chapters 3–4) due to the fact that after the pastor had the prophetic dream with the lion, they relocated moving from the city of Cambridge to the South End in Boston and had to "cross" the Charles River. The overarching biblical narratives of these congregations have a direct impact in the process of self-definition and missional signature in each group.

Returning: Worship and the Building of Community

That same hour they got up and returned to Jerusalem; and they found the eleven and their companions gathered together. (Luke 24:33)

At the end of the Emmaus narrative, the plot has an unexpected twist. How is it possible that after a full day of traveling by foot, when it is well into the evening, and Cleopas and his companion have just arrived home after several days gone, they decide to return to Jerusalem? Were they not concerned by Jesus staying on the road hours earlier? And now at the same hour they get up and walk seven miles back to the city of Jerusalem! Perhaps the impact of what has happened to them that day is so striking that they are compelled by an urgent need to share it with their faith community. The cumulative effect of walking with Jesus, listening to his comments on the scriptures, and recognizing him in the gestures and words at the table cannot be contained within their hearts at a personal level. Biblical understanding and spiritual experiences are insufficient if they want to be a worshiping community. There needs to be community building around those experiences, and this is what takes place in Latino immigrant congregations. As the immigrants get settled in the new country and become members of these Protestant congregations, the spiritual processes at work beginning with the initial crisis and conversion, crystallize in a set of transformations affecting their sense of personal identity, their family systems, their interactions with other Latinos, and their understanding of their place within American society.

Many new arrivals face marriage problems such as divorce, separation, and conjugal infidelity during the initial years living in this country. Some of them also report that their children struggle with drugs, risky sexual behaviors, and rebellion. But as time passes and they experience conversion and spiritual growth through church participation, their families too begin to undergo deep transformation. For many men, whose wives and children are still in their countries of origin, the church becomes a tremendous support system to deal with loneliness and depression. Several other members find their spouses in the congregations and for them the church becomes a source of spiritual nurture along their life journey. One congregant summarizes her church life with these words: "in this church, I received the Lord, got baptized, got married, and presented my daughter."[324] The congregations have an essential role in restoring

---

[324] Most Latino Protestant churches do not practice the baptism of infants but instead children are "presented" to God in a special liturgy based in biblical passages such as 1 Samuel chapter 1, Luke chapter 2, and Mathew 19.

the fabric of social interactions that families have lost because of migration. The church becomes an extended family, a multigenerational and multi-ethnic community where children and adults can flourish developing their gifts and contributing to the community as a whole.

Most first-generation Latino immigrants are introduced to issues of identity, race, and nationality when they arrive to the United States. This does not mean that racial differences are not part of the social fabric of Latin American and Caribbean countries. However, the majority of interviewees "discovered" they were Latinos, Hispanics, people of color, blacks, or Guatemalans only after they interacted with the North American racialized culture. Furthermore, many of them have never before lived outside their countries and, suddenly find themselves attending congregations where multiple nationalities are represented. They become deeply aware of this multiculturalism and its complexity. However, ethnic identity, whether based on shared language or country of origin, does not seem to be as important as what one respondent refers to as "our identity in God." This spiritual identity makes unity possible. One pastor explains "we are culturally different. This is something we cannot ignore but I believe that in Christ Jesus we can reach unity in the spirit because we love each other, and love will break any cultural barrier."

At the core of this returning to community is the conviction that God is bringing Latinos to this land not just to be blessed by the freedom and economic prosperity of this country, but more importantly, to be a blessing, to procure peace for the cities (Jeremiah 29:7), where hundreds of congregations multiply every year. This returning to community is actualized when the members of these congregations begin to realize that God's plan for them and their families involves a spiritual responsibility that goes beyond the boundaries of their own ethno-cultural context.

Conclusion

In general, scholarly literature refers to the Latino worship experience as festive, emotional, and family oriented. Many describe Latino worship as a "fiesta," a sort of *Cinco de Mayo* liturgy. This kind of generalizations not only perpetuates cultural stereotypes about Latino culture, but even more concerning, it imposes categories and language used in marketing and publicity to caricaturize the rich variety of Latino religious expressions. In this brief survey of worship in four immigrant Protestant congregations in New England, it becomes evident that worship experiences and practices are multilayered, and that religious meaning is derived from socio-cultural context. In these communities, the individual and communal interpretations of the Christian message and mission are built using the blocks of migratory stories, denominational theological tendencies, and local demands. At the same time, there is enough diversity even within homogeneous groups to call for a respectful specificity when theorizing about Latino Protestant religious life. This study does not focus on describing the Latino "flavor" of common worship practices such as singing, praying, bible reading, or evangelizing because, after four years of research and more than 200 hours of participant observation and semi-formal interviews, it is conclusive that the popular notion of a characteristic Latino worship style–whether of music or liturgy- simply does not exist. On the surface, the liturgical expressions present in these congregations, are uniformly similar to contemporary trends in their Anglo counterparts in areas like musical genres, theological emphasis, and performative worship routines. What is notably unique in these communities is the appropriation and internalization of those external liturgical expressions. In these churches, Latino immigrants intertwine the weft of widespread liturgical manifestations and the wrap of very specific personal and communal religious interpretations of various experiences of migration, endured racism, and economic struggle. The result is the multicolor tapestry of Latino worship and faith practice which is revealed in its depth only when those two threads are kept in sight.

SECTION FOUR

Mission to Migrants

CHAPTER TEN

Mission to Migrants: Challenges and Tasks

Jonathan Y. Tan

To say that we are currently living in an age of global and transnational migration, whether voluntary or involuntary across continents and oceans is an understatement. At the start of the twenty-first century, the world is witnessing the growth of large-scale *internal* and *external* displacements that are made possible by affordable international travel, advanced telecommunications, and broadband internet. Without a doubt, migration is a contemporary global phenomenon that is deeply embedded in, as well as shaping and transforming the lives of millions around the world. This is borne out by the International Organization for Migration's *World Migration Report 2011*, which notes that about one billion people (or one in seven of the world's population) are migrants[325] and highlights that five of the top 10 emigration countries are located in Asia, namely India (#2), China (#4), Bangladesh (#6), Pakistan (#7), and the Philippines (#9).[326] As people move, they bring with them their cultures, religious traditions, and ways of living.

This chapter focuses on the contemporary issues, challenges, and tasks arising from mission to migrants across the globe. In particular, migration, whether voluntary or involuntary, documented or undocumented, is more than

---

[325] International Organization for Migration, *World Migration Report 2011* (Geneva: International Organization for Migration, 2011), 49.
[326] *World Migration Report*, 68, citing World Bank, *Migration and Remittances Factbook, 2011* (Washington, D. C: The World Bank, 2011), 3.

transnational or global population mobility *simpliciter.* Hence, this chapter highlights two categories of migrants – *permanent* and *transient* migrants, identifying the challenges and tasks, as well as opportunities for mission and ministry to both groups of migrants. The category of *permanent migrants* refers to migrants who make a *permanent* and *unidirectional* move from their homelands to new countries, whether they are economic migrants who could be documented or undocumented, refugees, or asylum seekers. In contrast, *transient migrants* are constantly on the move in search of opportunities for advancement and therefore, not looking to stay in a particular location permanently or for the long term.

Permanent Migrants

Challenges of Permanent Migration

Patterns of permanent migration include voluntary migration of young adults from rural to urban centers in search of jobs and economic opportunities, voluntary migration from economic depressed countries to economic booming countries (for example, Filipinos working across Asia and sending their remittances to their families in the Philippines, as well involuntary or forced migration in the form of massive waves of refugees and asylum seekers fleeing violence and persecution (for example, refugees fleeing Syria, Iraq, and Libya, Tamils leaving Sri Lanka, Rohingyas being forcibly expelled from Myanmar, as well as many Central Americans escaping violence and turmoil in their homelands). Indeed, migration can be voluntary (for example, economic migrants in search of job opportunities) or forced (for example, refugees, asylum seekers, and internally displaced persons who are fleeing persecution in their homelands, as is the case with Syria, Libya, Myanmar, and other troubled spots around the world).

At the same time, migration, whether voluntary or involuntary, is ambiguous; it is welcome by some and resented by others. On the one hand, the abundant array of ethnic restaurants, galleries, and festivals is often welcomed

230

because they add spice and zesty variety to otherwise staid lives. On the other hand, complaints of cultural assault, cultural relativization, and cultural pollution are growing increasingly frequent and strident. Indeed, migration becomes the xenophobic bogeyman that embodies the fear, uncertainty, and insecurity about a community's self-identity vis-à-vis others, leading to the absolutization of its ethnic and cultural identity against what it perceives as the threat of encroachment by others. In extreme cases, it can stir up feelings of xenophobia, ethnocentrism, racism, and nationalism, as we see with the likes of Donald Trump in the United States, the growing influence of far right politicians and parties in Europe as exemplified by Nigel Farage and the UK Independence Party, *Front National* in France, which was founded by Jean-Marie Le Pen and currently led by his daughter, Marine Le Pen, *Lega Nord* (Northern League) in Italy, as well as *Nationaldemokratische Partei Deutschlands* (National Democratic Party) and *Alternative für Deutschland* (Alternative for Germany) in Germany that have taken a stridently anti-migrant stance vis-à-vis Angela Merkel's decision to admit Syrian refugees into Germany.

Moreover, one also has to acknowledge the reality that today's large-scale globalized migration patterns are fueled and abetted by immense poverty, extreme social-economic imbalances, and violent ethnic and religious strife, as well as the insatiable demand for cheap labor and cheap products. The magnitude of this problem is especially dire in Asia. Many Asians are migrants, whether willingly or unwillingly as victims of human trafficking, war, and political violence. Involuntary migrants include not just refugees and asylum seekers from Syria and Iraq, Sri Lanka and Myanmar who are fleeing wars, social strife, economic upheavals, political instability, religious tensions, and persecution, but also the many economic migrants, especially vulnerable women and children, who are exploited and trafficked by underworld gangs, smuggling networks, and secret societies for cheap labor, including child labor in slave-like conditions, as well as sex trafficking. The sheer violence and abject dehumanization that many of these women and children experience reveal the dark underbelly of migration and calls for a concerted response on the part of everyone to redress these problems. Activists and advocates often highlight the commodification and exploitation of migration and human trafficking, resulting in the abuse and dehumanizing of the human person.

Thus, the principal focus of mission to permanent migrants will need to pay attention to the pastoral care of migrants in diasporic communities, whether they are internally displaced migrants or migrants who leave their homelands because of persecution[327] or for better economic opportunities abroad.[328] Permanent migrants, voluntary or involuntary often struggle for acceptance in their new homelands. As the late Indian theologian S. Arokiasamy explained, migration "reveals the vulnerability of people's lives, their insecurity, exploitation, joblessness, uprootedness, political uncertainty and humiliating treatment as outsiders or foreigners."[329] Writing from both personal experience and academic research, the Vietnamese American theologian Peter Phan draws attention to the "existential condition of a transnational immigrant and refugee," which includes "violent uprootedness, economic poverty, anxiety about the future, and the loss of national identity, political freedom, and personal dignity."[330] He observes that no matter how much migrants endeavor to make a new life for themselves in their newly adopted lands, they often remain marginal in their new worlds. As he explains, "being immigrant means being at the margin, or being in-between or being betwixt and between" two worlds, i.e., the native homeland and the

---

[327] See, for example, Daniel G. Groody, "Crossing the Divide: Foundations of a Theology of Migration and Refugees," *Theological Studies* 70 (2009). 638–67.

[328] For examples of the academic theological literature focusing on various dimensions and implications of these categories of migration, see Jennifer B. Sauders, Elena Fiddian-Qasmiyeh, and Susanna Snyder, eds., *Intersections of Religion and Migration: Issues at the Global Crossroads* (New York: Palgrave Macmillan, 2016); Elaine Padilla and Peter C. Phan, eds., *Christianities in Migration: The Global Perspective* (New York: Palgrave Macmillan, 2016); and Gemma Tulud Cruz, *Toward a Theology of Migration: Social Justice and Religious Experience* (New York: Palgrave Macmillan, 2014).

[329] Soosai Arokiasamy, *Asia: The Struggle for Life in the Midst of Death and Destruction*. FABC Papers No. 70 (Hong Kong: Federation of Asian Bishops' Conferences: 1995), 9.

[330] Peter C. Phan, "The Experience of Migration as Source of Intercultural Theology in the United States." In Peter C. Phan, *Christianity with an Asian Face: Asian American Theology in the Making* (Maryknoll, NY: Orbis Books, 2003), 8.

adopted country.[331] Drawing from his own experience as a refugee, Phan writes that the migrants' quest for self-identity is affected by their marginal status:

> To be betwixt and between is to be neither here nor there, to be neither this thing nor that. Spatially, it is to dwell at the periphery or at the boundaries… Socially, to be betwixt and between is to be part of a minority, a member of a marginal(ized) group. Culturally, it means not being fully integrated into and accepted by either cultural system, being a *mestizo*, a person of mixed race… Psychologically and spiritually, the person does not possess a well-defined and secure self-identity and is often marked with excessive impressionableness, rootlessness, and an inordinate desire for longing.[332]

Challenges of Religious Diversity and Pluralism

More importantly, human mobility also brings about the *movement* and *interaction* of many cultures and religions, resulting in increasing cultural diversity and religious pluralism across the world, as the majority community in host countries are often faced with the challenges of welcoming and integrating incoming migrant communities in their midst. Indeed, migration leads to an increasing cultural diversity and religious pluralism in different parts of the world. The American historian, Peter Stearns' characterization of migrations as "cultures in motion"[333] is especially apt here. In practical terms, as Syrian and Iraqi Muslims move to predominantly Christian Europe and North America, or Christian Filipinos work in the Arab Muslim nations of West Asia, the implications of migration for ecumenical and interfaith relations between the native majority and minority migrant communities can no longer be ignored.

---

[331] Peter C. Phan, "Asian Catholics in the United States: Challenges and Opportunities for the Church.?" *Mission Studies,* 16 no. 2 (1999): 151–174, 162–3.

[332] Peter C. Phan, "Betwixt and Between: Doing Theology with Memory and Imagination." In *Journeys at the Margin: Toward an Autobiographical Theology in American-Asian Theology,* eds. Peter C. Phan and Jung Young Lee (Collegeville, MN: Liturgical Press, 1999), 113.

[333] Peter N. Stearns, *Cultures in Motion: Mapping Key Contacts and Their Imprints in World History* (New Haven: Yale University Press, 2001).

Maryknoll missioner and missiologist, William LaRousse expresses the relationship between migration and religious diversity succinctly when he points out that migration not only "brings Christians into contact with other believers but it also brings other believers into contact with Christians."[334] On this issue, Jehu Hanciles is emphatic that "every Christian migrant is a potential missionary."[335] Likewise, Stephen Bevans writes that Christian mission "done in the light of migration is a radical commitment to the marginalized."[336] In particular, Bevans speaks highly of migrant Christians witnessing "by their lives of faith and by their vital and vibrant church communities," as well as by their indigenous churches, social justice efforts, peacemaking initiatives, and outreach efforts to their hosts.[337] More specifically, Bevans also outlines the important roles that migrant Christians can play as agents of reconciliation:

> Migrant Christians can engage in interreligious dialogue at every level, especially with members of their own cultural and ethnic groups, and they are perhaps the best church agents in the ministry of reconciliation among their own congregations. In addition, they can be bridges between their own migrant communities and the host communities, as various personal, cultural, political, and ecclesial actions of reconciliation are needed.[338]

At the same time, many communities are confronted with the complex reality of cultural diversity and religious pluralism that is brought about by a relentless onslaught of people constantly on the move for social, political, or economic reasons. Not surprisingly, both the migrants and their host communities are often ill prepared to handle the inevitable cultural shock that

---

[334] William LaRousse, "'Go... and Make Disciples of All Nations': Migration and Mission.?" In *Faith on the Move: Toward a Theology of Migration in Asia*, eds. Baggio, Fabio and Agnes M. Brazal (Manila: Ateneo de Manila University Press, 2008), 155.

[335] Jehu J. Hanciles, *Beyond Christendom: Globalization, African Migration, and the Transformation of the West* (Maryknoll, NY: Orbis Books, 2008), 6.

[336] Stephen Bevans, "Migration and Mission: Pastoral Challenges, Theological Insights." In *Contemporary Issues of Migration and Theology*, eds. Elaine Padilla and Peter C. Phan (New York: Palgrave Macmillan, 2013), 171.

[337] Bevans, Ibid., 168.

[338] Bevans, Ibid., 168.

arises when different social, cultural, ethical, and religious dimensions are brought together in an explosive mix. Maryknoll missioner James H. Kroeger points out the reality that migrants are often "not only culturally alienated, but also religiously marginalized; frequently, they are relegated to the status of belonging to a minority, 'foreign' religion" in situations where they "follow a religious tradition different from their host country."[339] Indeed, both the migrants and their host communities are often ill prepared to handle the inevitable cultural shock that arises when different social, cultural, ethical, and religious dimensions are brought together in an explosive mix. The Jesuit theologian Thomas Michel describes it as follows:

> There is often the culture shock of moving from a simultaneously supportive and restrictive village society; where ethical and religious values are handed on and enforced by the community, to the secularized, individualistic, highly mobile world of industrialized societies. There are hence, the difficulties of social integration, often compounded by feelings of being unwanted or unaccepted by the host societies.[340]

According to Michel, many migrants come from countries where "their religions were not merely faith commitments, but also determined familial and social relationships and shaped the rhythm and structure of daily life, as well as the moral and value systems which they had known and live by" As these migrants move to more pluralistic and secular environments, they "have difficulty finding mosques, temples, or other places of prayer, centers for gathering during their free time, and the lack of facilities for following the dietary prescriptions of their faith."[341]

---

[339] James H. Kroeger, "Living Faith in a Strange Land: Migration and Interreligious Dialogue." In Fabio Baggio and Agnes M. Brazal, eds., *Faith on the Move: Toward a Theology of Migration in Asia* (Manila: Ateneo de Manila University Press, 2008), 225–226.

[340] Thomas Michel, "The Church and Migrants of Other Faiths.?" *Seminarium* 37 no. 4 (1985): 182.

[341] Michel, Ibid., 182.

Pastoral Responses

Within Roman Catholic circles, both Pope John Paul II and the Pontifical Council for the Pastoral Care of Migrants and Itinerant Peoples' 2004 Instruction, *Erga migrantes caritas Christi* speak of the need for outreach to migrants as part of the task of doing Christian mission, especially the pastoral care of Christian migrants in diasporic communities globally. In his 1996 World Migration Day Message on Undocumented Migrants, Pope John Paul II insisted that "a migrant's irregular legal status cannot allow him/her to lose his/her dignity, since he/she is endowed with inalienable rights, which can neither be violated nor ignored."[342] Pope John Paul II was also adamant that the Church should defend the rights of the undocumented migrants:

> In the Church no one is a stranger, and the Church is not foreign to anyone, anywhere. As a sacrament of unity and thus a sign and a binding force for the whole human race, the Church is the place where illegal immigrants should be recognized and accepted as brothers and sisters. ...
> Solidarity means taking responsibility for those in trouble. For Christians, the migrant is not merely an individual to be respected in accordance with the norms established by law, but a person whose presence challenges them and whose needs become an obligation for their responsibility. "What have you done to your brother?" (cf. Gn 4:9). The answer should not be limited to what is imposed by law, but should be made in the manner of solidarity.[343]

Pope Benedict XVI made a similar point when he called on Christians "to open their arms and hearts to every person, from whatever nation they come" in his address to the 2006 assembly of the Pontifical Council for the Pastoral Care of Migrants and Itinerant Peoples on the theme of "Migration and Itinerancy from and towards Islamic Majority Countries."[344]

---

[342] John Paul II, "Message for World Migration Day on Undocumented Migrants?" (1996). http://www.vatican.va/holy_father/john_paul_ii/messages/migration/documents/hf_jp-ii_mes_25071995_undocumented_migrants_en.html.

[343] John Paul II, "Message for World Migration Day on Undocumented Migrants."

[344] Benedict XVI, "Address of May 15, 2006 to the Plenary Assembly of the Pontifical Council for Migrants and Travelers.?" *L'Osservatore Romano* (May 24, 2006): 9.

Similarly, the Pontifical Council for the Pastoral Care of Migrants and Itinerant Peoples' 2004 Instruction, *Erga migrantes caritas Christi* calls on local churches to welcome, provide help and hospitality to, as well as seek to integrate migrants within their local communities regardless of their religions (n. 42).[345] It speaks of the Catholic Church's mission to non-Christian migrants as, first and foremost, "the witness of Christian charity, which itself has an evangelizing value that may open hearts for the explicit proclamation of the gospel when this is done with due Christian prudence and full respect for the freedom of the other" (n. 59). These suggestions echo what Pope John Paul II had previously said in his 2001 Message for World Migrants Day on the theme of "Immigration and Its Link to Interreligious Dialogue":

> The parish represents the place in which people can work a true pedagogy for meeting people of different religious convictions and cultures; ... the parish community can become a training ground of hospitality, a place where people can exchange experiences and gifts. This can only bolster a peaceful shared existence, preventing the flare-up of tension with immigrants who bring other religious beliefs with them. ... Every day, in many parts of the world, immigrants, refugees and displaced people turn to Catholic organizations and parishes seeking support, and they are welcome irrespective of their cultural or religious affiliation.[346]

This point that Pope John Paul II made is also echoed by *Erga migrantes caritas Christi*, which suggests that:

> The ordinary Catholic faithful and pastoral workers in local Churches should receive solid formation and information on other religions so as to overcome prejudices, prevail over religious relativism and avoid unjustified suspicions and fears that hamper dialogue and erect barriers, even provoking violence or misunderstanding. (n. 69)

---

[345] Pontifical Council for the Pastoral Care of Migrants and Itinerant Peoples, Erga migrantes caritas Christi (2004). http://www.vatican.va/roman_curia/pontifical_councils/migrants/documents/rc_pc_migrants_doc_20040514_erga-migrantes-caritas-christi_en.html.

[346] John Paul II, "Immigration and Its Link to Interreligious Dialogue," *The Pope Speaks* 47 no. 3 (2001): 134–5.

More recently, in his apostolic exhortation on the call to holiness in today's world, *Gaudete et exsultatde*[347] Pope Francis criticizes Catholics who regard the situation of migrants as a "lesser" or "secondary issue" compared to the "grave bioethical questions," insisting that "a politician looking for votes might say such a thing is understandable, but not a Christian, for whom the only proper attitude is to stand in the shoes of those brothers and sisters of ours who risk their lives to offer a future to their children" (n. 102). Pope Francis continues, citing Exod. 22:21, Lev. 19:33–34, and Isa. 58:7–8 with approval:

> A similar approach is found in the Old Testament: "You shall not wrong a stranger or oppress him, for you yourselves were strangers in the land of Egypt" (Exod. 22:21). "When a stranger resides with you in your land, you shall not oppress him. The stranger who resides with you shall be to you as a citizen among you; and you shall love him as yourself; for you were strangers in the land of Egypt" (Lev. 19:33–34). This is not a notion invented by some Pope, or a momentary fad. In today's world too, we are called to follow the path of spiritual wisdom proposed by the prophet Isaiah to show what is pleasing to God. "Is it not to share your bread with the hungry and bring the homeless poor into your house; when you see the naked, to cover him, and not to hide yourself from you own kin? Then your light shall break forth like the dawn." (Isa. 58:7-8) (n. 103)

Transient Migrants

Since the beginning of the twenty first century, sociologists have begun to pay attention to a new category of migration called "transient migrants" as distinct from "permanent migration," and which emerges as the result of transnational forces that shape recurrent migrations rather than a singular, linear, and unidirectional migration. In a seminal essay entitled "From International

---

[347] Pope Francis, *Apostolic Exhortation on the Call to Holiness in Today's World, Gaudete et exsultate* (2018). http://w2.vatican.va/content/franscesco/en/apost_exhortations/documents/papa-francesco_esortazione-ap_20180319_gaudete-et-exsultate.html.

Migration to Transnational Diaspora,"[348] Korean American sociologist John Lie argues that the classic immigration narrative of a "singular, break from the old country to the new nation" is no longer tenable or viable in view of a world that is becoming increasingly global and transnational.[349] Lie argues as follows:

> It is no longer assumed that immigrants make a sharp break from their homelands. Rather pre-immigration networks, cultures, and capital remain salient. The sojourn itself is neither unidirectional nor final. Multiple, circular and return migrations, rather than a single great journey from one sedentary space to another, occur across transnational spaces. People's movements, in other words, follow multifarious trajectories and sustain diverse networks.[350]

More importantly, Lie suggests that transnational and global forces subvert the "unidirectionality of migrant passage; circles, returns, and multiple movements follow the waxing and waning structures of opportunities and networks."[351]

It is in this context of recurrent transnational migrations that the Asian Australian sociologist Catherine Gomes has coined the terms "transient migration" and "transient mobility" to focus attention on those "transient migrants" who are constantly on the move and not looking to stay in a particular location permanently or for the long term. In an essay that Gomes and I co-authored together, Gomes uses the terms "transient migrants," "transient migration," and "transient mobility" to refer to the global and transnational

---

[348] John Lie, "From International Migration to Transnational Diaspora," *Contemporary Sociology* 24 no. 4 (1995): 303–306.

[349] Lie, Ibid., 303. See also Linda Basch, Nina Glick Schiller, and Cristina Szanton-Blanc, eds., *Nations Unbound: Transnational Unbound: Transnational Projects, Postcolonial Predicaments, and Deterritorialized Nation-States* (Langhorne, PA: Gordon and Breach Publishers, 1994) and Nina Glick Schiller, Linda Basch, and Cristina Szanton-Blanc, eds., *Towards a Transnational Perspective on Migration: Race, Class, Ethnicity, and Nationalism Reconsidered* (New York: The New York Academy of Sciences, 1992).

[350] Lie, Ibid., 304.

[351] Lie, Ibid., 305.

movements of people for work, study, and lifestyle including skilled professionals and students in pursuit of international education.[352]

On the one hand, the concept of transient migrants is not new. Indeed, existing theological scholarship has rightfully focused attention on *unskilled* transient migrants, especially foreign domestic workers and discussing important theological implications and pastoral responses to their lack of agency, ill treatment, and poor working conditions.[353] On the other hand, theologians have paid comparatively little attention to the growing transient migration and mobility of educated skilled professionals and international students. In global financial hubs like Singapore and Hong Kong, transient migrants comprise a significant proportion of the population. For example, of 1.6 million of the 5.47 million in Singapore, that is close to 30 per cent of Singapore's population are non-resident migrants.[354] Increasingly, transient migrant Christians are overshadowing local Christians in Hong Kong, Taiwan, and Japan, judging from the growing number of English, Tagalog, and Bahasa Indonesia services in these places, compared to services in local languages such as Cantonese, Mandarin, or Japanese.

---

[352] Catherine Gomes and Jonathan Y. Tan, "Christianity as a Culture of Mobility: A Case Study of Asian Transient Migrants in Singapore," *Kritika Kultura* 25 (2015):215–244, which has been revised and expanded as Catherine Gomes and Jonathan Tan, "Christianity: A Culture of Mobility?" In Catherine Gomes, *Transient Mobility and Middle Class Identity: Media and Migration in Australia and Singapore* (Singapore: Palgrave Macmillan, 2017), 185–208. The discussion that follows in this section summarizes and discusses the key ideas and conclusions that are taken from our co-authored 2015 and 2017 essays. See also Catherine Gomes, "Liking It, Not Loving It: International Students in Singapore and Their Navigation of Everyday Life in Transience." In Catherine Gomes, ed., *The Asia-Pacific in the Age of Transnational Mobility: The Search for Community and Identity on and through Social Media* (London: Anthem Press, 2016), 87–116. Cf. Aihwa Ong, *Flexible Citizenship: The Cultural Location of Transnationality* (Durham, NC: Duke University Press, 1999) and Aihwa Ong and Donald Nonini, eds., *Ungrounded Empires: The Cultural Politics of Modern Chinese Transnationalism* (New York: Routledge, 1997).

[353] For example, see Gemma Tulud Cruz, *Toward a Theology of Migration: Social Justice and Religious Experience* (New York: Palgrave Macmillan, 2014) and her earlier work, *An Intercultural Theology of Migration: Pilgrims in the Wilderness* (Leiden: Brill, 2010), as well as Rhacel Salazar Parreñas, *Servants of Globalization: Women, Migration, and Domestic Work* (Stanford: Stanford University Press, 2001).

[354] Gomes and Tan, "Christianity as a Culture of Mobility," 219.

Transient Migrants and Christianity

More significantly, these educated transient migrants, whether skilled professionals or international students, comprise one of the prime drivers of the growth of World Christianity without borders as they move across cities, countries, and continents in search of the next professional job assignment or higher education prospects. In this regard, Gomes' fieldwork among transient migrants in Singapore and Melbourne,[355] who were either skilled professionals or university-going international students reveal the active role that Christianity plays in the identity constructions and social networking for many of these transient migrants. Gomes herself noted that while she and her research assistants did not specifically go out to investigate Christianity among transient migrants, they discovered that "the Christian faith featured prominently in the answers of a number of respondents" in Singapore, with more than one third, that is 30 out of 88 of the respondents identified as Christian.[356] In our analysis of the interviews of these respondents, we came to the following conclusion:

> The results revealed that Asian foreign talent transient migrants who identified themselves as Christian turn to Christianity as a way of coping with everyday life in transience. On one level, the Christian groups they join allow them to create a sense of community while being away from the home nation. *This sense of community, however, is with other Asian foreign transient migrants, rather than with locals,* such as sharing the same nationality and ethnicity dominate. The results of this study contribute to ongoing intersecting discussions on the (transient) migration experience, community and Christianity.[357]

---

[355] This fieldwork in Singapore and Melbourne provided the ethnographic data for our co-authored 2015 and 2017 essays.

[356] Gomes and Tan, "Christianity as a Culture of Mobility," 225.

[357] Gomes and Tan, Ibid., 226, *emphasis added.*

We also noted how Christianity provided a framework for these transient migrants to develop resilience in order to cope with the various challenges of transience that they experience in their lives:

> Respondents [in Singapore] noted that they actively struck up friendships with people in order to help cope with the traumas of their voluntary uprootedness, with Christianity being a key feature in this quest. Of the thirty participants interviewed, a quarter of them alleviated these conditions by making friends with people from their respective churches. While a few participants were already Christian before coming to Singapore such as the Filipino Catholics and Indonesian Christians, others found Christianity while living in the island-state.[358]

It came as no surprise that transient migrants, whether Christians and converts to Christianity, chose to join congregations with fellow transient migrants rather than with local Singaporeans, experiencing a "community in transience" with fellow Christian transient migrants.[359] In other words, for many, if not the majority of the transient migrants in Singapore who embraced Christianity and made it a part of their identity constructions as transient migrants, their Christian faith becomes an important and defining aspect of who they are, affording them an opportunity to maintain their own Christian identity apart from Singaporean Christians. Gomes' ethnographic study of international students in Melbourne, Australia also reveal similar developments:

> Melbourne … is home to several significant churches catering to international students, including the Cross Culture Church. Situated in the heart of the city, the Cross Culture Church, which belongs to the Churches of Christ denomination, has services in English and Mandarin and one of its pastors is dedicated to ministering specifically to international students. … Even the serviced apartment complex Arrow on Swanston, which almost exclusively caters to international students during semester sessions,

---

[358] Gomes and Tan, Ibid., 228.
[359] Gomes and Tan, Ibid., 227.

has church facilities in its basement and likewise holds regular Sunday services.[360]

Transient Migrants in the Gulf Region of West Asia

Another region that has witnessed rapid growth in transient migrant Christians is West Asia, where transient migrant professionals in the petroleum, engineering, and construction, as well as hospitality sectors are contributing to the rapid growth of Christianity in a region dominated by Islam. In his March 8, 2014 article in the Boston Globe, columnist John L. Allen, Jr. notes that the Arab peninsula is witnessing dramatic Catholic growth rates driven, not by Arab converts, but by transient migrants who are foreign expatriates with no rights to permanent residency or citizenship: "The result is a Catholic population on the peninsula estimated at around 2.5 million. Kuwait and Qatar are home to between 350,000 and 400,000 Catholics, Bahrain has about 140,000 and Saudi Arabia itself has 1.5 million."[361] The bulk of these Catholics transient migrants are Filipino Catholics.[362] John Allen also reported that King Hamad bin Isa Al Khalifah of Bahrain agreed to donate land for the construction of a Catholic church to be called "Our Lady of Arabia" for use by the Catholic transient migrants in Bahrain. Up to this point, there is no church in Bahrain and Catholic transient migrants needed to go to one of the European embassies or gather in a private home or on the grounds of foreign-owned oil companies for masses.[363] In this vein, it is interesting to note that the largest Catholic parish church worldwide is not in Europe or North America, but in Dubai—Saint Mary's Church in Dubai has over 300,000 parishioners, all of whom are transient migrants working in Dubai, with 35–40 weekend masses in 12 languages and over 80,000 hosts distributed weekly. In 2014, the nightly Simbang Gabi services

---

[360] Gomes and Tan, Ibid., 188.
[361] John L. Allen, Jr., "Catholicism growing in heart of Muslim World," *Boston Globe* (March 8, 2014) http://www.bostonglobe.com/news/world/2014/03/08/catholicism-growing-heart-muslim-world/LxIiUYwSlro7Zl6ugvVQJM/story.html.
[362] See Agnes M. Brazal and Randy Odchigue, "Cyberchurch and Filipin@ Migrants in the Middle East," in Susanna Snyder, Joshua Ralston, and Agnes M. Brazal, eds., *Church in an Age of Global Migration: A Moving Body* (New York: Palgrave Macmillan, 2016), 187–200.
[363] Allen, "Catholicism growing in heart of Muslim World."

at Saint Mary's Dubai leading up to Christmas drew crowds of more than 15,000 Filipino Catholics each night, resulting in the services being held in the church's parking lot.[364]

Transient Migrants and the Catholic Charismatic Renewal Movement

Unlike Dubai and Bahrain, Saudi Arabia, with the largest concentration of Catholic transient migrants, many of whom are Filipino Catholics, have not granted permission for the building of churches, whether Catholic or Protestant. In this ecclesial vacuum, the Catholic Charismatic Renewal Movement (CCRM) generally, and the Gulf Catholic Charismatic Renewal Services (GCCRS) in particular, as well as individual Catholic charismatic groups such as the Filipino El Shaddai.[365] Catholic Charismatic movement play a very important role for the maintenance and nourishment of the faith life of these Catholic transient migrants. In this situation, charismatic prayer groups not only empower transient migrant lay Catholics as prophets, exorcists, healers, and lay leaders, but also enable them to transcend political borders and circumvent legal restrictions on churches and clergy presence. This has enabled transient migrant Christian lay leaders to assume leadership and responsibility for keeping the Christian faith alive and strong among their fellow transient migrant Christians in Saudi Arabia and across the Gulf region.

The Catholic Charismatic movement's empowerment of lay leadership and participation has kindled the fire that has led to its explosive growth across the globe generally, and in Asia in particular. In Asia, the Charismatic movement

---

[364] The information and statistics on Saint Mary's Church in Dubai come from personal communication with Filipino American theologian, Ricky Manalo, who visited this church in December 2014 and observed the weekend liturgies and Simbang Gabi celebrations.

[365] Established in 1981 by Mike Velarde, El Shaddai has spread like wildfire among Filipino Catholics in the Philippines as well as in the global Filipino diaspora, garnering a following of about 11 million within 15 years, with chapters in nearly every province in the Philippines and more than 35 countries around the world. For an in-depth examination of El Shaddai, its growth and impact for Filipino Catholicism, see Katharine L. Wiegele, *Investing in Miracles: El Shaddai and the Transformation of Popular Catholicism in the Philippines* (Honolulu: University of Hawai'i Press, 2005).

has swept through much of Asia and transforming Asian Christianity in general, and Asian Catholics in particular. Asia joins Africa and Latin America has having a sizeable number of Pentecostal and Charismatic Christians. The Roman Catholic Charismatic Renewal movement took root in Asia in the late 1960s, in the aftermath of the Second Vatican Council (1962–1965) that transformed the Roman Catholic Church in general, and the Asian Catholic Church in particular. Since the charismatic movement caught fire among Asian Catholics in the 1970s, it has experienced tremendous growth throughout Asia. According to the latest statistics compiled by the Vatican-backed International Catholic Charismatic Renewal Services (ICCRS), there are nearly 14,000 charismatic prayer groups in the Asian Church, with an estimated 15 per cent of Asian Catholics involved in the Catholic Charismatic Renewal Movement ("CCRM"). Indeed, Asia comes second after Latin America, which has an estimated 16 per cent of Catholics involved in the CCRM.[366]

The CCRM in Asia received a big boost in 1994 with the formation of the Catholic Charismatic Council for Asia-Pacific under the aegis of the ICCRS. As a result of the efforts of various local leaders in building and promoting the CCRM within various regions of Asia, the tremendous growth of the CCRM throughout Asia caught the attention of the ICCRS, which established the ICCRS Sub-Committee for Asia-Oceania (ISAO) in December 2006 at a meeting in Singapore that drew participants from fourteen countries in the Asia-Oceania region. The ISAO organized the First Asia-Oceania Catholic Charismatic Renewal Leaders' Conference in Jakarta, Indonesia from September 14–18, 2008, which drew 525 CCRM leaders from 21 countries in the Asia-Oceania region and marked an important milestone in the awakening of the Spirit in the revival of the Asian Catholic Church. This was followed by the establishment of the Gulf Catholic Charismatic Renewal Services (GCCRS) and an inaugural conference

---

[366] The statistics are taken from the Vice President of ICCRS, Cyril John's paper, "Lay Movements and New Communities in the life and Mission of the Church in Asia: Experiences from the Catholic Charismatic Renewal," which he presented at the Congress of Asian Catholic Laity, which met from August 31 to September 5, 2010 in Seoul, South Korea.

from December 7–9, 2008 that drew 1,800 leaders from Bahrain, Kuwait, Oman, Qatar, Saudi Arabia, and the United Arab Emirates under the banner "Let the Fire Fall Again" The sizeable numbers of leaders from West Asia/Gulf Region is testimony to how lay Catholic Charismatic leaders have organized and nourished the faith of their Catholic transient migrants in the absence of churches and clergy to maintain the traditional Catholic sacramental life. This 2008 conference paved the way for Asia to have the honor of hosting in South Korea from June 2–9, 2009, the International Catholic Charismatic Leaders' Conference. This was the first time that this global conference was held outside of Italy in Asia. Drawing participants from 43 countries around the world, this conference culminated in a charismatic prayer rally that drew around 50,000 participants. This was an important milestone and coming of age for the CCRM in Asia, enabling Asia to take its place alongside Latin America and Africa as regions where the CCRM is growing and thriving.[367]

Transient Migrants and Online Communities: A New Way of Being Church?

In response to the restrictions on churches and clergy, transient migrant Christians in the Gulf Region of West Asia are also breaking boundaries when they create online communities and form "cyberchurch" to circumvent legal restrictions on churches and clergy. Digital presence and online communities that are shaped by social media and mediated by livestreaming and messaging apps are redefining the traditional boundaries of Christianity and paving way for a global and transnational World Christianity that is also being realized in virtual and online communities.

Agnes M. Brazal and Randy Odchigue's exploratory essay, "Cyberchurch and Filipin@ Migrants in the Middle East"[368] describes how

---

[367] John, "Lay Movements and New Communities."

[368] Brazal, Agnes M. and Randy Odchigue, "Cyberchurch and Filipin@ Migrants in the Middle East." In Susanna Snyder, Joshua Ralston, and Agnes M. Brazal, eds., *Church in an Age of Global Migration: A Moving Body* (New York: Palgrave Macmillan, 2016), 187–200.

Filipino transient migrants[369] create online faith communities and utilize Facebook, YouTube videos, livestreaming of Sunday Eucharist and other presented, email lists and discussion groups, and other online resources to stay in touch with fellow Christians and practice their Christian faith in the absence of churches and clergy.[370] In other words, the transient Christian identity of these Filipino transient migrants in the Gulf Region that Brazal and Odchigue surveyed are making use of social media and other online tools to create online communities of faith that transcend geographical borders and political restrictions of churches operating in those regions. This paradigm shift toward online or virtual communities of faith is redefining what it means to be Christian, as well as demonstrating a new of being church that breaks the traditional geographical parochial boundaries and clerical leadership of such churches.

This turn by transient migrants towards online communities that define and nourish their transient migrant and Christian faith identities is not limited to transient migrants in the Gulf Region of West Asia. We see the same developments in the transient migrants in Singapore and Melbourne that Catherine Gomes surveyed. For example, an Indonesian information technology in Singapore speaks of nourishing his Christian faith through online downloads and Christian Youtube channels featuring pastors and preachers.[371] Other examples illustrate how the transient Christian identity is often nourished and maintained by social media platforms such as Facebook and Instagram, as well as messaging apps such as Weibo, QQ, Renren and WeChat, all of which are popular with transient migrants from mainland China, as well as WhatsApp and Line for transient migrants generally.[372]

---

[369] Brazal and Odchigue surveyed eight Filipino transient migrants in the Gulf Region: four in Saudi Arabia who are a graphic artist, caregiver, mechanic, and engineer, and four in the United Arab Emirates who are an electrical engineer, company administrator, teacher, and machine operator, respectively. See Brazal and Odchigue, "Cyberchurch," 187–188.

[370] Brazal and Odchigue, "Cyberchurch," 190–191.

[371] Gomes and Tan, "Christianity as a Culture of Mobility," 226.

[372] See example and discussion in Gomes and Tan, "Christianity: A Culture of Mobility," 190.

Transient Migrants' Challenges to Mission and Ministry

In the past, the grounded geography of Christianity meant that Christianity is based on communities meeting in physical buildings that are built in specific geographical regions. Ecclesiologies and theologies of mission and pastoral ministries have been constructed, debated, and shaped by the needs and aspirations of faith communities who gather for worship, fellowship, and communal life in those buildings in specific geographical locations. The growth of transient migrant Christian communities poses new challenges and opportunities for virtual ecclesiologies and mission theologies. Those transient migrants who are educated professionals and international students who move to new cities in search of jobs and educational prospects often turn to Christianity and online communities as a means of finding meaning, networking, and constructing their own faith and social identities. One could certainly argue that online communities and digital resources nourish the *resilience* of these transient migrants in the face of the many challenges of living in transience.

On the one hand, the 1.5 million Catholics in Saudi Arabia cannot legally build a church or gather for Sunday Eucharist that is presided by an ordained priest. On the other hand, lay run Catholic Charismatic Renewal cell groups such as El Shaddai and individual transient migrant Catholics in Saudi Arabia and across the Gulf Region can turn to social media and online communities to create virtual or online church beyond the reach of Saudi law. Ironically, without social media and online communities, there is no church in Saudi Arabia. Indeed, social media and online communities are redefining the boundaries of World Christianity, reimagining ecclesiology, missional outreach, and pastoral ministry, as well as posing new questions for theology on the issues of faith and identity formation in transience.

More importantly, while transience may be *lo cotidiano* for transient migrants, it is still an experience in uprootedness, loneliness, and a yearning for home. Historically, as a universal religion that spread throughout the world

248

because of transnational movements, Christianity plays an important role in helping transient migrants make sense of themselves and their faith experiences in strange and unfamiliar settings.[373] Yet, just because transient migrants embrace Christianity and make Christianity a part of their identity, it does not necessarily signal their assimilation into the broader host society or acceptance by their fellow Christians in their host society. Taking transient migrant Christians in Singapore as an example, by embracing Christianity on their own terms, these transient migrants "have consciously forced religious identities in opposition to the discrimination they have encountered" despite their shared Christian faith with Singaporean Christians because they have "created institutions that reflect their concerns and cater to their own needs."[374] In other words, the World Christianity of transient migrants can and does exist alongside indigenous or local Christianity because of the differing worldviews and expectations of these transient migrants and the locals who are citizens and permanent residents. This would have profound implications for ecclesiology and catholicity, especially the tensions between a universal vision of faith, mission, and church vis-a-vis the particularity of diversity and pluralism. Indeed, Catherine Gomes and myself see this in the majority of the transient migrant Christians in Singapore, as we concluded:

> For many, if not the majority of these Asian foreign talent transient migrants who embrace their Christian faith and make it a part of their diasporic identity in Singapore, their Christian identity becomes an important and defining aspect of who they are, enabling them to communicate with Singaporean Christians, yet affording them the opportunity to carve out a niche where they can define their own identity apart from their fellow Singaporean Christians… leading to heterogenized, hybridized, and conflicting constructions of faith identity that simultaneously connect yet distance themselves from other Singaporean Christians. It is important to note that when Asian foreign talent transient migrants embrace a Christian faith identity, often

---

[373] Gomes and Tan, "Christianity as a Culture of Mobility," 233–234.
[374] Gomes and Tan, Ibid., 234.

with more fervour than they do in their homelands, this goes beyond mere nostalgic longing for home to encompass new opportunities for them to shape their own transnational, hybridized, and often contested multiplicity of identities in Singapore, where they are at best tolerated or at worse vilified by Singaporeans who express varying degrees of xenophobia against them.[375]

Conclusion

Migration in all its forms highlights the challenges and opportunities for missional engagement that go beyond past precedents to rethink and re-envision new strategies and ways of missional witness among migrants, whether voluntary or involuntary, permanent or transient, Christian or of other or no faith. Permanent migrants, whether voluntary or involuntary, face a host of challenges of adjusting to new life in a society that is different from their homelands. This demands that missioners and pastoral ministers equip themselves with the appropriate language skills, as well as cultural and emotional intelligence to engage with these migrants and help them transition and settle down.

The rise of digital frontiers and social media platforms means that diasporic communities can be either geographical and defined by physical communal and ecclesial structures or virtual and nourished by social media and other online platforms, as is the case with transient migrants across different parts of Asia. The fact that transient migrants turn to Christianity as part of their own identity construction as transient migrants in the face of xenophobic vilification by locals is both an opportunity and a challenge for local missioners working with these transient migrants. Just as printing transformed the medieval world and ushered in a new way of doing Christian mission through bibles, tracts, and pamphlets, so too, social media and other online platforms offer opportunities for new ways of engaging with migrants, permanent and transient, and especially the younger generation of migrants. This would require creative

---

[375] Gomes and Tan, Ibid., 234–235.

imagination on the part of missioners and pastoral ministers to utilize new approaches to engage with transient migrants who, by the very nature of their transience, would not put down deep roots in local communities, but nonetheless are still interested in the Good News of Jesus in response to their very transience.

CHAPTER ELEVEN

To, Among, and With Migrants

vănThanh Nguyễn, SVD

The island of Anguilla is a British overseas territory in the Eastern Caribbean, also referred to as the West Indies. Anguilla is one of the most northerly of the Leeward Islands, lying east of Puerto Rico and the Virgin Islands. It is a flat island of coral and limestone and is noted for its spectacular coral reefs and pristine beaches attracting many tourists. Consequently, the island's main source of revenue is tourism. On this attractive vacation spot, so far removed from Asia, lives a small population of Catholic Filipinos. They of course did not come from the other side of the globe for a vacation but rather for labor. About a dozen of these Filipino migrant workers belong to the choir of the St. Gerard's Roman Catholic Church. They actually established the Saturday choir and take charge of the music at every Sunday Vigil Mass. Some of them are married, but most are single. Their beautiful voices and upbeat songs, accompanied by drum and guitar, usually attract a good crowd. During the Communion meditation they normally sing a traditional Tagalog hymn to add more flavor to an already very cross-cultural liturgy. The members of the congregation are predominantly Caribbean with dark skin whose ancestors came from Africa. A few tourists from Europe or North America occasionally come to church. I, the visiting priest, who was born in Viet Nam but now live and work in the United States of America, was the main celebrant and preacher of that Vigil Mass. As I looked across the pews and witnessed the migrant Filipino workers singing and praising God with fervent joy and enthusiasm "in a foreign land" (Psalms 137:4), I was greatly moved with admiration and compassion. As migrant workers they have taken their religion with them and fervently give witness to their faith in songs and by serving at the local church. Although vulnerable and displaced from their homeland and family, they actively live out their faith commitment, contributing much and becoming a precious gift to this small and seemingly insignificant corner of the world.

The reality is that the migrant and refugee crisis has erupted exponentially and become one of the major factors shaping the world today. Indeed, we are living in a time when ethnic, cultural, and linguistic diversity is more evident than ever due to the worldwide phenomenon of migration. This can be an hour of great opportunities for the church and its evangelization. While Christian international migrants are the largest population of people on the move, over half of those on the move—over 110 million people—are from other religious traditions.[376] It goes without saying therefore that preaching *to*, *among*, and *with* migrants provides a great opportunity to engage in ecumenism, to enter into inter-religious dialogue, and thus promote healthy communion. However, contextual preaching is key! Accordingly, evangelizing in the context of the global crisis of migration is no longer an option but a pastoral responsibility. As it shall be made clear, fellowship through dialogue and prophecy or "prophetic dialogue" is an appropriate modality and characteristic of a proclaimer for the Christian Good News today, particularly in the context of migration. But first, let us examine the richness of the cultural diversity of our world and church in order to recognize and acknowledge the gift of the migrants, who are often messengers in disguise.

---

[376] See: http://www.pewforum.org/2012/03/08/religious-migration-exec/ (accessed January 12, 2018).

One Church, Many Faces

The United States of America was initially built on the backs of slaves from Africa and only later developed by predominantly European immigrants. Subsequently, Catholicism in the United States has benefited much from the multicultural "American" heritage. The mosaic of cultures is becoming increasingly more evident as the Catholic Church in the U.S. continues to welcome more immigrants from around the world, particularly from Latin America, Africa, and Asia. Hispanics, for example, comprise more than 35 percent of all Catholics in the U.S., and more than 20 percent of all Catholic parishes have Hispanic ministries. Recent studies suggest that the Latino composition will continue to grow for decades to come.[377]

Indeed, the face of the Catholic Church in the U.S. is changing, and it shall continue to be fashioned and enriched by newcomers, many of whom are Catholic immigrants.[378] This transformation however brings ethnic, cultural, and linguistic diversity in our liturgical and sacramental celebrations, influences our religious devotions, and even alters our theology and spirituality.[379] Different cultural practices and expressions of faith can cause tension and disturb the unity of the church. The reality of the church today might cause many Catholics to experience, more acutely perhaps than in previous times, an uneasy tension between unity and diversity. But the question is, "Is it a healthy tension that

---

[377] Approximately 42.5 million US residents who self-identify as non-Hispanic white are estimated to be Catholic, representing about 21.6 percent of the 196.8 million people. Hispanics therefore represent the single largest racial and ethnic group among Catholics in the USA. See Mark Gray, Mary Gautier, and Thomas Gaunt, "Cultural Diversity in the Catholic Church in the United States," a CARA Report, June 2014, 7; for online document, see: http://www.usccb.org/issues-and-action/cultural-diversity/upload/cultural-diversity-cara-report-phase-1.pdf (accessed on July 19, 2015).

[378] See many excellent articles found in this book: Peter C. Phan and Diana Hayes, ed., *Many Faces, One Church: Cultural Diversity and the American Catholic Experience* (Lanham, Maryland: A Sheed & Ward Book, 2005).

[379] See William V. D'Antonio, Michele Dillon and Mary L. Gautier, *American Catholics in Transition* (New York: Rowman & Littlefield Publishers, 2013); William Cenkner, ed., *The Multicultural Church: A New Landscape in U.S. Theologies* (New York: Paulist Press, 1996).

proves to be enriching or does it cause more misunderstanding and greater separation?"

Sometime ago I gave a recollection entitled "Celebrating Diversity in Unity" in Fort Wayne, Indiana. The topic came about because of the growing tensions that were being experienced in the parish. Like many Catholic parishes in the United States, St. Patrick Church is ethnically, culturally, and linguistically diverse. The community is made up of three distinct groups: Anglos, Hispanics, and Vietnamese. Different though they are, they try to work together respecting each other's cultural differences, but it has not always been easy. Different customs and practices naturally lead to conflict and tension. A simple issue such as which statue of Mary should be placed in the church, whether Our Lady of Fatima or Guadalupe or La Vang, can prove to be contentious and problematic. Fortunately, the pastoral team is also culturally diverse, helping to ease most tensions. The pastor is a Vietnamese American who is fluent in English and Vietnamese. Since the Hispanic population has grown significantly over the past few years, another priest, who happens to be an Anglo-American but speaks perfect Spanish, was brought in to help out with the growing demands of the parish. During the recollection, my talks were simultaneously translated into Vietnamese and Spanish. The closing Mass was celebrated in three languages, highlighting the richness of the community. While the people in this parish rub shoulders with each other and disagree on various issues, they nevertheless respect the others' customs and beliefs. They genuinely seek to be one body of Christ. They had gathered together to celebrate their diversity because they saw it as a gift and a blessing. As I walked out of the church that day, I noticed that all three statues of Our Lady were placed prominently in their respective locations. I must admit that the recollection was a great eye opener for me. Our church indeed has many faces, but she is still one, holy, Catholic Church, rich in diversity and traditions.

Diversity in Unity

Diversity is not only a contemporary phenomenon. The church has been diverse since the very beginning of its existence. It is true that the earliest followers of Jesus Christ were only Palestinian Jews, but soon after Pentecost, Hellenistic Jews also became followers. The list of people who were present at Pentecost indicates that people came from all over the Roman Empire; there were "Parthians, Medes, and Elamites, inhabitants of Mesopotamia, Judea and Cappadocia, Pontus and Asia, Phrygia and Pamphylia, Egypt and the districts of Libya near Cyrene, as well as travelers from Rome, both Jews and converts to Judaism, Cretans and Arabs" (Acts 2:9–11). The book of Acts also records that the Hellenist believers became numerous and caused a bit of tension within the community. Thus, the apostles had to choose seven deacons to attend to their own ethnic group (Acts 6:5–7). Eventually, the Gentiles too joined the mix. Through the success of the preaching of Paul and Barnabas, many Gentiles turned to the Lord. While Paul and Barnabas readily embraced the Gentile believers into the church without many restrictions, some Jewish believers forced the Gentile believers to follow the Mosaic Law, especially the circumcision ritual. In other words, Gentiles had to become proselytized or fully Jewish in order to be Christians. This obligation obviously would not allow Paul, Barnabas, and other missionaries to associate and have table fellowship with Gentiles. This rigid restriction would surely interfere with the missionary work of the church. The issue concerning the inclusion of the Gentiles, particularly enforcing circumcision, was no small matter for it could have divided or even destroyed the church (see Galatians 2:11–14 and Acts 15:1–2). The heated debate led to the convening of the Jerusalem Council, the first council of the church. Through the guidance of the Holy Spirit and the testimonies of Paul, Barnabas and Peter, the church imposed only minor conditions on Gentile converts (see Acts 15:1–29). The decision was monumental for the church's growth and development!

Since its very beginning, the church wisely recognized that unity was not a cause for uniformity, but rather that there could be diversity in unity. Diversity was not seen as a threat of disunity but viewed as a gift and a blessing that was fostered for the enrichment of the church. The church accepted that there were two different ways of spreading the gospel, one to the circumcised, entrusted to Peter, and the other to the uncircumcised, entrusted to Paul (Gal. 2:7–9). Nevertheless, it is faith in Jesus Christ that kept the church tied together as one body. Interestingly, Paul often used the image of the body and its members to confront the various party factions in the churches (see Rom.12 and 1 Cor. 12). Paul recognized that diversity is indispensable, like a body with many parts. Paul writes, "As a body is one though it has many parts, and all the parts of the body, though many, are one body, so also Christ. For in one Spirit we were all baptized into one body, whether Jews or Greeks, slaves or free persons, and we were all given to drink of one Spirit" (1 Cor. 12:12–13). Paul accepts the differences between the members as an enrichment of the body, and since each one is unique, the Spirit distributes gifts to each person as the Spirit chooses. Again, Paul says, "There are different kinds of spiritual gifts but the same Spirit; there are different forms of service but the same Lord; there are different workings but the same God who produces all of them in everyone. To each individual the manifestation of the Spirit is given for some benefit" (1 Cor. 12:4–7). Diversity that produces such marvelous gifts and comes from the Spirit can be embraced without disorder. Rather, unity is guaranteed by God, Jesus Christ, and the Holy Spirit through faith and love. The apostle Paul saw a deep bond of unity between particular churches. The preaching of a common gospel united all the believers. Furthermore, Baptism and the Eucharist also created and fostered communion among Christians. The words of the institution of the Lord's Supper, found both in Paul's letter (1 Cor. 11:23–26) and in the Gospels (Matt. 26:26–28; Mark 14:22–24; Luke 21:17–20), may infer that the Eucharist was fundamentally the same in Corinth as in Antioch or in Rome.

Then, as well as now, the Church is a *communion*, modeled on the love among Father, Son, and Holy Spirit. It seeks to imitate that communion and oneness in the Trinity. Moreover, the Church is catholic! In its universality, it welcomes and gathers all people without exception—"from every tribe and tongue, people and nation" (Rev. 5:9). It is a communion in diversity, not in uniformity.

Indeed, the church in America is experiencing the dawn of a new day. In 2007, the United States Conference of Catholic Bishops (USCCB) established several priorities for action. One of those priorities was the "recognition of cultural diversity."[380] The bishops were not just concerned with the practical matter of diversity but saw the issue as something "integral to the Church's very identity and mission." They said, "Proficiency in matters of culture and intercultural relations is an essential feature of the ongoing process of conversion by which the Gospel becomes life for people."[381] They stressed an urgent need to grow in knowledge and develop appropriate attitudes and skills for the purpose of carrying out the church's mission to evangelize. The push for appreciation of greater cultural diversity in the church has become part of the New Evangelization today. The bishops encouraged establishing programs for intercultural competencies. There is now a manual that is designed to help leaders in ministry to achieve a basic level of awareness and proficiency in the area of intercultural competency. The manual, Building Intercultural Competence for Ministers, is found online or can be obtained in print.[382] Needless to say, the most important step of promoting cultural diversity and evangelization is to recognize and acknowledge the gift of the migrant.

Migrants as Messengers

Based on the religious composition of international migrants, approximately 105 million international migrants are Christians.[383] Statistics

---

[380] See http://www.usccb.org/issues-and-action/cultural-diversity/.
[381] Ibid.
[382] See www.usccbpublishing.org.
[383] For the religious composition of internal migrants in 2010, see http://www.statista.com/statistics/221157/religious-composition-of-international-migrants/

indicate that Christian migrants or immigrants are the largest population on the move, totaling 49 percent of all international migrants on the planet. The two favorite destinations of Christian immigrants are North America (72 percent of 43 million immigrants) and Europe (57 percent of 40 million immigrants).[384] Noticeably, 85 percent of immigrants to Latin America and the Caribbean are Christians.[385] If every Christian migrant is a potential missionary, migration then could have enormous prospects and opportunities for evangelism. When Christian immigrants travel, they take their religion with them, or more personally, their God literally migrates with them.[386] As people in transition, who experience the pain of homelessness and displacement, so "they are usually open to new commitments and ready to assume faith in a personal way."[387] Jonathan Tan also notes, "In the context of Asia, the movement of peoples also brings about the movement of cultures and religions, resulting in increasing cultural diversity and religious pluralism across Asia, as the majority community in host countries are often faced with the challenges of welcoming and integrating incoming migrant communities."[388]

Jehu Hanciles correctly points out that "Christianity is a migratory religion, and migration movements have been a functional element in its

---

[accessed January 8, 2018]. See also http://www.pewforum.org/2012/03/08/religious-migration-exec/ [accessed January 8, 2018]. According to this figure, the top seven religious affiliations of international immigrants are as follows: Christian (105,670,000); Muslim (58,580,000); Unaffiliated (19,330,000); Hindu (10,700,000); other religions (9,110,000); Buddhist (7,310,000); and Jewish (3,650,000).

[384] For charts and other pertinent statistics, see http://www.statista.com/statistics/221384/immigration-to-north-america-by-religion/ (accessed January 8, 2018).

[385] See, http://www.statista.com/statistics/221400/immigration-to-latin-america-and-the-caribbean-by-religion/ (accessed January 8, 2018).

[386] When the Israelites travelled in the wilderness for forty years, God moved about with them and dwelled among his people in the tabernacle (Ex 25:8; 29; 45–46; Nm 1:50). Tabernacle means, "tent," "place of dwelling" or "sanctuary." It was a sacred place where God chose to meet the Israelites, and the people came together to worship and offer sacrifice during the forty years that they wandered in the desert.

[387] Samuel J. Escobar, "Mission Fields on the Move," *Christianity Today* (May 2010) 28–31, here 31.

[388] Jonathan Y. Tan, *Christian Mission among the Peoples of Asia* (Maryknoll, NY: Orbis Books, 2014) 174.

expansion."[389] Hanciles observes that the six ages or phases of Christian history that were identified by Andrew Walls were shaped in one way or another by migratory movements.[390] From the very beginning, Christian expansion and migratory movement were forcibly and intimately intertwined. In a more comprehensive study, Hanciles' book explores the massive consequential connection between migration and mission in the history of Christian missionary expansion, starting with the age of European migrations in the sixteenth century.[391] The book successfully demonstrates that migratory movement was and remains a prime factor in the global spread of Christianity, Islam, and other world religions. What he says in the concluding section of the book bears truth and wisdom, "Every Christian migrant is a potential missionary."[392]

This of course is not new. Migration was a key factor in the expansion of the church in the New Testament times.[393] In the book of Acts, the Evangelist Luke records numerous stories of Christian missions advanced in the context of migration. Early Hellenistic Christians who were scattered because of religious persecution founded churches in Samaria (8:1), Damascus (9:2), Phoenicia, Cyprus, and Antioch (11:19). In other cases, voluntary immigrants moved with a missionary purpose in mind. The efforts of Peter, John, and other itinerant missionaries succeeded in planting new communities in various towns throughout the regions of Judea, Galilee, and Samaria (9:31; 10:1–48). Paul,

---

[389] Jehu J. Hanciles, "Migration and Mission: Some Implications for the Twenty-first-Century Church," *Missiology* 27, no. 4 (Oct 2003) 146–153, here 149.

[390] *Ibid.*, 148–49. For a complete study, see Andrew F. Walls, *The Missionary Movement in Christian History: Studies in the Transmission of Faith* (Maryknoll, N.Y.: Orbis Books, 1996) 16–25. See also his helpful article, Andrew F. Walls, "Mission and Migration: The Diaspora Factor in Christian History," *Journal of African Christian Thought* 5.2 (Dec 2002) 3–11.

[391] Jehu J. Hanciles, *Beyond Christendom: Globalization, African Migration, and the Transformation of the West* (Maryknoll, N.Y.: Orbis Books, 2008) 157ff.

[392] *Ibid.*, 378.

[393] The link between migration and mission is already found in the life of Jesus. Jehu J. Hanciles states that "Jesus' life and ministry embodied the interconnection of mission, boundary-crossing movement, and the alienation of exile and migration." (*Beyond Christendom*, 150). For a brief survey of the theme of migration in the Bible, see vanThanh Nguyen, SVD, "Asia in Motion: A Biblical Reflection on Migration," *Asian Christian Review* 4, n. 2 (Winter 2010) 18–31, here 22–27.

Barnabas, and their traveling companions were sent out on various missionary journeys to establish and build up the Christian communities in Celicia, Illyricum, Asia Minor, Macedonia, and Achaia (Rom. 15:19, 23–24). Paul's list of farewell greetings in Romans 16 likewise gives us a glimpse of his successful mission endeavor, reaching all the way to the imperial capital. We are told that he even planned to travel to Spain (Rom. 15:24) to evangelize to the edge of the known world.

The story of Priscilla and Aquila illustrates that migration and mission were closely intertwined.[394] This Judean-Christ-believing-couple was constantly on the move for the cause of the gospel.[395] They first settled in Rome, were then forced to migrate to Corinth because of the Edict of Claudius in 49 C.E., relocated in Ephesus for the purpose of evangelization, and finally returned to Rome after Claudius' death in 54 C.E. They relocated both their home and their trade at least three times in three different locations. Their home was as movable as the tents that they erected. Yet, they never faltered in their commitment to preach the Gospel of Jesus Christ, risking everything because of their faith. Like any immigrant who experiences the trauma of displacement and marginalization, they knew the importance of being welcomed and finding shelter. Their homes became house churches. The case of Priscilla and Aquila is a good example for lay Christian immigrants scattered all over the globe to emulate, for their displacement, whether voluntary or involuntary, can serve as an opportunity for church planting, hospitality, mission, and evangelism. Furthermore, the story of Priscilla and Aquila also serves as a reminder for the church to realize that Christian migrants, voluntary and involuntary, can fall within the plan of God and become a key factor in the expansion of the church. Migrants therefore often turn out to be messengers or angels in disguise.

---

[394] See vanThanh Nguyen, "Migrants as Missionaries: The Case of Priscilla and Aquila," *Mission Studies* 30 (2013): 192–205.

[395] The references to Priscilla and Aquila appear six times in the New Testament: three times by Luke (Acts 18:1–3, 18–19, 26–27); twice by Paul (1 Cor 16:19; Rom 16:3); and once by a Deutero-Pauline (2 Tim 4:19).

Precious Gift of the Church

In his article, "Mission *among* Migrants, Mission *of* Migrants," Stephen Bevans makes at least two important points. First, the church's mission is among migrants because they represent the face of the "border Christ" who said, "I was a stranger and you welcomed me" (Matt. 25:35); second, migrants are also the *subjects* of the church's mission. Bevans says, "Christian migrants themselves have precious gifts to give to the church itself—to form it more fully into the body of Christ in the world."[396] Recognizing the "gift" of the migrants, the Catholic Church continually seeks ways to appropriately address the needs and pastoral care of the migrants and refugees. One of its pontifical documents states: "It should be led by the principle that no one, be they migrants, refugees or members of the local population, should be looked upon as a 'stranger,' but rather as a 'gift,' in parishes and other ecclesial communities. This is an authentic expression of the 'catholicity' of the Church."[397] Since migrants are precious gifts of the church, again Bevans correctly states, "The task of the local church is, therefore, not only to respond to migrants' need and to accompany them on their journey, but also to call and equip them for ministry, both within the church and within the world."[398]

Migrants are indeed a precious gift of our church, especially Asian Christian migrants, who normally bring their faith with them and bear witness of the Christian faith wherever they are. Their presence not only alters the

---

[396] Stephen Bevans, "Mission *among* Migrants, Mission *of* Migrants," in *A Promised Land, A Perilous Journey: Theological Perspectives on Migration,* edited by Daniel G. Groody and Gioacchino Campese (Notre Dame, IN: University of Notre Dame Press, 2008) 90.

[397] Pontifical Council for the Pastoral Care of the Migrants and Itinerant People, "Starting Afresh from Christ: Towards a Renewed Pastoral Care for Migrants and Refugees.?" Fifth World Congress on the Pastoral Care of Migrants and Refugees, (Rome, 2003) Part II, Pastoral Care, #9. See http://www.vatican.va/roman_curia/pontifical_councils/migrants/documents/rc_pc_migran ts_doc_2004001_Migrants_Vcongress_%20findoc_en.html (accessed July 9, 2015).

[398] Bevans, "Mission *among* Migrants," 101.

263

demographic landscape but also enhances the spirituality of the host countries.[399] Recognizing their precious gift to the U.S. Church, the Committee on Migration of the United States Conference of Catholic Bishops (USCCB) in 2001 wrote a wonderful document entitled, "Asian and Pacific Presence: Harmony in Faith." This pastoral letter affirms with loving assurance their presence and prominence in the U.S. Catholic Church. It states: "We pray that this pastoral statement will facilitate a fuller appreciation of their communities in our local churches and will encourage Asian and Pacific Catholics to take on active leadership roles in every level of church life."[400] The document celebrates numerous gifts and contributions in which Asian and Pacific Catholics have enriched the church communities over many decades. It further states, "The Church is blessed with Asian and Pacific pastors, social workers, educators, diocesan directors, and lay leaders who are actively and selflessly contributing to building the Kingdom of God in this country. The number of Asian and Pacific Catholics who have been given responsibility in church structures, or are well known in their fields of endeavor, is growing."[401]

Preaching in the Context of Global Migration

We are living in a time when ethnic, cultural, and linguistic diversity is more evident and intense than ever. Like it or not, the face of the church in the 21st century will continue to be even more ethnically diverse due to the

---

[399] According to a survey done in 2010, Asian Americans exhibit more religious commitment with 64 percent saying religion is very important in their lives, compared to 54 percent for white Americans. Also, 6 in 10 Asian Catholics say they attend Mass at least once per week, while only 4 in 10 white American Catholics say that. Another interesting statistic is that 61 percent of Asian Americans report that they pray daily, while 55 percent of white Americans are likely to do the same thing. See the 2011 survey done by the United States Conference of Catholic Bishops under the office of the Secretariat of Cultural Diversity in the Church of the Asian and Pacific affairs, which is available online: http://www.usccb.org/issues-and-action/cultural-diversity/asian-pacific-islander/demographics/upload/survey_demographics.pdf (accessed on January 10, 2018).

[400] *Asian and Pacific Presence: Harmony in Faith*, 1. For the online text; go to: http://www.usccb.org/issues-and-action/cultural-diversity/asian-pacific-islander/resources/upload/AP-Pastoral-Statement-English.pdf (accessed on January 10, 2018).

[401] *Ibid.*, 10.

worldwide phenomenon of migration.[402] Unlike the past, diversity is not a thing to overcome but rather an essential component to foster. This can be an hour of great opportunities for the church and its evangelization. At our Sunday celebrations, one cannot help but notice the cultural diversity of peoples represented in the pews. The Anglo, African, Asian, and Hispanic faces form a magnificent rainbow of colors. According to the 2014 statistics,[403] there are approximately 15.2 million people in the U.S. who self-identified as Asian, Native Hawaiian, or Pacific Islander, and about 2.9 million people, which is a little over 19 percent, are Catholics. The percentage of Christians in general and Catholics in particular is significantly higher among Asian Americans than in their native lands. For example, Vietnamese Catholics in the U.S. are estimated to number 483,000, which is about 27 percent of the 1.7 million Vietnamese in living in the U.S., while the percentage of Catholics in Viet Nam is only 8 percent.[404]

The face of the priesthood is also changing. On any given Sunday, thousands of foreign-born priests are preaching from the pulpit. While an exact count is not available, it is estimated that there are over 8,500 foreign-born priests currently serving in the U.S. Each year there are approximately 300 new international priests who come to North America to begin a new ministry.[405] The majority of these foreign-born priests come from Asia, Africa, and Latin America.[406] In the archdiocese of Los Angeles, for example, the Mass on any given weekend is conducted in forty-five different languages. Consequently, mono-cultural parishes are being replaced by "shared parishes" or "national

---

[402] vănThanh Nguyen and John M. Prior, eds., *God's People on the Move: Biblical and Global Perspectives on Migration and Mission*, (Eugene, OR: Pickwick Publications, 2014), xi.

[403] Gray, Gautier, and Gaunt, "Cultural Diversity," 7–8.

[404] *Ibid.*, 7.

[405] Aniedi Okure, "International Priests in the United States: An Update," *Seminary Journal* 1.1 (2012) 34–43, here 35.

[406] Interestingly the U.S. Catholic Church is becoming a mission-receiving church rather than a mission-sending church. This is a clear sign of "mission-in-reverse."

parishes,"[407] that is parishes in which more than one language, racial or cultural group worship together as one Christian community. As "shared," "national" or "multicultural" parishes become the norm, everyone must be prepared to embrace the reality of our church and learn to appreciate its extraordinary variety. Preachers, ministers, and pastoral workers are especially encouraged to prepare themselves to work in diverse environments and to foster the right knowledge, attitudes, and skills to be effective in the diverse vineyard of the Lord. Furthermore, to effectively proclaim the message of God's reign and salvation to all people, particularly to, among, and with migrants, whose number has reached over 244 million and still rising,[408] one needs to preach in context.

What exactly is contextual preaching? Allow me to turn to Stephen Bevans' famous quote saying, "There is no 'theology' as such—no 'universal theology'—there are only contextual theologies."[409] Recently Bevans, who co-authored with Ricky Manalo, writes, "Just as there is no such thing as 'theology' but only 'contextual theology,' so there is no such thing as 'preaching.' There is only 'contextual preaching.' Only preaching that makes an effort to communicate to real people in real situations is preaching that is worthy of the name."[410] The reality is that the migrant and refugee crisis has exploded exponentially and become one of the major factors shaping our world. The document Erga Migrantes Caritas Christi astutely observes, "In fact nearly all countries are now faced with the eruption of the migration phenomenon in one aspect or another; it affects their social, economic, political and religious life and is becoming more

---

[407] Mark Stelzer, "A New Ecclesial Reality and A New Way of Doing Theology: Heralding A New Pentecost," in *Many Faces, One Church: Cultural Diversity and the American Catholic Experience*, ed. Peter C. Phan and Dianna Hayes, (Lanham, Maryland: A Sheed & Ward Book, 2005), 13.

[408] Elizabeth W. Collier and Charles R. Strain, *Global Migration: What's Happening, Why, and A Just Response* (Winona, MN: Anselm Academic, 2017), 8.

[409] Stephen B. Bevans, *An Introduction to Theology in Global Perspective* (Maryknoll, NY: Orbis Books, 2009), 4.

[410] Stephen Bevans and Ricky Manalo, "Contextual Preaching," in *A Handbook for Catholic Preaching*, edited by Edward Foley (General Editor), (Collegeville, MN: Liturgical Press, 2016), 234.

and more a permanent structural phenomenon" (EMCC, no. 1).[411] Consequently, preaching in the context of the global crisis of migration is "not an option but a pastoral imperative."[412]

While nearly half of the world's international migrants are Christians, fifty-one percent are not Christians. The religious composition of international migrants is as follows: Muslims make up the second-largest share of people on the move, about 27 percent (nearly 60 million); Hindus 5 percent (nearly 11 million); Buddhists 3 percent (about 7 million); Jews 2 percent (more than 3.6 million); adherents of other faiths, such as Sikhs, Jains, Taoists, and other traditional religions, 4 percent (over 9 million); and those unaffiliated, for example atheists or agnostics, 9 percent (over 19 million).[413] It goes without saying that preaching *to*, *among*, and *with* migrants gives us a great opportunity to enter into inter-religious dialogue and promote communion. The document *Erga Migrantes Caritas Christi* states:

> Today's migrations constitute the greatest movement of persons, if not of peoples, of all time. They bring us into contact with men and women, our brothers and sisters, who for economic, cultural, political or religious reasons have left or have been compelled to leave their homes and end up, for the most part, in refugee camps, in a soulless megalopolis and in slums on the outskirts of cities, where they often share the marginalisation of the unemployed, the ill-adjusted youth, and abandoned women.
>
> In the Christian community born of Pentecost, migration is an integral part of the Church's life, clearly expresses its universality, promotes communion within it, and influences

---

[411] The document, *Erga Migrantes Caritas Christi*, which is translated as "The Love of Christ towards migrants?" (aka *EMCC*) is written by the Pontifical Council for the Pastoral Care of Migrants and Itinerant People in 2004 from Vatican City See, http://www.vatican.va/roman_curia/pontifical_councils/migrants/documents/rc_pc_migran ts_doc_20040514_erga-migrantes-caritas-christi_en.html (accessed January 10, 2018). It is an official instruction from the Catholic Church in response to the crisis of international migration.

[412] Bevans and Manalo, "Contextual Preaching", 242.

[413] http://www.pewforum.org/2012/03/08/religious-migration-exec/ (accessed January 10, 2018).

its growth. Migration thus offers the *Church* an historic opportunity to prove its four characteristic marks: the Church is *one* because in a certain sense it also expresses the unity of the whole human family; it is *holy* also to make all people holy and that God's name may be sanctified in them; it is *catholic* furthermore in its openness to diversity that is to be harmonised; and it is likewise *apostolic* because it is also committed to evangelise the whole human person and all people.

It is thus clear that the Church's missionary calling is not determined only by geographic distances but by differences of culture and religion. "Mission" is thus going out to every person to proclaim Jesus Christ and, in Christ and the Church, to bring him into communion with all humanity. (*EMCC*, no. 96-97)

Communion through Prophetic Dialogue

Christian preachers are "builders" and "deacons" of communion because they seek to embark on the journey of fellowship with all people (*EMCC*, no. 98-99). Their primary task is promoting "fraternal dialogue and mutual respect, the living testimony of love and welcome thus constitute in themselves the first and indispensable form of evangelization" (*EMCC*, no. 99). For such ideal communion to be achieved, sincere and humble dialogue among all people and religions must take place. Highlighting the importance of dialogue, Pope Francis says:

> Evangelization also involves the path of dialogue. For the Church today, three areas of dialogue stand out where she needs to be present in order to promote full human development and to pursue the common good: dialogue with states, dialogue with society – including dialogue with cultures and the sciences – and dialogue with other believers who are not part of the Catholic Church. (*EG*, 238)

Edmund Chia, a theologian from Malaysia notes that throughout the thirty years of the existence of the Federation of Asian Bishops' Conferences (FABC) the theme of dialogue surfaced at practically every assembly and appeared in every document. Chia writes, "Dialogue is the way of being Church in Asia. Dialogue is also the method for doing theology in Asia. In short, dialogue is the life and mode of the Asian Church."[414] Not surprisingly, the FABC emphasizes three areas of dialogue: with the Asian poor, with their cultures, and with their religions. This "triple dialogue" is the modality in which the church in Asia carries out its "evangelizing mission and thus becomes the local church."[415] At every moment of the triple dialogue, a fourfold element is drawn into the conversation:

> a. The *dialogue of life,* where people strive to live in an open and neighborly spirit, sharing their joys and sorrows, their human problems, and preoccupations.

> b. The *dialogue of action*, in which Christians and others collaborate for the integral development and liberation of people.

> c. The *dialogue of theological exchange*, where specialists seek to deepen their understanding of their respective religious heritages, and to appreciate each other's spiritual values.

> d. The *dialogue of religious experience*, where persons, rooted in their own religious traditions, share their spiritual riches, for instance, with regard to prayer and contemplation, faith, and ways of searching for God or the Absolute.[416]

Recognizing the importance of communion through dialogue, the Asian Bishops encouraged the presbyters to be formed and well trained to carry out the

---

[414] Edmund Chia, *Towards a Theology of Dialogue* (Bangkok, Thailand, 2003), 230. Chia served as executive secretary of interreligious dialogue for the Asian Bishops' Conference from 1996–2004.

[415] Peter C. Phan, *In Our Tongues: Perspectives from Asia on Mission and Inculturation* (Maryknoll, NY: Orbis Books, 2003), 18. See also Peter Phan's latest book, *The Joy of Religious Pluralism: A Personal Journey* (Maryknoll, NY: Orbis Books, 2017). In *Joy of Religious Pluralism*, Phan relates his story of the questions raised by the Congregation for the Doctrine of the Faith about his understanding of the salvific role of Christ and the Church. In this "page-turner," Phan explains the "errors and ambiguities" that were identified by the Vatican in his book, *Being Religious Interreligiously*. I highly recommend everyone to read Phan's book, *The Joy of Religious Pluralism*.

[416] See *For All the Peoples of Asia*, FABC Documents from 1992–1996, volume 2, edited by Franz-Josef Eilers (Manila: Claretian Publications, 1997), 21–26. This citation is quoted in Phan, *In Our Tongues*, 19.

triple dialogue when working and serving in an Asian context. According to the Asian Bishops, the role of the presbyter is

> To inspire, to encourage, to foster initiatives, and to help charisms to develop. After the pattern of Christ the Good Shepherd, whose saving action he makes present to his flock, the presbyter is sensitive to its diverse needs, especially those of the underprivileged and the poor. He is quick to come to their assistance and to be present to them in moments of crisis, not content with showing solicitude but being deeply involved in their life and sharing their lot. His one concern is to form his community into a living sign of the presence in the world of the Risen Lord Who assumes and heals all human situations and brings to fulfillment all hopes and aspirations. The *prophetic* role of the presbyter, then, consists in building up a committed Christian *fellowship* as a *prophetic* sign of the future kingdom already operative in the world.[417] (emphasis added)

Interestingly, the way of being and ministering in the church, whether in Asian contexts or elsewhere, is seeking *communion* through *dialogue* and *prophecy*. In other words, dialogue alone is not enough but both dialogue and prophecy are important characteristics of evangelization in the context of migration. To put it in another way, Christians carry out the mission of the church when they live and minister in "prophetic dialogue."[418] This term or concept has been well developed by Stephen Bevans and Roger Schroeder. Their book, titled *Prophetic Dialogue: Reflections on Christian Mission Today*, has further clarified this important characteristic and has greatly contributed to the field of mission theology. Consequently, communion or fellowship through "prophetic dialogue" is an appropriate modality and characteristic of a messenger or proclaimer of the Christian Good News today, particularly in the context of global migration.

---

[417] *For All the Peoples of Asia*, FABC Documents from 1970–1991, volume 1, edited by Gaudencio B. Rosales and C. G. Arevalo (Manila: Claretian Publications, 1997), 86.
[418] Stephen B. Bevans and Roger P. Schroeder, *Prophetic Dialogue: Reflections on Christian Mission Today* (Maryknoll, NY: Orbis Books, 2011), 59.

Conclusion

I would like to conclude by highlighting how Pope Francis is a prime model of one who practices contextual preaching *to*, *among*, and *with* migrants. In *Evangelii Gaudium*, Pope Francis notes that a good preacher not only has to contemplate "the word" but also "the people" (*EG*, no. 154). The people that Pope Francis has in mind are the vulnerable. And who are the most vulnerable people on the planet today? They are the millions of migrants and refugees, many of whom are women and children. Pope Francis writes, "Migrants present a particular challenge for me, since I am the pastor of a Church without frontiers, a Church which considers herself mother to all" (*EG*, 210). With heartfelt concern, Pope Francis challenges all Christians saying, "Jesus, the evangelizer par excellence and the Gospel in person, identifies especially with the little ones (cf. Matt. 25:40). This reminds us Christians that we are called to care for the vulnerable of the earth" (*EG*, 209). Whether these migrants and refugees are Christians, Buddhists, or Muslims, Pope Francis reaches out to and advocates for all of them with genuine concern and heartfelt compassion. He has consistently engaged in respectful ecumenism and inter-religious dialogue to foster and establish universal fellowship and communion by means of genuine dialogue and prophecy. Over the course of this pontificate Pope Francis has delivered numerous speeches, sermons, and instructions on the pastoral care of migrants.[419] He repeatedly summons Christians and nations to welcome these migrants and refugees as one would welcome God's messengers. More than just ornaments on a tree, migrants are lives fashioned in the image of God and are Christ Jesus himself, often disguised in the most vulnerable and the least. "On immigration and the poor," one reporter writes, "Pope Francis walks his talk!"[420] There is a tapestry of concrete gestures showing that when it comes to

---

[419] For message on World Day of Migrants and Refugees, see https://w2.vatican.va/content/francesco/en/messages/migration.index.html (accessed January 12, 2018).
[420] See https://cruxnow.com/vatican/2017/02/17/immigrants-poor-pope-francis-walks-talk/ (accessed on January 12, 2018).

responding to the immigration crisis, Pope Francis has led not only with words, but also by example. As the leader of a worldwide (catholic) church, Pope Francis has been a great builder and deacon of communion who lives and preaches "with the smell of his sheep."[421]

---

[421] *Evangelii Gaudium*, no. 24. In his address to the world's priests at the Chrism Mass on Holy Thursday, March 28, 2013, Pope Francis also said, "The priest who seldom goes out of himself ... misses out on the best of our people, on what can stir the depths of his priestly heart. ... This is precisely the reason why some priests grow dissatisfied, lose heart and become in a sense collectors of antiquities or novelties—Instead of being shepherds living with 'the smell of the sheep.' This is what I am asking you—be shepherds with the smell of sheep." See: http://w2.vatican.va/content/francesco/en/homilies/2013/documents/papa-francesco_20130328_messa-crismale.html (accessed on January 12, 2018).

SECTION FIVE

Refugees

CHAPTER TWELVE

Refugees in the Urban Wilderness: Plight of Refugees in Landing Cities and Opportunities for Response

Michael D. Crane

Perceptions about refugees have been colored by popular culture portrayals of refugees in rural camps with basic needs provided by relief agencies. Today, more than half of the world's refugees are based in cities and are responsible for their own shelter and sustenance. In many instances, refugees seeking resettlement must first go to a city in a third country where they are screened by the United Nations for resettlement. This process takes a number of years and involves a unique set of challenges. In this article, the author examines the realities faced by refugees/asylum seekers in these landing cities and explores opportunities for response by the church.

During the time of the pharaohs, the people of Israel grew large in number and became a threat to the Egyptians. In response to this perceived threat, the Egyptians turned the people of Israel into slaves and oppressed them terribly (Exod. 1:8–22). Moses led Israel out of Egypt and brought this nation of refugees to the Promised Land, but not without first going through the wilderness for forty years. Much happened during these years in the wilderness that would forever impact who Israel is. Their time in the wilderness was challenging in so many ways, but it was also a catalyst to reliance on God and the formation of his people. When we tell the story of Israel making their way to the Promised Land without mention of the wilderness, we do a disservice to the church. The story of Israel in the wilderness offers an example that helps us understand the plight of many refugees today.

Refugees are displaced from the nation they have known as home. And, as they await resettlement in a land that holds much promise, many must endure years in cities where they remain an unwelcomed presence. Most likely your perceptions about the refugee life are skewed by a combination of news media and Hollywood. Judging by comments observed on social media, it seems that many people anticipate that refugees simply hop in a dingy and arrive in the United States. However, increasingly, asylum seekers take up residence in a global city and apply for recognition as refugee, awaiting resettlement in a third country. This is a rigorous, arduous process that takes years.

My wife and I said goodbye to good friends, Hannah and Roger, who left our city to be resettled in North America. They arrived in our city seeking asylum for religious reasons but faced terrible difficulties for over five years as they progressed through the refugee process. Work, transportation, and even education for the children is full of challenges. As in many locations, they were given legal status as refugees, but not given the freedom to survive for five years. As we will cover in this chapter, refugees in landing cities often have restrictions on working, education, and sometimes even remaining in the city. Philip Marfleet notes the new urban reality faced by many refugees when he says, "More and more refugees are city dwellers whose existence is denied by governments and agencies."[422]

The population of those forcibly displaced around the world is at an all-time high (80 million as of mid-2020).[423] Only a few countries will accept refugees for long-term resettlement, but many of those countries are inaccessible to the asylum seeker. Facing few options, many asylum seekers are taking up residence in "landing cities" that allow refugees on a temporary basis. A limited

---

[422] Philip Marfleet, "'Forgotten,' 'Hidden': Predicaments of the Urban Refugee," *Refuge* 24, no. 1 (2007): 36.

[423] United Nations High Commissioner for Refugees, "UNHCR-Refugee Statistics," UNHCR, accessed January 17, 2021, https://www.unhcr.org/refugee-statistics/.

number of refugees are resettled in other countries. Most migration is south-south migration.[424] This leaves hundreds of thousands of refugees in limbo in cities where their legal status is ambiguous at best. While there is a lot written about work with refugees in resettlement countries,[425] there is very little written on work with refugees in this time of transition in landing cities. In this article, we seek to understand the realities these asylum seekers/refugees face in these landing cities and suggest opportunities for response.

Before we drill down deeper into the notion of urban refugees and the realities they face, it is important to clarify our terminology. According to the UN, a refugee is "someone who has been forced to flee his or her country because of persecution, war, or violence."[426] An asylum seeker is one who seeks recognition as a refugee as he or she seeks safe harbor in another nation.[427] An asylum seeker appeals to the United Nations High Commissioner of Refugees (UNHCR) office to become officially recognized as a refugee. This process is described in more detail in this article. These "landing cities" described in this article are the points of first arrival for the asylum seeker after fleeing the country of origin. These cities are officially transitory homes for the refugees as they seek to move to a resettlement country. Resettlement countries are ones that are

---

[424] Mechteld Jansen, "Christian Migrants and the Theology of Space and Place," in *Contested Spaces, Common Ground: Space and Power Structures in Contemporary Multireligious Societies,* ed. Ulrich Winkler, Lidia Rodriguez Fernandez, and Oddbjorn Leirvik (Leiden; Boston: Brill Rodopi, 2017), 148.

[425] Enoch Wan and Anthony Casey, *Church Planting among Immigrants in US Urban Centers: The "Where", "Why", And "How" of Diaspora Missiology in Action* (Portland, OR: Institute of Diaspora Studies, 2014); Enoch Wan and Thanh Trung Le, *Mobilizing Vietnamese Diaspora for the Kingdom* (Portland, OR: Institute of Diaspora Studies, 2014); Yaw Attah Edu-Bekoe and Enoch Wan, *Scattered Africans Keep Coming: A Case Study of Diaspora Missiology on Ghanaian Diaspora and Congregations in the USA* (Portland, OR: Institute of Diaspora Studies, 2013).

[426] "What Is a Refugee," *USA for UNHCR* (blog), 2016, http://www.unrefugees.org/what-is-a-refugee/.

[427] United Nations High Commissioner for Refugees, "Asylum-Seekers," UNHCR, 2016, http://www.unhcr.org/asylum-seekers.html.

signatories to the 1951 Refugee Convention and which allow refugees to settle long-term with a path to permanent residency or citizenship.[428]

The Changing Nature of the Refugee

I was raised in Southeast Asia from the 1970s through the early 1990s. In the aftermath of the Vietnam War, there were many refugees fleeing Vietnam on boats and being forced to live in designated camps. Their whole life was relegated to those camps. Movies most often depict this kind of refugee life, rows of tents in a dusty, no-man's-land surrounded by barbed wire. While many millions of refugees still live this way, more and more are arriving in cities to seek asylum. They have much more freedom to roam than those fenced in in more traditional refugee camps. The United Nations now reports that more than half of the world's refugees are based in cities.[429] This is a significant shift, as just ten years ago only 18% of the world's refugees were urban.[430] The challenges faced by these urban refugees differ somewhat from those based in camps.

I met one brother and sister from Central Asia for a curry lunch in Kuala Lumpur. They were planning to fly to Jakarta the next day with the goal of boarding a boat that would take them to Australia. They had done their research and felt that their best option for securing long-term escape from persecution in their home country was to take the chance in a boat arranged by a coyote (human smuggler) to Australia. With the increase of mobility and accessibility of information, desperate people have options for escape. Some still take boats that drift prayerfully towards a welcoming and hospitable land mass. Others travel over land to their destination city. And many now fly on commercial airlines to a

---

[428] Brad Coath et al., "'You Took Me In': Seeking Transformation for Migrant Workers, Refugees, and Asylum Seekers," in *Signs of Hope in the City: Renewing Urban Mission, Embracing Radical Hope*, ed. Graham Hill (Melbourne: ISUM, 2015), 67.

[429] Baher Kamal, "Now 1 in 2 World's Refugees Live in Urban Areas | Inter Press Service," Inter Press Service, May 29, 2016, http://www.ipsnews.net/2016/05/now-1-in-2-worlds-refugees-live-in-urban-area/.

[430] Karen Jacobsen, "Refugees and Asylum Seekers in Urban Areas: A Livelihoods Perspective," *Journal of Refugee Studies* 19, no. 3 (August 2006): 273–86.

city they know will receive them, at least initially, as tourists. As a result, global cities all over the world have growing refugee populations. Of note in this study are Istanbul, Amman, Bangkok, Kuala Lumpur, Nairobi, and Johannesburg.

Many have a preconceived notion that a refugee should be poor, uneducated, and helpless in some manner. This brother and sister were both already studying for their bachelor's degrees and were from a middle-class background. Their chosen path to fly to Jakarta and then take a boat to Australia was a terribly treacherous one, and I tried everything I could to persuade them not to proceed with their plan. These boats that take desperate refugees to another country are organized by criminals, called coyotes, who exploit their clients by charging many thousands of dollars. In some cases, the coyotes take the money and disappear without ever delivering on the boat. If the refugees do make it on the boat, they are generally packed beyond capacity on a vessel that is under-maintained. Just a month before I met this brother and sister, one such boat from Jakarta bound for Australia sank with no survivors. If the boat defies the odds and makes it safely to Australia, chances are the Australian government will arrest them and send them to a remote island to be placed in detention. Would such young, educated, middle class individuals risk such peril if it weren't already a matter of life and death?

From Seeking Asylum to Resettled Refugee

Typically, refugees do not have the option of fleeing to a country that will allow them to settle and become citizens of the new nation. Very few nations receive refugees for long-term settlement. "Mass movements of refugees are seldom welcome, unless they fulfill a specific economic or ideological function, and states may go to great lengths to exclude incomers and/or to isolate them from the wider society."[431]

---

[431] Marfleet, "'Forgotten,' 'Hidden': Predicaments of the Urban Refugee," 36.

In ideal circumstances, refugees are permitted to return to their nation of origin after the conflict has subsided. Less than one percent of refugees are sent to a third nation for resettlement.[432] Such a small percentage is resettled because the few nations who receive refugees have annual quotas permitted each year. There are a number of key issues asylum seekers face as they seek to be recognized as refugees.

Interviewing with UNHCR

One friend arose early one weekday morning to beat the crowds at the UNHCR office. He was lining up to make an appointment for his first interview to receive refugee status. They gave him an appointment card with a date two years in the future. This was to be only the first of three interviews with the UNHCR. We have known several who have waited months or years for their appointment only to have it cancelled because there was no translator that day. Others have had trouble with translators mistranslating their answers to the UNHCR representative. The future of those seeking asylum rests on these interviews.

Those from the UNHCR office have the unenviable job of discerning between those who are truly refugees and those who see an opportunity to live in a developed nation. We have seen some asylum seekers ask churches to be baptized so they can claim religious persecution. Strangely enough, a UNHCR representative will be quizzing asylum seekers claiming to be Christians escaping persecution on finer points of Christian theology even though they themselves may not be Christians.

Once an asylum seeker proves to have a legitimate case after a series of interviews and background checks, the UNHCR will grant him or her refugee status. In some countries this gives limited protection and permission to remain in the city in which they have sought asylum while awaiting resettlement. But the waiting list to be resettled is long, which means thousands of refugees are forced

---

[432] United Nations High Commissioner for Refugees, "Resettlement," UNHCR, 2016, http://www.unhcr.org/resettlement.html.

to wait for several years before they can move (and those are the lucky few who are actually accepted by a country for resettlement; most of them will languish indefinitely in the landing city). For example, in Kuala Lumpur there are more than 150,000 registered refugees and only a few thousand will be resettled this year. Every year the list grows longer.

After being recognized as refugees by the UNHCR, they are then matched up with a resettlement country. The resettlement country will conduct a series of interviews and background checks. In the case of the United States, the refugee is interviewed by the State department, and then several agencies perform strenuous background checks. This process can sometimes take a number of years. As an added stress, the refugee has little idea when or if they will know something about their resettlement. Planned limbo is one thing; unpredictable limbo is even more difficult.

Education for Refugee Children

Many refugees arrive as families with school-aged children. If a family arrives with a ten-year-old daughter and they have to wait six years before they are resettled, those six years are critical for that daughter in terms of education and stability. In most of these landing cities, refugee children are not permitted in the government-run schools. In response, in some landing cities, churches and social organizations have started learning centers all over the city. The UN helps with a small amount of funding, and the rest is supported by volunteer teachers and donations. The NGO International Rescue Committee did a study on refugees from Myanmar in Kuala Lumpur. In this study of 1000 households: 84% of children ages 6-11 are in some kind of learning program. 37% of children ages 12–18 are in a learning program. "Refugee youth between the ages of 11 and 18 in Malaysia are at high risk of missing out on the opportunity to obtain an education."[433] We have known two girls who dropped out of these schools as they reached adolescence because they were drawing too much attention from local police as they traveled from home to school. As refugees, they have no certainty of their rights being honored.

Employment Opportunities

In a number of landing cities, refugees are not allowed to work officially. This is a challenge for most refugees because the length of the interview and resettlement process takes several years. Those in refugee camps have basic needs (lodging, food, medical care, simple education) met, but urban refugees must pay for their own rent, food, and any education for their children. Very few refugees have enough financial savings to see them through years of living in a global city. Therefore, most urban refugees must work illegally.

I have met refugees who were once doctors, engineers, and academicians in their former countries who now come to cities like Istanbul, Bangkok, and Jakarta with no other choice but to work in simple jobs for long hours. Many work for wages paid under the table. I have seen several places where employers exploit refugee labor, knowing their desperation. I met one Syrian refugee working at a retail kiosk. The owner of a competing kiosk called the immigration authorities and soon this Syrian man was put in a detention center. After his time in the detention center, he trembles at the thought of working again and being exposed to the authorities.

Every description I have heard about the detention centers is horrifying. In most cases, however, local business owners will not even hire a refugee to begin with. This is especially true of refugees who look different from the local population. For example, African refugees in Bangkok find it nearly impossible

---

[433] Amy A. Smith, *In Search of Survival and Sanctuary in the City: Refugees from Myanmar/Burma in Kuala Lumpur, Malaysia* (Kuala Lumpur, Malaysia: IRC, 2012), 11, http://www.rescue.org/resource-file/search-survival-and-sanctuary-city-refugees-myanmarburma-kuala-lumpur-malaysia-decembe.

to find work because they stand out as obviously not Thai nationals (den Otter, 2007, 49).[434]

The refugees I have met have desperately wanted to work and provide for their families. Aside from the legal obstacles to working, refugees often have to learn another language to work and adjust to different cultural norms of work. Those that do manage to find work often have to endure long hours and few, if any, days off. Even commuting to work is rife with danger due to random police check points causing many refugees to remain in a confined urban area for fear of detainment.

Whether it is navigating the interview process or finding employment and education, urban refugees face nearly overwhelming obstacles as they search for a life free from oppression.

Unsettled Refugees

Many, if not most, refugees are never resettled in a third country. With nearly 20 million recognized refugees around the world, there simply are not enough countries willing to receive refugees for resettlement. With only 80,000 refugees being resettled each year, Brad Coath notes "it doesn't take a degree in mathematics to realize that that's like trying to pour an entire beach worth of sand through an egg timer."[435] This means there are thousands of refugees who will remain in the cities mentioned in this article for decades or even the rest of their lives. When the phenomenon of the urban refugees became more prevalent in the late 1990s, the UNHCR issued a report that indicated that these "spontaneous" or "self-settled" refugees were illegal and were circumventing the process designed for those coming from rural settings.[436]

---

[434] Vera den Otter, "Urban Asylum Seekers and Refugees in Thailand," *Forced Migration Review* 28 (2007): 49.

[435] Coath et al., "'You Took Me In': Seeking Transformation for Migrant Workers, Refugees, and Asylum Seekers," 66.

[436] Marfleet, "'Forgotten,' 'Hidden': Predicaments of the Urban Refugee," 40.

For many refugees, returning to their country of origin is not a possibility. But this leaves refugees in legal limbo because they are no longer recognized as citizens of any nation. This even includes children born in the landing cities, as very few nations will automatically recognize the citizenship of those born within their borders. This means these refugee families never gain legal freedom to work and enter children into government sponsored schools. This means life continues on the margins of society.

The situation for refugees differs in each city. In cities like Bangkok or Jakarta, it is very difficult for refugees to ever create a sustainable future due to government restrictions.[437] Cities like Nairobi or Cairo have developed neighborhoods of refugees from Somalia, Ethiopia, and South Sudan that create their own micro-economy.[438] Other cities, like Istanbul, demonstrate a higher level of tolerance for these refugee communities.[439]

There are also a number of factors that can derail a resettlement. The stress families endure sometimes leads to divorces or other family splits. At times single refugees have children with refugees from other nations or with citizens of the host nation. This sometimes leads to a paperwork gridlock that never gets resolved. If the refugee wants to stay with the child, they need to remain in the landing city, legal or not.

---

[437] den Otter, "Urban Asylum Seekers and Refugees in Thailand," 50; Alice M. Nah, "Refugees and Space in Urban Areas in Malaysia," *Forced Migration Review* 34 (2010): 29–31.

[438] Pascale Ghazaleh, "In 'closed File' Limbo: Displaced Sudanese in a Cairo Slum," *Forced Migration Review* 16 (2003): 24–26; Flavie Halais, "What It Means for Cities Now That More than Half the World's Refugees Live in Urban Areas," Citiscope, May 27, 2016, http://citiscope.org/story/2016/what-it-means-cities-now-more-half-worlds-refugees-live-urban-areas?utm_source=Citiscope&utm_campaign=d36ef17853-Mailchimp_2016_05_27&utm_medium=email&utm_term=0_ce992dbfef-d36ef17853-118051765.

[439] John H., "Refugees in Istanbul- Personal Correspondence," April 25, 2016.

Other issues that can slow things down for a refugee awaiting resettlement include health issues,[440] legal issues,[441] or a failure to be cleared by the third nation.[442] One family we know ended up in a lawsuit, being sued by a citizen of the host country at which point the refugee process became stalled. Refugees often flee their country of origin with very little, sometimes just the clothes on their backs. I am aware of some refugee minors who fled their home country after their parents were killed and made their way through Southeast Asian jungles to get to Bangkok or Kuala Lumpur. The dilemma for UNHCR is they have no paper trail to verify their stories.

Refugees in these extended holding patterns have no choice but to join the informal economy of the landing cities. If they have families, they need to find ways for children to have documentation and education. For some this means changing their status from refugee to obtaining another type of visa (i.e. student or employment visas). Others remain in legal ambiguity, always facing the threat of being sent to a detention center or expelled from the country.

Opportunities to Serve

From the first chapters of Genesis through the rest of the Bible, we have accounts of people who are displaced because of humanity's sinful condition.[443] Abraham was asked by God to leave his home and go to a land with other occupants. We have already seen how the nation of Israel became refugees after they were delivered from Egyptian slavery. And in Matthew 2, Jesus and his family became refugees when Herod ordered the massacre of all children under the age of two. In other words, the notion of refugees is not a foreign concept in

---

[440] Sahana Basavapatna, "Access to Health Care for Refugees in New Delhi," *Refugee Watch Online* (blog), March 19, 2009, http://refugeewatchonline.blogspot.com/2009/03/access-to-health-care-for-refugees-in.html.

[441] Anita Fabos and Gaim Kibreab, "Urban Refugees: Introduction," *Refuge* 24, no. 1 (2007): 3–10.

[442] Ghazaleh, "In 'closed File' Limbo: Displaced Sudanese in a Cairo Slum."

[443] Frederick A. Norwood, *Strangers and Exiles: A History of Religious Refugees, Vol. I* (Nashville: Abingdon Press, 1969).

the Bible (pardon the pun). "The biblical mandate to care for refugees is clear and binding."[444]

God's people are clearly told to love the sojourner/stranger (noted by Hebrew terms *ger* and *towshab* used over 100 times in the Old Testament) in their midst. There are a number of passages calling God's people to welcome the strangers among us, to show mercy, and even to love them as our own family (Lev. 19:9–10, 19, 34; 23:22; Deut. 24:19; Heb. 13:2, etc.). These commands to love the stranger is rooted in the nature of God, who is love (1 John 4:8) and loves sojourners specifically (Deut. 10:18; Psalm 9:9). Space does not permit a detailed survey of the biblical passages that inform ministry among refugees, so I draw on Anthony Casey's conclusion: "God's care for the foreigner is so strong throughout Scripture, that regardless of the political laws of our (or any country), Christians must care for the foreigner among us while we have a chance."[445] Broadly speaking, there are three areas of response for the church: social justice, physical welfare, and spiritual welfare.

Social Justice

In many of these cities there is a risk in helping refugees. Since many of the landing cities are in countries that are not signatories to the 1951 Refugee Convention, the international community has little input into refugee rights in those countries. For example, refugees in Malaysia or Thailand have no legal status. This means Malaysian or Thai citizens who help refugees are themselves in grey legal area. However, if the biblical calling is to help refugees, that overrides earthly legality.

One important way the church in these landing cities can respond is through advocacy both via legal channels as well as at a grassroots level.

---

[444] Peter Vimalasekaran, "Strategies for Reaching Refugees," in *Scattered and Gathered: A Global Compendium of Diaspora Missiology*, ed. Sadiri Joy Tira and Tetsunao Yamamori, Regnum Studies in Mission (Oxford: Regnum Books, 2016), 216.

[445] Anthony Casey, "Caring for the Stranger in Our Midst: Biblical and Practical Guidelines for Local Church Ministry in the Midst of a Refugee Crisis" (Evangelical Missiological Society: Regional Meeting, Wake Forest, N. C., 2016), 16.

Refugees, due to their limited legal status, have few options to appeal to the government structures of the host countries. Christian lawyers and political representatives can work for changes in laws, as well as strive to shine a light on police and immigration exploitation, which is so rampant in many of the landing cities. When there are specific legal cases involving refugees, Christian lawyers can provide counsel and representation.

On a grassroots level, the church can help other citizens understand the plight of urban refugees and call for a change in how the public treats refugees. Refugees are often exploited by landlords, employers, and other power-holders. The church should take the lead in promoting just rental agreements, adherence to employment laws, and safe passage for refugees throughout the city. Even in multicultural cities like these landing cities, many people operate out of xenophobia and a lack of trust (Bauman, 2016, p. 13).[446] Christians can be advocates for refugees as a viable segment of the city's population.

Physical and Social Welfare

A clear aspect of the biblical mandate to care for the sojourners among us regards seeing to their physical and social needs. The church in each of these cities is blessed with many resources that can be used for these who have been forced from their homelands. Refugees often do not have the means with which to see to their own needs due to language obstacles, legal restrictions, and a lack of funds. The church can respond in a number of ways.

The starting point is to gain an understanding of the needs. One easy way to do this is to network with the local UNHCR office, NGOs, and local aid organizations. The needs of these refugees is far beyond what any organization can handle; therefore, an offer of help is usually welcomed. Through collaboration, the impact on refugee lives is multiplied.[447] Once there is an understanding of the needs, the church can assess her resources that will help

---

[446] Zygmunt Bauman, *Strangers at Our Door* (Malden, MA: Polity, 2016), 13.

[447] Coath et al., "'You Took Me In': Seeking Transformation for Migrant Workers, Refugees, and Asylum Seekers," 76.

meet the needs. Similar to serving in any under-resourced community, it is best to work collaboratively with the community to ensure the help rendered is actually helpful.[448]

The church should consider helping with needs that are not easily met by individuals. Some ministries try to deliver a small amount of food to refugee families, but they would rather be able to work to earn their own income. Churches can provide help in finding work (the church in a city is a surprisingly vast network), vocational training, and teaching the trade language(s) necessary to work in the city. Christian business owners might consider hiring refugees and ensuring fare wages and work hours.

Another way the church can help is through education. In Kuala Lumpur there are over a hundred rag-tag schools/learning centers for refugee children. During the years refugees spend in landing cities, they need educational alternatives for the children. Many churches are already involved in several ways. Some churches provide classroom space for refugee children to study. In addition, Christians can volunteer to teach the kids or help secure schoolbooks and other necessities for these schools. If children miss five years of education, it could be devastating for their adjustment in the resettlement country.[449]

There are many other services the church can provide.[450] Medical and dental needs are always important. Many refugees need help negotiating fair rental agreements and finding apartments near public transportation. In some cases, refugees need help navigating the UN's interview process and accessing services being offered by various NGOs. But one of the greatest gifts you can give a refugee is your friendship. Throughout the process with UNHCR and government agencies, refugees are treated like paperwork in need of a number of

---

[448] See Brian Fikkert and Steve Corbett, *When Helping Hurts: Alleviating Poverty Without Hurting the Poor. . .and Ourselves* (Chicago: Moody Publishers, 2009), 2009.

[449] See further: Michael D. Crane, "The Vital Role of Faith Communities in the Lives of Urban Refugees," *International Journal of Interreligious and Intercultural Studies* 3, no. 2 (2020): 31, https://doi.org/10.32795/ijiis.vol3.iss2.2020.708.

[450] See Andrew Ng and Michael Crane, "Models of Ministry with the Transient Poor," *Evangelical Missions Quarterly* 51, no. 1 (January 2015): 58–67.

signatures. What better way to introduce a small dose of dignity into the life of a refugee than offering genuine friendship?

Spiritual Welfare

The church is called to make disciples of every nation (Matt. 28:18–20). This mandate certainly includes seeing to the spiritual welfare of refugees. Deuteronomy clearly indicates we are to include refugees and other people in transition in our spiritual community (31:12). Similar to the physical and social welfare of refugees, the church needs to first spend time understanding the spiritual needs of a refugee community. Some refugees come from places where gospel witness is suppressed, and the greatest need is evangelism. Other refugees come from a deeply rooted Christian background. And yet others are fleeing persecution due to their Christian faith. In every case we want to make disciples and foster healthy churches. But in each case the starting point will differ.

Refugees coming from places where there is very little gospel witness will need people who can lovingly and patiently share the gospel with them. This can be a wonderful opportunity to share the gospel with those from countries few Christians can enter. We do need to be mindful that persecution can persist even within a particular community which has fled to a landing city. If people from a particular nation repeatedly come to a particular city, churches should be ready with Bibles and other materials in the refugee's language. Those who come to faith in Jesus may then be able to share the gospel among their own people.

Those who are Christians leaving an environment of heavy persecution may lack sufficient discipleship. We worked with one young man who was involved in distributing Christian literature in his home country and, when he discovered he was going to be arrested, left immediately. When my wife and I met with him, we soon discovered he knew very little about the Christian faith even though he was being persecuted for it. This time of transition for refugees can be a critical time of discipleship. There is a need for mature Christians willing to invest their time with these refugees.

Other refugees come from places where the church is already quite developed. For example, in Southeast Asia there are many refugees coming from tribes in Myanmar that are majority Christian (i.e., Chin, Karen, and Kachin tribes all have heavily Christian populations). For many refugees, the distractions and temptations of city life can draw people away from spiritual vitality. There is a need for the planting of healthy churches and biblically solid leadership development.[451] I have found that refugee churches can become wonderful partners in trying to engage the rest of the city with the gospel. And refugee churches become an important community hub that serves the greater refugee community.[452]

Whether we are sharing the gospel with someone who is hearing for the first time or equipping a mature Christian with leadership skills, there are vital opportunities to make disciples who make disciples (2 Tim. 2:2). The church must be careful that it does not focus on either the physical needs or the spiritual needs alone. Loving the refugees in our midst means showing concern about them physically *and* spiritually. But we also need to remember that other organizations might do a better job of addressing their physical needs, but the church has a responsibility to meet the spiritual needs. This time of transition can be pivotal for refugees' spiritual growth. Returning to the example of Israel in the wilderness, Bruce Waltke observes: "In short, lacking normal human structures of society and life and confronted with the hostility of the environment and enemies, Israel finds its life in God."[453]

Conclusion

At a time when more than half of the world's refugees are urban, it is important for the church to understand their process of going from their original

---

[451] Michael D. Crane, "Equipping the Transient for Ministry in a Global City," *The New Urban World Journal* 3, no. 1 (May 2014): 7–15.

[452] David Ley, "The Immigrant Church as an Urban Service Hub," *Urban Studies* 45, no. 10 (September 1, 2008): 2057–74, https://doi.org/10.1177/0042098008094873.

[453] Bruce K. Waltke, *An Old Testament Theology: An Exegetical, Canonical, and Thematic Approach* (Grand Rapids, MI: Zondervan, 2007), 540.

home country to a landing city and then, sometimes, on to a resettlement country. While the church has been involved with refugees in resettlement countries, there is a great need for the church to minister among refugees in these landing cities. The church can play an important role in ministering to people that have undergone severe pain and hardship. The church can minister best by first understanding the realities of refugees in these landing cities. With a firm grasp of the biblical mandate to love refugees in our midst, we must respond to address physical, social, and spiritual needs while simultaneously addressing issues of injustice directed at refugees. As refugees struggle through the urban wilderness while waiting for their eventual new home, this can be a critical time to learn how to rely on God.

CHAPTER THIRTEEN

Unrecognized Refugees: Children, Youth, and Mothers Fleeing Violence in Central America

Alexia Salvatiera

The 9-year-old girl had arrived from El Salvador two days before. Her mother was listening desperately to a lawyer giving an orientation to a group of women about how to file their own asylum applications. I had given the girl a coloring book and she was making beauty with careful strokes while she told me a horror story about the beating of her brother by the *Marasalvatrucha* and the police. "Sangre salio de su cabeza, de su boca, de sus oidos, mucha sangre" (Blood came out of his head, his mouth, his ears, lots of blood) she said with wide eyes. And then she whispered, "Pero ya estamos bien. Vamos a quedarnos aqui" (But now we are ok; we are going to stay here.")

Since the human rights crisis heated up in Central America in 2014, thousands of little girls just like her have not been ok. The Obama administration struggled with the political jeopardy of appearing to be too welcoming to refugees and asylum-seekers. In small and subtle ways, they failed to protect many of these children. Behind the scenes, however, they did invest in a multinational collaboration which within the first year of its existence had already begun to have some impact on the crisis itself. In 2015, El Salvador reached the level of 108.5 murders out of 100,000 residents, vying with Honduras and Syria for the most murders per capita in the world.[454] (In comparison, the U.S. hovers around 2-3.) In 2016, the murder rate went down significantly in El Salvador and the number of asylum seekers fleeing lessened correspondingly. However, during the Trump administration, these efforts ceased and the murder rates went back up. Next came a flood of restrictions; over 400 changes in the immigration system from new regulations or executive orders, all of them restrictive and a number aimed directly at reducing or even ending political asylum. The separation of children from their parents at the border was a horror story that was widely publicized. Lesser known changes were equally if not more destructive. Eliminating gang-related or domestic-violence related asylum claims (even though asylum is designed for situations in which governments are unable to protect citizens as well as government which directly persecute them); Reducing the personnel covering asylum cases and forcing families to wait in Mexico for years before their cases would be heard; Requiring that people fleeing Honduras or El Salvador would have to seek for asylum in Guatemala (a country from which people have received asylum) before being able to petition in the U.S.; sealing the border during COVID for an indefinite period of time with no benchmarks for re-opening.

Now we are in a new moment where the Biden administration seems to be listening to the cries of Central Americans. The question is how deeply they will hear and how quickly they will respond. Let's begin by listening ourselves to some of the stories: First, I want you to meet the boys:

Josue is the grandson of Trinidad, the manager of the Lutheran Guest House in San Salvador. It is the place that you will stay if you come to El Salvador on a short-term mission trip with the Lutheran Church of El Salvador. When Josue was at high school one day, two members of the *Marasalvatrucha* (also known as MS-13) approached him and told him that he would become a member or die. MS-13 is often referred to as a gang but that may be a misnomer;

---

[454] Center for American Progress, Report, 2/24/2016

it is one of the most powerful international mafias that has ever existed. It earns most of its money from trafficking – guns, drugs, people – and from the extortion of small businesses ($600 million in 2015.) They are controlling increasingly large territories of Central America's Northern Triangle (Honduras, El Salvador, Guatemala.) The *Marasalvatrucha* recruits by force. Their threats are not idle. Josue is a Christian and he did not want to become a member of the MS-13. He ran home for his father's protection, knowing that his father was spiritually and physically strong. His father had just returned from his shift as a bus driver; he stepped outside and said to Josue's pursuers; "You cannot have my son" One of the MS-13 took out his gun and murdered Josue's father in front of his eyes. The next morning, Josue ran for relatives in the US.

> Lucas' uncle was killed by a gang in Guatemala; his brother was beat up a year after that by the same gang. After his brother was beat up, he left for the United States. One day Lucas was walking to church and the same gang approached him, beat him up, cut off his fingertips and told him this is the last time they would be beating him up. The next time they would kill him. He left for the states shortly after that. He has four brothers and one has just been detained at the Texas border. His lawyer, in cross examination asked him if he would stop going to church if he went back. He said that he would never stop going to church because his love for God was too great. The judge has asked for more evidence.

Jose is 17 years old, from El Salvador. When he was 16, in his first year at the National University studying electrical engineering, the gangs in his neighborhood began threatening him and his family. They wanted him to join their gang, but he resisted. Finally, they told him that if he did not join, they would kill him, or his family, or both. His parents put him on the journey to the United States, where he has two uncles. He spent two months traveling across Guatemala and Mexico, many times hiding from the police; other times hiding from Mexican gangs. He finally reached the US where he was detained for a month in the "Refrigerator" at a detention center in Texas. The temperature was a constant 60 degrees and he had only a blanket and his underwear. No shoes and socks; no shirt or pants. It was miserably cold. He only got one meal a day, usually a white-bread sandwich with a piece of baloney in between—dry. Finally, he was allowed to travel to Los Angeles where he is now staying with his uncles and going to high school. His court date has not been set yet. He fears being returned to El Salvador, as he is sure he will be killed as soon as he arrives.

The gangs/mafias in Central America do not pressure girls to join. They pressure girls in other ways. Here is a story from a group of United States journalists on a 2015 fact-finding tour[455]:

> The girl is dead. She's 15 years old and her name is Marcela. Witnesses tell us she was executed by a gang member. We can't see her face. All we can see is her plaid pants and gray T-shirt. Her family is across the street in a pickup truck. We can't tell you their names because it would put them in danger. Marcela's mother is too upset to talk. So, we talk to her grandmother. She says Marcela left the house that morning with her sister. The two worked in downtown San Salvador, the capitol of El Salvador, making tortillas. The grandmother tells us that Marcela's boyfriend was a bus driver in a gang-controlled neighborhood. First, he got threats. "Help the gang or we'll kill you." Then he disappeared. Then Marcela started getting threats. And now this: Marcela's body, lying on the ground, while people drive to work. We find the police investigator on the case. He says Marcela was attacked from behind and shot twice in the head. He says Marcela's sister witnessed the killing. She's now in police protection. We ask him why a gang member would kill a 15-year-old girl. He speculates that it's because she didn't want to be someone's girlfriend or didn't want to do something for that gang. Is this normal, we ask? Does it happen to young women a lot? It happens every day, he says. The police later release Marcela's sister from their protection, even though local reporters tell us the gangs will probably go after her now. The family tells us their only option is to leave the country, ideally for the U.S. But they've got about $200 to their name. It's not nearly enough to pay a smuggler.

---

[455] National Public Radio, October 5, 2015.

Here are two stories of girls that we met in immigration courts.

Jasmine is 17 years old, originally from Guatemala. She is an unaccompanied minor who is under the care on her aunt, whom she met when she arrived to the United States. Jasmine appeared in court for the second time without a lawyer. The judge gave her an extension once again to give her a chance to look for an attorney. During her court session the judge decided to go off the record and have a conversation with her about her current living situation. It appears that Jasmine has found herself a boyfriend who is much older than her. Because of tensions in her aunt's home, she decided to move out of her aunt's house and go live with him. For this reason, there are some organizations that are unable to help her since she is no longer under her legal guardian's protection. She is pregnant and no longer attends school. Like many other kids Jasmine seems to not understand exactly what she is facing.

Testimony of "Maria", 17 years old,

I left Guatemala after both of my parents were murdered by gang members. My father was a humble farmer who was gunned down while he was working in the fields. No one knows why he was targeted. A few years later, I was home with my mother and my four siblings when a masked man holding a shotgun broke into our home. The man demanded all of the money we had in the house, but we didn't have enough for him, so he shot and killed my mother in front of all of us. That was the hardest thing in my life, seeing my mother killed in front of me. I have a sister who is close to my age, but our other three siblings are very young. My sister and I didn't know how we were going to take care of them. After our mom was killed, my sister and I decided to move to another part of Guatemala. We knew that gang members will often break into houses where young women are staying alone and rape them, and we didn't want to stay in the place where we had seen our mother killed. We tried to make ends meet in another part of Guatemala, but we couldn't make enough to take care of our little brother and sisters. All of us were so affected by our parents' death but we weren't able to afford any kind of therapy; we could barely afford enough to eat. We never felt safe wherever we went. So, we decided to come to the

United States so that our younger siblings could feel safe, get an education, and have a better life than what my sister and I could offer them after our parents were taken away from us.

If the children come alone, they are meant to be covered under the Wilbur Wilberforce Anti-Trafficking Act of 2008. The Act requires that unaccompanied minors arriving from non-contiguous countries receive a full legal assessment for potential asylum. Instead of going straight to immigration court, their case can first be heard at the Asylum Office, a less hostile environment. However, legal representation is still necessary for most Central Americans to win an asylum case. The Asylum laws are rooted in a response to the refugee crisis of World War II. Almost all of the nations in the world, horrified by the Holocaust, signed a United Nations High Commission on Refugees agreement in 1948 to welcome individuals and families fleeing violent persecution in their home countries[456]. If they apply for refuge in a center overseas, they can become official refugees, eligible for a variety of resettlement benefits. If they instead apply for refuge at the border, they can become asylees; the criteria for refugee status or asylum status is the same but there are no resettlement benefits for asylum recipients. However, this system is designed primarily to identify governments that are persecuting their citizens as a result of their race, religion, class, or political associations. Children running from gangs have to prove that their government could not protect them.

In 2015, when the numbers of children and youth fleeing Central America jumped from 9,000 a year to 70,000 over 18 months, voices in the press criticized parents who could send their children on this dangerous journey unaccompanied. However, if the parents accompanied their children, those children cease to be covered by the Act. Both mothers and children end up

---

[456] Article 14 of the 1948 Universal Declaration of Human Rights, UNHCR

facing an adversarial immigration court. Hear a testimony from one of the mothers:

> I cannot return to El Salvador or the MS-13 gang will kidnap my daughter and kill me. I come from a humble background and worked hard to open my own small store to support my family. MS-13 started taking over my neighborhood, and everyone lived in fear of the gang members. The gang members would come into my store and take things without paying. They would also ask for money almost daily and raise the amount they demanded constantly. They were demanding more than what I could give, so I was forced to close my store. The MS-13 gang was very angry that I closed the store and demanded $7,000 or they would kidnap my 8 year old daughter. They said she was very pretty and they could do a lot of things with her. They also said that if I were to go to the police, they would kill me and my other children. I would not have gone to the police anyway because they are connected with the gangs and often tell the gang members when victims report crimes. The gangs have killed many people who have tried to cooperate with the police. I know I can't go anywhere else in El Salvador because MS-13 is everywhere, and others who have tried to flee to other parts of the country following similar threats have been found and killed. After the gangs threatened to kidnap my daughter, I could not send her to school anymore. We fled to the United States and asked for protection at the border. We were detained in freezing cold rooms and given very little food to eat. The gangs have now started targeting my mother, and I am afraid that she will be hurt or killed because I left.

It is hard to listen to these stories. Most people, even most Christians, want to cover their ears, to run away in horror. It is easy to feel overwhelmed. One more terrible need. One more burden to take on—or not. Privilege means being able to choose your burdens. If you are born in this country and you are not related to anyone from Central America, you don't ever have to think about what is happening in Central America or to Central Americans.

However, that's not the Jesus way. I became a Christian in the Jesus Movement of the '70s. Part of the attraction of Jesus to me was his compassion.

(Jesus looked at the crowds and had compassion on them Matt. 9:36). Compassion is not pity. (Pity would have held no attraction for me.) Compassion is an English or Spanish word consisting of two Latin word, "passio" – to feel or to suffer, and "com" – with. Jesus feels our pain as if it were his pain, our hopes and dreams as if they were his hopes and dreams. When everyone else is running away from the suffering, Jesus is running toward the suffering of others, with healing in his hands.

Of course, there is a step that Jesus takes in Matthew 9 before he has compassion, a critically important step. He looks at the crowds. He looks deep into people's hearts and he see why they are suffering. He looks deep into their lives and he sees the dreams they long for. We do not really have a compassion problem in the church, but we often have a vision problem. We don't see the suffering of the people around us very clearly – let alone people who are far away. If we are to share Christ's compassion, we must see through his eyes.

Hebrews 13:2 tells us that we must not neglect to show hospitality to strangers because by doing so, we may entertain angels. The word for angel in Koine Greek does not merely refer to celestial beings. It refers to any messenger of God, sent to bring a blessing. Jesus does not just see people through the lens of their need; he sees the potential gift of the person in front of him. He sees the possible divine messenger. He also sees the connection between us. If we have one heavenly Father, we are all brothers and sisters. We cannot cease to be family; we can just be functional or dysfunctional family, healthy or unhealthy family. In healthy and functional families, family members are responsible to and for each other. We are our "brother's keeper."

If Central Americans are believers, then we are even more than just members of a common family. We are members of the same body, the Body of Christ. We need to feel the pain in our arms and legs. Lepers do not feel the pain in their extremities – but Jesus cures lepers. For us to be fully alive as the Body, we must feel and live our connection. John 17:21 tells us that the world knows that Jesus has come because of the unity of his followers. This has to mean more than Methodists and Baptists getting together. (I have noticed that denominational ecumenism doesn't seem to convince the world that the Messiah has come.) If our compassion does not cross the boundaries of national identity, we are not followers of the One who loved friend and foe alike.

It is only from that place of seeing and having compassion that we can move to the next step of effective action. What do we need to do for the Central American children, youth and mothers seeking refuge?

First, we have to accompany them. Our Guardian Angels project sends volunteers into the courts in T-Shirts marked by an iconic picture of a guardian angel. We monitor the court process to make sure that the rights of the children and mothers are respected. (Our presence effectively stopped "rocket docket", the process of rushing children and youth through the court process in order to deport them.) We also refer these mothers and children to lawyers when possible or to our pro se legal clinic where lawyers can coach them in submitting their own initial application. Of course, we also pray for them and sometimes with them.

A hopeful story: In the midst of an economic recession several years ago, Sandra came from El Salvador to work and send money home to her family. She left little Christian with her family. When he was 12, he left for school one day only to find out that his school was now in gang territory and that they would not let him enter. Determined to attend school, he recruited his aunt to walk him to school. The gang members stabbed her. Terrified, he cowered in the house until his uncle took him north to the border. He was placed with his mother and she took him to court. The judge gave her a list of lawyers; the least expensive asked for an initial installment of $1,200. Sandra earns less than $1,000 a month making "pupusas" (a Central American popular dish). She could not afford a lawyer. Desperate, she returned to court and asked for time to save the money. The judge scolded her and sent her and Christian into the hallway. Terrified and crying, she was tapped on the shoulder by Guillermo, a Guardian Angels volunteer. He returned with her to court and told the judge that the

Guardian Angels would find her a pro bono lawyer. They found the lawyer; she took on Christian's case and he has now been granted asylum. Sandra says that Christian is doing very well in school, with the goal of becoming a lawyer, and he has great faith. "We now believe in guardian angels" Sandra says.

Of course, there are not enough legal resources to provide pro bono services to all of the Central American children, youth and mothers that need them. The UCARE coalition (managed by Clergy and Laity United for Economic Justice – CLUE) is a local collaboration of faith leaders and non-profit organizations, including legal services providers. The UCARE coalition is determined to develop and advocate for more legal resources. There is a court case by a number of non-profit legal services providers attempting to obtain free and affordable legal representation for asylum-seekers, particularly for minors seeking refuge. Our Guardian Angels in their courtwatch activities gather evidence for this court case. However, we have also all come together to start the Pro Se Clinic at the Carecen offices (a Central American Resource Center dating back to the 1980's.) The Clinic accompanies the families in taking the first steps of their legal process without legal representation. The Guardian Angels try to encourage the families to go to the Pro Se clinic rather than falling prey to the "tiburones" (sharks) – lawyers or notary publics who claim that they will represent the families for whatever money they can muster but who actually do nothing to win their cases (so that the people will be deported, and they can just keep the money.)

However, none of these activities will actually solve the broader problem. We need to engage the problem at its roots.

In Matthew 9, Jesus does not only see individuals; he sees the crowd. We understand the problem and the solution differently if we do not only see individuals but also see the crowd. It is not enough to help a few individual Central Americans if it is possible to impact Central America. The first foreign aid response by the federal government to this crisis was to increase funding to the Mexican government to stop the children and youth from arriving at our border. For about a year, this was a successful strategy from the viewpoint of the US government; while the same numbers were leaving, far fewer were arriving at our border. I met teenage girls, of course, who had fled rape by MS-13 only to be raped by the Mexican police. This was not a humane or effective solution from our perspective. We then joined many others around the country in advocating for our foreign aid funding to go towards international policing and international development. When the civil wars ended in Central America in the early '90s, there was no Marshall plan. (The Marshall plan after WWII provided resources to Germany for economic development.) The Obama administration began to move in this direction, with some encouraging results, but much more needed to be done – and now, we will have to build again from the bottom up.[457] This will take advocacy. Advocacy is democracy at work, citizens calling on our representatives to represent our true values and beliefs. In a democracy, advocacy is an exercise in the stewardship of our influence. When we advocate in a way that is biblically based, we actually minister to our legislators, calling on the better angels of their nature to decide and act in ways that are pleasing to God.

That little 9-year-old Salvadoran girl is one of us. She is God's child; she is our little sister. Josue, Luis, Jose, Jasmine, Maria...all of them are our family members and many are fellow members of the Body of Christ. May we do all that is in our power to keep them safe from harm—just as we would for ourselves and our families. May we follow the Lord who calls us to love our neighbor as ourselves, and the stranger as the native-born.

---

[457] 750 million was allocated in December of 2015 for international policing and development in the Northern Triangle, significantly less than the administration had requested.

CHAPTER FOURTEEN

Strangers or Co-Pilgrims? Interreligious Dialogues among Migrants in the U.S.

Anh Q. Tran

Introduction

Immigration has been a salient feature of the U.S. population. In every age since the foundation of the country, migrants have constituted the backbone of America. They have come to realize the American dream, living in a new land, learning a new language, experiencing a new culture, and being forced to adjust to an unfamiliar environment–in some cases, drastically different from their home countries. Many have suffered from disorientation and uprootedness. Researchers have noted the language barrier, cultural challenge, social adjustment, and economic disadvantage of migrants and refugees in the U.S. However, few scholars have discussed their religious situation, especially in the case of non-Christian migrants living in the U.S.[458]

This essay explores the religious relationships among immigrant groups in the U.S. I argue that religious pluralism itself may be the fact of life in American society but the intermingling between different religious groups among migrants does not happen frequently. The primary interfaith dynamic is the

---

[458] A few exceptions are Diana Eck, *A New Religious America: How a "Christian Country" Has Become the World's Most Religiously Diverse Nation* (San Francisco: HarperCollins, 2001), Richard Alba, Albert J Raboteu and Josh DeWind, eds, *Immigration and Religion in America: Comparative and Historical Perspectives* (New York: NYU Press, 2009).

engagement between Christians and non-Christians rather than among members of other religions, as the reader shall see later in this essay.

In this essay, I will first review the religious history of the U.S. migrants, providing a contextual understanding of their religious exchanges and engagements with one another. Next, I discuss the dynamics of interreligious dialogues and then apply them to the specific interchanges among the immigrants, especially between Christians and Muslims, Buddhists, and Hindus. Finally, I will comment on the phenomenon of interfaith marriages and multiple religious belonging that would be an inevitable outcome of the current scene of living and working together.

In a New Land

The United States has been the home of immigrants since its foundation. Unlike other developed countries, American society has been and is still characterized by its religiosity. Americans tend to profess a faith and go to religious services regularly.

Historically, religious participation is an important factor in immigration assimilation and integration. Ethnic churches provided the social structure to support and sustain the immigrants, providing mutual assistance and support for the first-generation migrants and their children.

Before the 1960s, the religious scene in the U.S. was relatively simple. It was made up of Protestants, Catholics, and Jews. Protestantism was the dominant faith of the country, and its followers were mostly white, non-Hispanic people. Catholicism increased rapidly in the nineteenth and early twentieth century because of large immigrant groups from Ireland, Germany, Italy, Poland, and later, other European countries. It was considered the religion of the immigrant and foreigner, and for the most part, Hispanic Catholicism in the Southwest was unaccounted in the mainstream narrative. Before World War II, the Jewish population was relatively small and localized, mostly in cities on the east coast.

Oriental religions such as Buddhism, Hinduism, Chinese and Japanese religions also existed. But they were mostly confined within the respective ethnic population and did not influence American society. The immigration policy of the nineteenth and early twentieth centuries, such as the Chinese Exclusion Act of 1882 and the Immigration Act of 1924, excludes most Asians and Middle Easterners. Therefore, Americans have limited experience of the religions of the East.

The American religious scene changed rapidly in the late 1960s. President Johnson's Immigration and Nationality Act of 1965 allowed larger numbers of immigrants from non-European non-Anglo-Saxon countries to settle in the U.S. These new immigrants have brought with them religious practices from their home countries. Unlike other immigrant groups before them, they were not forced to assimilate into the mainstream religious scene of the U.S. In other words, they would have tended to keep their religious faith and practices rather than convert to Christianity, the dominant religion in America.

Coupled with the American interests in Orientalism and New Age spirituality between the 1960s and 1980s, the religions practiced in ethnic groups, such as Hinduism and Buddhism, attract followers from the main white population and gradually made religious pluralism in the U.S. a reality. Since 1975, political conflict and war around the world also brought to the U.S. many refugees and migrants from Asia, the Middle East, and sub-Saharan Africa, and these trends continue today.

The largest non-Christian religious adherents among recent immigrants since 1965 have been Muslims, Buddhists, and Hindus. Even though being the largest non-Christian religion, the Jewish population is very much American-born and no longer represents the religion of the newcomers as it was before World War II. In the following sections, I will briefly describe the history of the three major non-Christian groups in the U.S the Muslims, the Buddhists, and the Hindus, before turning to the subject of interreligious dialogues.

Who are the American Muslims?

With about 1.6 billion Muslims around the globe, Islam is the second major world religion, after Christianity. Since the rise of Islam in the seventh century, the Christian-Muslim history of engagements was for the most part a struggle for power, influence, and domination, both in military expeditions and cultural expansions. The long historical enmity began with the Muslim conquest of North Africa, followed by the Crusades against the Turkish forces in the Holy land, and the capture of Constantinople by the Ottoman Empire in the fifteenth century. The Arab world was occupied, and its lands were divided by the British and French powers after the Ottoman Empire was defeated in World War I. In modern times, the Israel-Arab conflict since 1948 has caused suspicion and resentment among Muslims as they perceive that Western powers are pro-Israel.

Historically, the first Muslims came to the U.S. from Africa and among the African slaves. Domestically, Islam gradually grew among African Americans as a form of resistance against the religion of the slave owners. Modern Muslim immigrants only came after World War I from Turkey and increasingly in the late 1980s from the Middle East and Sub-Saharan Africa. There are about 3.3 million Muslims in the U.S., or about 1% of the population (2015 data);[459] among them 66% are immigrants and 17% are their children. They are also a diverse group: 38% are White, 28% are Black, and 28% are Asian.[460]

Who are the American Buddhists?

Buddhism started as a monastic movement in the sixth century BCE in northern India. Its founder, prince Siddhartha Gautama, left the court life around the age of 30, searching for the ultimate meaning of life. Wandering in search of the solution to the dissatisfaction that plagued human life, he tried many ascetical

---

[459] Pew Research Center, *A New Estimate of Muslim Population* (2016). https://www.pewresearch.org/fact-tank/2016/01/06/a-new-estimate-of-the-u-s-muslim-population/.

[460] Pew Research Center, *Muslims-Religion in America: U.S. Religious Data, Demographics and Statistics* (2014). https://www.pewforum.org/religious-landscape-study/religious-tradition/muslim/.

practices until he attained enlightenment through deep meditation under a tree. He realized the transient nature of the phenomenal world and the emptiness of all reality, including the self that causes suffering. He then taught this truth to his followers and founded a religious tradition that broke with the ritualized Brahmanism of his days. In subsequent centuries, Buddhism spread throughout India and beyond, to Central, East, and Southeast Asia. There are three major families of Buddhist traditions: Mahayana, Theravada, and Vajrayana.

Asian immigrants to the U.S. in the nineteenth century brought Buddhism to America. Before World War II, the most active Buddhist organization is of Japanese Pure Land Buddhism (Jodo Shinshu) that founded the Buddhist Churches of America for Japanese immigrants. Japanese Zen teachers also taught the practice in the early twentieth century, but Zen only became popular since the 1950s. Later on, Chinese, Tibetan, and Theravadan masters also taught Buddhism and gained followers among Americans. Going beyond its ethnic origin, Buddhism appeals to the counterculture of the 1960s and the subsequent New Age movement.

Reliable statistics about U.S. Buddhists are difficult to find. Since Buddhism does not require any formal conversion, the numbers are only an estimation. It is safe to claim that the majority of Buddhist immigrants are from East and Southeast Asia.[461] About 0.7% of the U.S. population (about 2.1 million) declared themselves Buddhist (Pew 2012 data).[462] Among them, 44% of Buddhists are White, 33% are Asian, and 12% are Latino.[463]

Who are the American Hindus?

Unlike other religions, Hinduism has no founder and no common creed or unified practice. The term was coined by Western academics in the eighteenth

---

[461] The U.S. is home to Buddhists of different Asian origins: Chinese, Japanese, Korean, Vietnamese, Sri Lankan, Thai, Cambodian, and Burmese.

[462] Pew Research Center, *Asian Americans: A Mosaic of Faith* (2012). https://www.pewforum.org/2012/07/19/asian-americans-a-mosaic-of-faiths-overview/.

[463] Pew Research Center, *Buddhists-Religion in America: U.S. Religious Data, Demographics and Statistics* (2014). https://www.pewforum.org/religious-landscape-study/religious-tradition/buddhist/.

century to loosely describe the beliefs of the Hindustan (India). Later, Hindu nationalists adopted the name to differentiate their religious practices from Jainism, Sikhism, and Islam. Within Hinduism, there are various local devotions and philosophies held together by a common cosmology and purpose of life. Doctrinally, it teaches a form of pantheism–the Divine or Great Self is both within and transcends beings and objects in the universe–and the followers seek to realize that union with the Divine through rituals, devotions, meditations, or works.

Americans learned about Hinduism when Swami Vivekananda spoke at the World's Parliament of Religion in Chicago in 1893. In the early twentieth century, all immigrants from India, including the Sikhs, were mistakenly referred to as "Hindoo." The Immigration Act of 1924 prohibited the immigration of Asians, including Middle Easterners and Indians. Hindu believers immigrated to the U.S. in large numbers after 1965, when the Immigration and Nationality Act was passed. They are mainly from South Asia, Southeast Asia, the Gulf countries, and other places. Also, during the 1960s, Hindu teachers came into contact with the American mainstream and, through their disciples, spread the religion in the U.S. through movements such as the International Society for Krishna Consciousness (ISKON).

Hinduism now is the fourth largest non-Christian faith group, composing about 0.7% of the American population (Pew 2015 data).[464] Although 87% are first-generation Asian immigrants, 7% of Hindus are converts among the white, black, and Latino Americans.

The Catholic Church and Interreligious Dialogue

The Catholic engagement in interreligious dialogue started as a post-Holocaust self-examination of the Christian and Jewish relations. At the Second

---

[464] Pew Research Center, *America Changing Religious Landscape* (2014). https://www.pewforum.org/2015/05/12/americas-changing-religious-landscape/.

Vatican Council (1962-1965), the Church looked at its relations with non-Christians, starting with the Jews and eventually extending to other religious traditions. At several places in its sixteen documents, the council expresses a positive and sympathetic understanding of world religions.

Paragraph 16 of the council's *Dogmatic Constitution on the Church* (*Lumen Gentium*) speaks of the salvation of Jews, Muslims, and others in sympathetic words. Jews are considered the "people most dear to God" for God does not take back his promise to their forefathers (cf. Roman 11:28–29). Muslims are also included in the plan of salvation because they "acknowledge the Creator," "profess to hold the faith of Abraham," and along with Christians "adore the one and merciful God, who on the last day will judge mankind [*sic*]" For the rest of humanity, God is not "far distant from those who in shadows and images seek the unknown God, for it is He who gives to all men life and breath and all things, and as Saviour wills that all men [*sic*] be saved."[465] (LG 16).

In the *Declaration on the Relation of the Church to Non-Christian Religions* (*Nostra Aetate*), after discussing the merits of Hinduism and Buddhism, the council emphatically declares:

> Likewise, other religions found everywhere try to counter
> the restlessness of the human heart, each in its own manner,
> by proposing "ways," comprising teachings, rules of life,
> and sacred rites. The Catholic Church rejects nothing that is
> true and holy in these religions. She regards with sincere
> reverence those ways of conduct and of life, those precepts
> and teachings which, though differing in many aspects from
> the ones she holds and sets forth, nonetheless often reflect
> a ray of that Truth which enlightens all men [sic]. (NA 2)

Although ecumenism and missionary activities were more prominent at Vatican II, the Catholic Church wanted to engage in interreligious dialogue with believers of other religions. Already in 1964, before the council adjourned, Pope

---

[465] The quotations from Church documents are taken from the Vatican website: www.vatican.org. I leave the "non-inclusive" language as it is since it is the official translation.

Paul VI established the Vatican Secretariat for Non-Christians to coordinate interreligious engagements and activities among Roman Catholics, specifically with Muslims, Hindus and Buddhists.[466] Since then, the work of interreligious dialogue has become a regular activity of the Church, even though it was controversial at first.

The challenge for many Catholics (and to some extent other Christians) is the nature and purpose of interreligious dialogue. Is interfaith dialogue a "preparation for the Gospel"? Is dialogue a replacement for evangelization? Is the purpose of dialogue to witness to the truth of one's faith, or simply to build friendly relations? How to show genuine respect for the adherents of another religion, and at the same time try to proclaim the Gospel to them? Is it worth the effort if the dialogue results in friendly conversations that minimize disagreements? Would it lead to doctrinal relativism? Such questions naturally arose from the experience of ecumenical and interfaith dialogues, where sometimes reaching doctrinal agreement is not possible.

After 20 years of interreligious engagement, the Secretariat for Non-Christians, an office of the Vatican, issued a reflection on the attitude of the Church toward followers of other religions, emphasizing the dual nature of dialogue and mission in a 1984 document that features these concepts in its title. *Dialogue and Mission* clarifies the meaning of interreligious dialogue as "not only discussion but also includes all positive and constructive interreligious relations with individuals and communities of other faiths which are directed at mutual understanding and enrichment" (DM 3). Then in 1991, the same office, under a new name, the Pontifical Council for Interreligious Dialogue (PCID), published an expanded version of the earlier directive entitled Dialogue and Proclamation. In this document, the Church lays out the rules for effective dialogue (part I) and proclamation (part II), which Catholic participants in dialogue must hold

---

[466] Interestingly enough, this office does not cover the Jewish-Catholic relations, which is under a separate committee, reporting to the Pontifical Council for Christian Unity.

together. In the first part, the PCID distinguished and updated the four forms of dialogue, spelled out in *Dialogue and Mission* earlier.

a) The *dialogue of life*, where people strive to live in an open and neighborly spirit, sharing their joys and sorrows, their human problems and preoccupations.

b) The *dialogue of action*, in which Christians and others collaborate for the integral development and liberation of people.

c) The *dialogue of theological exchange*, where specialists seek to deepen their understanding of their respective religious heritages, and to appreciate each other's spiritual values.

d) The *dialogue of religious experience*, where persons, rooted in their own religious traditions, share their spiritual riches, for instance, with regard to prayer and contemplation, faith and ways of searching for God or the Absolute. (DP 42, cf. DM 17)

These four forms of dialogue are the guidelines for Catholic engagements with different religious communities and at different levels. It is clear from the document that not all dialogues take the same form and with the same goal.

Learning from the experience of those who engage in interreligious dialogue, the PCID spells out the necessary dispositions to a fruitful dialogue, namely keeping a balanced attitude, having a religious conviction, being open to the truth, as well as the new dimensions of faith (DP 47–50). In addition, the document names a number of factors that impede dialogue, among which are insufficient grounding in one's own faith, lack of knowledge and understanding of the belief and practices of other religions, burdens of the past, a wrong understanding of notions like conversion, a lack of conviction on the merit of dialogue, suspicion of other's motives, holding a polemical spirit, or intolerance due to the political and religious climate in which one lives (see DP 52). Nevertheless, as the document says, "despite the difficulties, the Church's commitment to dialogue remains firm and irreversible" (DP 54). Although this directive is addressed to Catholics, other Christians and members of other religious traditions could also find the principles and guidelines here helpful in building and maintaining religious conversations.

Principles of Interreligious Dialogue

As a whole, interreligious dialogue presupposes a mutual understanding of one's religious attitude toward another. Scholars of religious studies have identified at least three forms of religious views that one could hold. From a conservative to a liberal range, they are religious exclusivists, inclusivists, and pluralists. The classification depends on their emphasis on which end of the dialogue and proclamation spectrum they stand.[467]

On the conservative side, *religious exclusivists* favor the conversion of others into their own faith. They generally hold that their religion is the only valid way to God or the Transcendent, and that everyone else is in error. This view has strong historical precedents in places with a dominant religion, and religious minorities are tolerated at best, such as Medieval Europe or the Arab world today. Naturally, this type of attitude makes interreligious dialogue quite difficult and challenging, since the purpose of dialogue is to win arguments and convert the others to their side.

Religious inclusivists would prefer to convince other believers of the merits of their religions but not as forcefully as the exclusivists. They are more opened and engaging in interreligious relations for the sake of collaboration and mutual enrichments but will not compromise on the privilege of their beliefs. The official Catholic position on religions certainly belongs to this camp when it insists on both dialogue and proclamation as equal ends.

On the liberal end of the spectrum, the *religious pluralists* argue for multiple paths to God or religious Truth. Their premise is that all religions lead to the same place. There is no real merit to claim that one religion is better than another. The differences between religions are due to their historical contexts

---

[467] For an introduction to these typologies see Alan Race, *Thinking about Religious Pluralism: The Shaping of Theology of Religions for Our Times* (Minneapolis: Fortress Press, 2015).

and origins; various religions were born out of different cultural and linguistic environments from particular peoples. As such, to compare the merits of Hinduism to Islam or Christianity to Buddhism does not make sense. Everyone thus should be allowed to follow a religion according to his or her choice.

A variation of religious pluralism is *religious particularism.* Unlike the universal-oriented pluralists who postulate a common core or essence of religion, particularists insist on the differences between religions. The religions are not various expressions of one Truth; instead, they have different religious ends. This post-modernist approach to religions dispels any illusion that the differences in beliefs and practices can be ignored or minimized. Particular views are not compatible when we put them side by side.

When people from two or three traditions are engaged in interreligious dialogue, they must keep in mind their implicit religious views about the other dialogue partners—whether they approach the others from an exclusivist, inclusivist, pluralist, or particularist perspective. Awareness of one's religious attitude toward others help to keep the conversation honest and open, as well as clarifying the goal of dialogue. Interreligious dialogue should lead to a better understanding of the religious others, promote religious tolerance and acceptance, foster co-existence and collaboration, and form friendships. It is not a leveling of religious identities, since mutual enrichment can be achieved through interreligious dialogue.

In the U.S., religion is viewed as personal and private. In daily life, few people want to engage in interreligious dialogue unless it happens pro-actively. The word "dialogue" might put off some people since it could mean verbal exchanges, debates, and discussion. Perhaps, a better term to describe the dialogical dynamic between members of two (or more) religions is "interreligious engagement."

In interreligious engagement, the aim is to witness one's own beliefs, religious way of life or practices, and foster a common exploration for life's questions and search for religious meaning. Its goal is not to change religions or win adherents but a change of attitude and view of the others–a conversion at a deeper level. Of the four types of interreligious engagement (or dialogue) proposed by the Catholic Church, each will have a different interfaith goal. The *dialogue of life* aims to foster peaceful co-existence and friendship. The dialogue of action leads to finding a common value and building a better world through collaboration. The *dialogue of religious experience* gives mutual aids and enrichment for one's spiritual life. And the dialogue of theological or doctrinal exchanges promotes a deeper understanding of one's own and the other's religious tradition.

It is important to note the dialogue of theological exchanges is the last, not the first type of dialogue one should engage in. It is better done by specialists, presuming an informed understanding and fair assessment of the other tradition as well as one's own. It is the most challenging of the four types of dialogue since one has to overcome his or her bias and the difference of beliefs and worldviews. The person must also hold a humble attitude, *speaking from* his or her tradition and not *for* the tradition.

Interfaith Dialoguing between Christians and Muslims, Hindus and Buddhists

In the following sections, I offer an overview of the present situation of interreligious dialogue among the four largest religions of the immigrants: Christianity, Islam, Hinduism, and Buddhism. I would admit that the dialogues do not happen on equal footing. As Christianity, with all its denominations, remains the dominant religion in the U.S., the dialogue will naturally fall to the side of Christian versus others. Specifically, I speak as a Catholic Christian and Asian immigrant who has experienced dialogues with Muslims, Hindus, and Buddhists, both in Asia and in the U.S.

Muslim-Christian Dialogue

The Muslim-Christian dialogue in the U.S. often takes place in academia, advocate groups, and policymakers. In terms of theological exchanges, the doctrinal disputes between Christians and Muslims center on each faith's understanding of Jesus. Although the two religions consider Jesus to be the Messiah, their views on the person of Christ are on the opposite ends. In essence, Muslims see Jesus as no more than a great messenger of God, not God's Son or God the Son as Christian would claim. They consider the doctrine of Trinity a denial of the Oneness of God and thus a grave sin. Besides, they do not understand the Christian refusal to accept Muhammad as the Prophet who succeeded Jesus to proclaim the final revelation. On the other hand, Christians are puzzled when Muslims fail to acknowledge the divinity of Christ as declared by the Council Nicaea in 325. Many Christians also take issue with Muslims when the latter denies the crucifixion and resurrection of Christ.

The doctrinal disputes are based on their understanding of the life and works of Jesus based on the Gospel and the Quranic accounts. In a polemical tension, Muslims view the Gospel as a distortion or corruption of the original message of God, while Christians consider the Quran to be an apocryphal work. Both sides accuse the other of being infidels. In recent years, as the two faiths learn more about the other doctrinal views, their positions are softening somewhat, recognizing the different traditions in the Biblical and Quranic accounts. In addition, Mary the Mother of Jesus is honored by both traditions, and she often serves as a bridge in doctrinal exchanges, which does not get recognized often.

In addition to these historical and doctrinal disputes, Muslim-Christian dialogue suffers from entanglements with politics in the Middle East and the rise of Islamic fundamentalism. The catastrophe of September 11, 2001 casts in the mind of many Americans that Islam is a religion of violence, its treatment of women is oppressive, and many customs in the Islamic laws (*shariah*) violate human rights and undermine democracy. Among policymakers, the dialogue focuses on human development, women's rights, and the common threat of religious violence, fundamentalism, and secularism. Because of its checkered history, Muslim-Christian dialogue requires a lot of patience and goodwill. It is happening slowly within the immigrant community.

Hindu-Christian Dialogue

Contemporary Christian-Hindu relations are a mixed affair among the immigrants from India. In their country of origin, Christians comprise a small but visible minority, and they are more activity in dialoguing with the Hindus, Sikhs, and other members of Indian religions at many levels. In contrast, dialogues between American Hindus and Christians tend to be confined to the academic level surrounding the philosophical issues and yogic practice, often facilitated by Hindu converts. Outside of intellectual exchanges, there is little engagement between members of the two faiths, especially at the level of religious ritual and festivity as it is done in India, except for some Hindu-Christian ashram experiences.

Hindu immigrants on the ground are not so interested in interreligious dialogue. As a whole, they are more secularized than their homeland counterparts. 88% of the Hindu population believes in God, but only 25% think that religion is very important in their lives, and 60% occasionally attend religious services (Pew 2014 data).[468] The religious demography is also diverse among the South Asians themselves: there are Indian Christian, Hindu, Sikh, and Muslim communities, and they seem to keep their religions private.

Buddhist-Christian Dialogue

Compared to a dialogue between Christians and Muslims or Hindus, interreligious exchanges between Christians and Buddhists are the most fascinating. Since Buddhism has adapted to various cultures, including Western ones, one can find many opportunities to engage in dialogue. One key feature of

---

[468] Pew Research Center, *Hindus-Religion in America: U.S. Religious Data, Demographics and Statistics* (2014). https://www.pewforum.org/religious-landscape-study/religious-tradition/hindu/.

Buddhism is its adaptability, known as "skillful means" (*upaya*) that could harmonize opposite beliefs and practices. As time went on, there were many schools of Buddhism, all claiming to originate from the Buddha's teachings. Within the Buddhist world, there are mutually exclusive sects and endless debates between schools and lineages. However, in the absence of a central authority, multiple forms of Buddhism flourished.

Buddhist Christian dialogue take many forms, from the intellectual exchanges between scholars of religions to the shared experiences of genuine practitioners, from the cordial meetings of leaders of the faith, the celebration of each side's holidays to the collaboration in projects for common ethical concerns, and forming interreligious friendships. Doctrinally, the two faiths have fundamental differences that cannot be reconciled. Christianity is a monotheistic faith in a Creator, and Buddhism is a non-theistic philosophy of life with multiple world-realms and endless cycles of birth-and-death. In terms of salvation, Buddhists rely more on a self-effort to work out one's karma, and see no need for an external interference from a Deity, whereas the notion of grace and faith is at the core of Christian theology.

Doctrinally, Buddhists and Christians are farthest from each other, but there are many similarities and overlap in their religious practices. Both traditions have parallel structures of sacred texts, codes of ethical conduct, prayers and rituals, spiritual practices, and religious teachers and clergy. The Society of Buddhist-Christian studies has an annual meeting and actively engages Buddhist and Christian scholars in various philosophical, textual, and ritual comparisons. No less fruitful are the exchanges of spiritual experiences between Buddhist and Christian monks and nuns. The popularity of Asian monks such as the Dalai Lama and Thich Nhat Hanh adds to the American interests in Buddhist practices and contributes to the forming of Western Buddhism.

Not as visible as the above forms of dialogue, the dialogue of life occurs among Buddhists and Christians on a familial and personal level, especially among Asian immigrants. Since Christianity is a minority religion in Asia, within the ethnic communities, co-existence and collaboration happen naturally between people of the two different faith communities. Since Buddhism is more inclusive and less doctrinal, the dialogues are more on the day-to-day experience where mutual learning and enrichment can happen. From a practical perspective, Christians often participate in Buddhist meditation sessions, even if they do not acknowledge the religious root of such practices.

Christians in Dialogue with Chinese and Japanese Religions

Even though the textbooks on world religions often mention Confucianism, Daoism, and Shintoism as the major faith of the East Asian people, few carry it to the soils of America. Most Chinese and Japanese migrants to the U.S. see these religions of their native land as cultural practices than living religious traditions to be continued. In Chinatowns across the major cities in the U.S., there is an occasional Chinese temple that houses folk religious practices.

Since there are few professed followers of these traditions, most of the dialogues take the form of comparative religious studies or philosophy at the university level, where researchers and professors study, discuss, and debate on ancient texts. The dialogue comprises of intellectual exercises that enhance cultural exchanges between the U.S. and China or Japan, but have little relevance for the average Chinese or Japanese migrants.

Religious Identity and Belonging

The American religious scene is less secularized than Europe, partly because even though there is a separation of Church and State, the U.S. government still supports religious institutions as non-profit organizations, protected by religious rights and tax-exemptions. Thus, belonging to a religious institution has both an advantage and disadvantage.

At a general level, there is a considerable difference and expectation of religious membership among the world religions. Western religions such as Judaism, Christianity, and Islam consider themselves communal religions, bound by a common religious identity. Membership and boundary are quite clear. The faithful are expected to keep religious observance and attend service. On the contrary, most Oriental religions like Hinduism, Buddhism, Chinese and Japanese religions are considered personal devotion in a traditionally multiple religious society. Their members are free to keep or change their religious adherence at will.

The question of religious identity

Living in an open society like the U.S., where religion is considered a personal and private affair, entails less pressure for a person to declare or adhere to their religious practice. A new immigrant to the U.S. naturally feels a need for support and often joins a church, mosque, temple, or religious organization that they feel they belong to. The question for an immigrant may not be which religion to embrace but how many, or none.

On the one end, an immigrant will follow the religious tradition as it was practiced in their country of origin. The ethnic community purchases an old church and converts its space for religious usage. When they have enough financial means and supports, they will build their own religious building according to the traditional architecture and style found in their homelands. Still, a number of adaptations must be done to adjust to life in the U.S. Hindu, Buddhist, and other temples often change their religious days and rituals to the weekend and often model their services after a Christian church. These religious centers also function as a cultural center to teach their children about the language, history, and culture of their ethnicity.

Many ethnic communities choose this way of belonging, something akin to the ethnic churches of nineteenth-century America. In such a situation, religious exchanges and dialogues beyond their immediate community happen at a cultural level when they host visitors and friends in religious festivals that often are displays of cultural elements.

On the other end, there are those immigrants who do not feel the need to maintain their original religious commitment. They might have different priorities in building a new life in the U.S., so that spiritual practices and

321

belonging might not be the most pressing ones. Some also escape the religious oppression of their own country and not ready to take on a similar or different religious identity. Furthermore, the reluctance to identify with institutional religions is coupled with post-modern thinking about rejecting all absolute claims.

In the U.S., religion is synthesized according to personal taste and judgment, leading a person to either a multi-religious practice or none. Some immigrants will employ a functional approach to religion. They do not feel the need to belong to a particular religion or find identity in it. There is a situational and complementary, often compartmentalized, orientation. For example, most contemporary Japanese will see themselves as practicing different religious traditions but belonging to none at all. The only criterion is the enhancement of "my" potentiality.

Multi-religious belonging is a contemporary phenomenon where an individual identifies with two or more religions. It is a function of globalization where the free circulation of beliefs is detached from any tradition, a religious supermarket where belief without belonging is embraced.

The multi-religious practice or belonging is frowned upon by monotheist religions as syncretism or religious relativism. It is ultimately a question of religious identity and belonging. Christians and Muslims insist on an exclusive religious identity and explicit membership, even within their own traditions. According to their views, the community gives us religious orientation and belonging; we do not choose a religion, we accept one, and the boundary is clear. If one cannot be both a Catholic and Baptist or Sunni and Shiite, then the idea of multi-religious belonging is an anathema.

However, in discussing the complex dynamic of multi-religious belonging, one needs to separate the two levels of belonging. At a personal level, a person might incorporate religious practice from different traditions that would enrich one's spiritual life and thus feel that they belong to more than one religious home. This dynamic happens with people who grew up in a mixed-religion family as a result of interfaith marriage. However, at a social level and institutional commitment, it is challenging to maintain dual or multiple citizenship in two or more religious traditions. There is always an asymmetry of belonging. Just like language proficiency, there will be primary and secondary identities and expressions of worldviews, values, feelings, and beliefs.

On the opposite end of the multi-religious belonging is the "spiritual but not religious" attitude. Some immigrants, in particular, those who grow up in China, Vietnam or other highly secularized countries do not often have a religious commitment, and may remain that way. They are not necessarily anti-religion; and some might have spiritual needs but have no experience of belonging to any religious community or institution, and see no need to belong to one. These people might be curious about religion and open to a religious dialogue if an opportunity comes.

Interfaith marriage

The immigrants' religious identity will be most visible when it is displayed on a personal level, especially within marriage and family. Interfaith marriage is the coming together of two persons of different faith traditions to becoming one in a family. Historically, interfaith marriages were rare, but now they are becoming more common. As the world is getting smaller, more personal engagements of people with different backgrounds, including religious faith, are happening. In a culturally and religiously diverse society such as the U.S., the number of interfaith marriages is increasing, and this trend is expected to continue. In 1960, 81% of couples were married to a member of the same religion; that figure dropped to 61% in 2014.[469]

The norms and practices of interfaith marriage vary from one religious community to another. Among Christians, "marriage outside of the faith" varies from denomination to denomination. Only 25% of Catholics and Evangelical

---

[469] Pew Research Center, *America's Changing Religious Landscape: Religious Switching and Intermarriage* (2015). https://www.pewforum.org/2015/05/12/chapter-2-religious-switching-and-intermarriage/#interfaith-marriage-commonplace.

Protestants have a spouse or partner of another religion. The figure increases for Black Protestants (35%), Mainline Protestants (41%) and Orthodox (47%). Islam takes a much more stringent view. Islamic law allows a man to take a non-Muslim wife, but a woman should marry a Muslim. Thus only 21% married non-Muslims. Practicing Hindus and Sikhs, for the most part, prefer arranged marriages, and therefore, interfaith marriage is mostly a non-practice (only 9%). On the other hand, Buddhists do not have a strong view about the religious nature of marriage, and thus, are the most open to interfaith marriage (61%).[470]

Interfaith marriage, like interracial marriage, challenges the cultural or religious endogamy common among immigrants to preserve their cultural identity. In interreligious marriage, boundaries are being pushed with regard to acceptance of different religious customs. During the dating period, many couples do not bring up the topic of religions and do not have sufficient knowledge about the partner's faith. In marriage preparation, the religious leader might give fine sermons on interreligious harmony. Still, after the wedding, an interfaith couple must find a middle ground between conflicting religious beliefs and practices in daily life. Often some compromise could be made during the early phase of marriage when the spouses are adjusting to each other's religious beliefs and practices of the spouses.

However, tension might arise when it comes to the faith of children. Would the child follow the religion of the father, or mother, or both? For many immigrants, marriage is not only between two individuals but also between two extended families to some extent. In many cases, the couple might feel pressure from their families to maintain their offspring's religious identity. In strong patrilineal cultures, a father's faith might be a dominant factor, especially among Muslims and Hindus. Even though the Christian mother might wish for the child to be reared in the Christian faith, the reality might not be that simple. Catholics likewise are strongly encouraged to do everything possible to ensure that a child

---

[470] Ibid.

is baptized and raised as a Catholic. On the other hand, most Buddhists would not insist that their children must become Buddhist; they see religion as a journey of discovery and not something that can be imposed.

Conclusion

Whatever one's view of religion, the relationship between migration and faith is complicated. There is a dynamic of power difference, religious and cultural identity.

American religious diversity remains, to use a metaphor, a salad bowl, rather than genuinely integrated into U.S. ideal of "one nation indivisible" For the most part, immigrant adherents from other faiths–whether Muslims, Hindus, Buddhists, or others -- have little exchanges and interaction among themselves. Up to the present, religions exist to serve the needs of their respective ethnic groups. If interreligious dialogues and engagements have occurred, it is mostly a majority-minority group interchange: Christian-Muslim, Christian-Buddhist, Christian-Hindu, Christian-Confucian, and so forth.

Admittedly, there are some efforts to expand these bilateral dialogues into multiple religious engagements such as Muslim-Jewish-Christian, Jewish-Buddhist-Christian, or Christian-Hindu-Buddhist. However, these types of multiple-constituent dialogues (or tri-logues) are often academic exercises that occur mostly on university campuses but not yet at the congregational level. Within the family, interfaith marriage is becoming a means to promote interreligious engagement. The practice can be healthy and fruitful in a multi-religious society, such as the U.S., especially if it does not create discord between the families.

American society is built upon and sustained by immigrants. As long as people from all parts of the world continue to settle in the U.S., the dynamic of interreligious engagements will shape how we can co-exist and collaborate to build this country for all its inhabitants. Religious harmony is a key component to peace-building, and the tasks of interreligious dialogue among immigrants, in whatever form, will continue to be relevant, both in life and in politics.

SELECTED BIBLIOGRAPHY

Ahn John J. and Jill Middlemas, eds. *By the Irrigation Canals of Babylon: Approaches to the Study of the Exile*. London: Bloomsbury T&T Clark, 2012.

Anderson, Bernard. *From Creation to New Creation*. Minneapolis: Fortress Press, 1994.

Appadurai, Arjun. *Modernity at Large: Cultural Dimensions of Globalization*. Minneapolis: University of Minnesota Press, 1996.

Aponte, Edwin D. *¡Santo! Varieties of Latino/a Spirituality*. Maryknoll, NY: Orbis, 2012.

Banner, Stuart. *How the Indians Lost Their Land: Law and Power on the Frontier*. Cambridge: Harvard University Press, 2005.

Basch, Linda, Nina Glick Schiller, and Cristina Szanton Blanc. *Nations Unbound: Transnational Projects, Postcolonial Predicaments, and Deterritorialized Nation-States*. Langhome: Gordon and Breach, Publishers, 1994.

Basavapatna, Sahana. "Access to Health Care for Refugees in New Delhi." *Refugee Watch Online* (blog), March 19, 2009. http://refugeewatchonline.blogspot.com/2009/03/access-to-health-care-for-refugees-in.html.

Bauman, Stephen, Matthew Soerens, and Issam Smeir. *Seeking Refuge: On the Shores of the Global Refugee Crisis*. Chicago: Moody Publishers, 2016.

Bauman, Zygmunt. *Strangers at Our Door*. Malden, MA: Polity, 2016.

Bedford, Nancy E. "To Speak of God from More than one Place: Theological Reflections from the Experience of Migration." In *Latin American Liberation Theology: The New Generation*, edited by Ivan Petrella, 95-118. Maryknoll, NY: Orbis, 2005.

Bevans, Stephen B. *An Introduction to Theology in Global Perspective*. Maryknoll, NY: Orbis Books, 2009.

_____. "Mission among Migrants, Mission of Migrants." In *A Promised Land, A Perilous Journey: Theological Perspectives on Migration*, edited by Daniel G. Groody and Gioacchino Campese, 89-102. Notre Dame, IN: University of Notre Dame Press, 2008.

Bevans, Stephen and Ricky Manalo. "Contextual Preaching." In *A Handbook for Catholic Preaching*, edited by Edward Foley, 233-242. Collegeville, MN: Liturgical Press, 2016.

Bevans, Stephen B. and Roger P. Schroeder. *Prophetic Dialogue: Reflections on Christian Mission Today*. Maryknoll, NY: Orbis Books, 2011.

Beavis, Mary Ann and HyeRan Kim-Cragg. *What Does the Bible Say? A Critical Conversation with Popular Culture in a Biblically Illiterate World*. Eugene, OR: Cascade Books, 2017.

Black, Kathy. *Culturally-Conscious Worship*. St. Louis: Chalice Press, 2000.

Boda, Mark J., Frank Ritchel Ames, John Ahn, and Mark Leuchter, eds. *The Prophets Speak on Forced Migration*. Atlanta: SBL Press, 2015.

Ceja, Miguel. Chicana College Aspirations and the Role of Parents: Developing Educational Resiliency. *Journal of Hispanic Higher Education*. 3 (2004) 338–62.

Capps, Michael Fix, Jeffrey S. Passel, Jason Ost, and Dan Perex-Lopez. "A Profile of Low-Wage Immigrant Workforce." Urban Institute, Brief No. 4 (November, 2003).

Carroll R., M. Daniel. *Christians at the Border: Immigration, the Church, and the Bible*. Grand Rapids: Baker Academic, 2008.

Chavez, Leo R. *Shadowed Lives: Undocumented Immigrants in American Society*. Belmont: Wadsworth, 2013.

_____. *The Latino Threat: Constructing Immigrants, Citizens, and the Nation*. Stanford: Stanford University Press, 2013.

Cenkner, William, ed. *The Multicultural Church: A New Landscape in U.S. Theologies*. New York: Paulist Press, 1996.

Chia, Edmund. *Towards a Theology of Dialogue*. Bangkok, Thailand, 2003.

Coath, Brad, Angela Akamine, Laurie Krepp, Hwa Hui-En, and Andy Sparkes. "'You Took Me In': Seeking Transformation for Migrant Workers, Refugees, and Asylum Seekers." In *Signs of Hope in the City: Renewing Urban Mission, Embracing Radical Hope*, edited by Graham Hill, 65–81. Melbourne: ISUM, 2015.

Collier Elizabeth W. and Charles R. Strain. *Global Migration: What's Happening, Why, and A Just Response*. Winona, MN: Anselm Academic, 2017.

Cornille, Catherine, ed. *Many Mansions: Multiple Religious Belonging and Christian Identity*. Maryknoll, NY: Orbis Books, 2002):

Crane, Michael D. "Equipping the Transient for Ministry in a Global City." *The New Urban World Journal* 3, no. 1 (May 2014): 7–15.

_____. "The Vital Role of Faith Communities in the Lives of Urban Refugees." *International Journal of Interreligious and Intercultural Studies* 3, no. 2 (2020): 25–37. https://doi.org/10.32795/ijiis.vol3.iss2.2020.708.

Curin, Philip D. *The Atlantic Slave Trade: A Census*. Madison, WI: University of Wisconsin Press, 1972.

Dalai Lama. *Toward a true kinship of Faiths*. New York: Doubleday, 2010.

D'Antonio, William V. Michele Dillon and Mary L. Gautier, *American Catholics in Transition*. New York: Rowman & Littlefield Publishers, 2013.

Duck, Ruth. *Worship for the Whole People of God: Vital Worship for the 21st Century*. Louisville: Westminster/John Knox, 2013.

Eck, Diana. *A New Religious America: How a "Christian Country" Has Become the World's Religiously Most Diverse Nation*. San Francisco: HarperSanFrancisco, 2002.

Edu-Bekoe, Yaw Attah, and Enoch Wan. *Scattered Africans Keep Coming: A Case Study of Diaspora Missiology on Ghanaian Diaspora and Congregations in the USA*. Portland, OR: Institute of Diaspora Studies, 2013.

Ehle, John. *Trail of Tears: The Rise and Fall of the Cherokee Nation*. New York: Anchor Books, 1988.

Escobar, Samuel J. "Mission Fields on the Move." *Christianity Today* (May 2010): 28-31

Fabos, Anita, and Gaim Kibreab. "Urban Refugees: Introduction." *Refuge* 24, no. 1 (2007): 3–10.

Fikkert, Brian, and Steve Corbett. *When Helping Hurts: Alleviating Poverty Without Hurting the Poor. . .and Ourselves*. Chicago: Moody Publishers, 2009.

Foley, Edward. *From Age to Age: How Christians Have Celebrated the Eucharist*. Louisville: Westminster/John Knox Press, 2013.

Geertz, Clifford. *The Interpretation of Cultures*. New York: Basic Books, 2000.

Glazer, Nathan and Daniel P. Moynihan. *Beyond the Melting Pot*. Cambridge: M.I.T. Press, 1964.

Ghazaleh, Pascale. "In 'closed File' Limbo: Displaced Sudanese in a Cairo Slum." *Forced Migration Review* 16 (2003): 24–26.

Groody Daniel G. "Crossing the Divide: Foundations of a Theology of Migration and Refugees." In *And You Welcome Me: Migration and Catholic Social Teaching*, edited by Donald Kerwin and Jill Marie Gershultz. Lanham, MD: Lexington Books, 2009.

Halais, Flavie. "What It Means for Cities Now That More than Half the World's Refugees Live in Urban Areas." Citiscope, May 27, 2016. http://citiscope.org/story/2016/what-it-means-cities-now-more-half-worlds-refugees-live-urban-areas?utm_source=Citiscope&utm_campaign=d36ef17853-Mailchimp_2016_05_27&utm_medium=email&utm_term=0_ce992dbfef-d36ef17853-118051765.

Hanciles, Jehu J. "Migration and Mission: Some Implications for the Twenty-first-Century Church," *Missiology* 27, no. 4 (Oct 2003): 146-153.

_____. *Beyond Christendom: Globalization, African Migration, and the Transformation of the West*. Maryknoll, N.Y: Orbis Books, 2008.

Haney, Ian. *White By Law: The Legal Construction of Race*. New York: New York University Press, 2006.

Heft, James L., ed. *Catholicism and Interreligious Dialogue*. New York: Oxford University Press, 2012.

Hetzel, Peter G., Pablo A Jimenez and Emmet G. Price III. "Lean into Liberation Love: The Origins of Evangelical Liberation Theology at Gordon-Conwell Center for Urban Ministerial Education," In *Evangelical Theologies of Liberation and Justice*, edited by Mae Elise Cannon and Andrea Smith. Downers Grove, IL: InterVarsity Press, 2019.

Heyman, Josiah. *Finding a Moral Heart for U.S. Immigration Policy: An Anthropological Perspective*. Arlington: American Ethnological Society Monograph Series, Number 7, 1998.

Himes, Matthew J. and Kenneth R. Himes. *Fullness of Faith: The Public Significance of Theology*. New York: Paulist Press, 1993.

Hing, Bill Ong. *Deporting Our Souls: Values, Morality, and Immigration Policy*. Cambridge: Cambridge University Press, 2006.

Hsu, Madeline. *Dreaming of Gold, Dreaming of Home: Transnationalism and Migration Between the United States and South China, 1882-1943*. Stanford: Stanford University Press, 2000.

Irfan A. Omar, ed., *A Muslim View of Christianity: Essays on Dialogue* by Mahmoud Ayoub. Maryknoll, NY: Orbis 2007.

Jacobsen, Karen. "Refugees and Asylum Seekers in Urban Areas: A Livelihoods Perspective." *Journal of Refugee Studies* 19, no. 3 (August 2006): 273–86.

Jacobson, Matthew Frye. *Whiteness of a Different Color: European Immigrants and the Alchemy of Race.* Cambridge: Harvard University Press, 1998.

Jansen, Mechteld. "Christian Migrants and the Theology of Space and Place." In *Contested Spaces, Common Ground: Space and Power Structures in Contemporary Multireligious Societies,* edited by Ulrich Winkler, Lidia Rodriguez Fernandez, and Oddbjorn Leirvik, 147–61. Leiden; Boston: Brill Rodopi, 2017.

Jimenez, Pablo A. "Hispanics in the Movement." In *The Encyclopedia of the Stone-Campbell Movement,* edited by Douglas A Foster, Paul M. Blowers, Anthony L. Dunnavant, and D. Newell Williams. Grand Rapids: Eerdmans, 2004.

Jordon, Winthrop D. The White Man's Burden: Historical Origins of Racism in the United States. London: Oxford University Press, 1974.

Kamal, Baher. "Now 1 in 2 World's Refugees Live in Urban Areas | Inter Press Service." Inter Press Service, May 29, 2016. http://www.ipsnews.net/2016/05/now-1-in-2-worlds-refugees-live-in-urban-area/.

King, C. Richard. *Redskins: Insult and Brand.* Lincoln, NE: University of Nebraska Press, 2016.

Kim, Matthew D. *Preaching with Cultural Intelligence: Understanding the People who Hear our Sermons.* Downers Grove, IL: InterVarsity, 2017.

Kim-Cragg, HyRan. "Through Senses and Sharing: How Liturgy Meets Food,:" *Liturgy* 32, no. 2 (Apr-June 2017): 34-41.

Knitter, Paul F. *Introducing Theologies of Religions.* Maryknoll, NY: Orbis Books, 2002.

Lefebure, Leo D. *Transforming Interreligious Relations: Catholic Responses to Religious Pluralism in the United States.* Maryknoll, NY: Orbis Books, 2020.

Leong, David P. *Street Signs: Toward a Missional Theology of Urban Cultural Engagement.* Eugene, OR: Pickwick Publications, 2012.

Ley, David. "The Immigrant Church as an Urban Service Hub." *Urban Studies* 45, no. 10 (September 1, 2008): 2057–74. https://doi.org/10.1177/0042098008094873.

Lewellen, Ted C. *The Anthropology of Globalization*. Westport: Bergin and Garvey, 2002.

Looney, Jared. *Crossroads of the Nations*. Skyforest, CA: Urban Loft Publishers, 2015.

Marfleet, Philip. "'Forgotten,' 'Hidden': Predicaments of the Urban Refugee." *Refuge* 24, no. 1 (2007): 36–45.

McCurdy, David, J. Spradley, and Dianna Shandy. *The Cultural Experience: Ethnography in Complex Society*. Long Grove: Waveland Press, 2005.

Meyers, Ched and Matthew Colwell. *Our God is Undocumented*. Maryknoll, NY: Orbis, 2012.

Mulder, Mark T., Aida I. Ramos and Gerardo Marti. *Latino Protestants in America: Growing and Diverse*. Lanham, MD: Rowman & Littlefield, 2017.

Nah, Alice M. "Refugees and Space in Urban Areas in Malaysia." *Forced Migration Review* 34 (2010): 29–31.

Ng, Andrew, and Michael Crane. "Models of Ministry with the Transient Poor." *Evangelical Missions Quarterly* 51, no. 1 (January 2015): 58–67.

Nguyen, vanThanh, SVD. "Asia in Motion: A Biblical Reflection on Migration," *Asian Christian Review* 4, n. 2 (Winter 2010): 18-31.

_____. "Migrants as Missionaries: The Case of Priscilla and Aquila," *Mission Studies* 30, no. 2 (2013): 192-205.

_____. *Strangers, Migrants, and Refugees*. Hyde Park, NY: New City Press, 2021.

Nguyen, vanThanh and John M. Prior, eds. *God's People on the Move: Biblical and Global Perspectives on Migration and Mission*. Eugene, OR: Pickwick Publications, 2014.

Norwood, Frederick A. *Strangers and Exiles: A History of Religious Refugees, Vol. I*. Nashville: Abingdon Press, 1969.

Obed, Bustenay. *Mass Deportations and Deportees in the Neo-Assyrian Empire*. Wiesbaden: Dr. Ludwig Reichert Verlag, 1979.

Okure, Aniedi. "International Priests in the United States: An Update," *Seminary Journal* 1, no. 1 (2012): 34–43.

Otter, Vera den. "Urban Asylum Seekers and Refugees in Thailand." *Forced Migration Review* 28 (2007): 49–50.

Padilla, Elaine. "Border Crossing and Exile: A Latina's Theological Encounter with Shekhinah." *Cross Currents*, 60, no. 4 (December 2010): 526–548.

Padilla, Elaine and Peter C. Phan, eds. *Contemporary Issues of Migration and Theology.* New York: Palgrave/Macmillan, 2013.

Phan, Peter C. *In Our Tongues: Perspectives from Asia on Mission and Inculturation.* Maryknoll, NY: Orbis Books, 2003.

_____. "Migration in the Patristic Era" In *A Promised Land, a Perilous Journey: Theological Perspectives on Migration*, edited by Daniel G. Goody and Gioacchino Campese. Notre Dame: University of Notre Dame Press, 2008.

_____. "Deus Migrator–God the Migrant: Migration Theology and Theology of Migration" *Theological Studies* 77/4 (November 2016): 845–868.

_____. *The Joy of Religious Pluralism: A Personal Journey.* Maryknoll, NY: Orbis Books, 2017.

Phan, Peter C. and Diana Hayes, ed. *Many Faces, One Church: Cultural Diversity and the American Catholic Experience.* Lanham, Maryland: A Sheed & Ward Book, 2005.

Pilch, John J. *A Cultural Handbook to the Bible.* Grand Rapids, MI: Eerdmans, 2012.

Romero, Robert Chao. "Migration as Grace" *International Journal of Urban Transformation*, Vol 1, 10–35, October, 2016.

_____. *Brown Church: Five Centuries of Latina/o Social Justice, Theology, and Identity.* Downers Grove, IL: InterVarsity Press, 2020.

Rynkiewich, Michael. *Soul, Self, and Society: A Postmodern Anthropology for Mission in a Postcolonial World.* Eugene, OR: Cascade Books, 2011.

Sarna, Nahum. *Exploring Exodus: The Origins of Biblical Israel.* New York: Schocken Books, 1986.

Saxton, Alexander. *The Indispensable Enemy: Labor and Anti-Chinese Movement in California.* Berkeley: The University of California Press, 1971.

Schreiter, Robert J. *Constructing Local Theologies.* Maryknoll: Orbis Books, 1985.

Shiller, Nina Glick, Linda Basch, and Cristina Szanton Blanc, eds. *Towards a Transnational Perspective on Migration: Race, Class, Ethnicity, and Nationalism Reconsidered.* New York: The New York Academy of Sciences, 1992.

Smith, Amy A. *In Search of Survival and Sanctuary in the City: Refugees from Myanmar/Burma in Kuala Lumpur, Malaysia.* Kuala Lumpur, Malaysia: IRC, 2012. http://www.rescue.org/resource-file/search-survival-and-sanctuary-city-refugees-myanmarburma-kuala-lumpur-malaysia-decembe.

Snyder, Susanna. "Introduction." In *Church in an Age of Global Migration: A Moving Body.* Edited by Susanna Snyder, Joshua Ralston, and Agnes M. Brazal. New York: Palgrave/Macmillan, 2016.

Soerens, Matthew and Jenny Hwang Yang. *Welcoming the Stranger: Justice, Compassion, and Truth in the Immigration Debate.* Downers Grove: InterVarsity Press, 2010.

Stelzer, Mark. "A New Ecclesial Reality and A New Way of Doing Theology: Heralding A New Pentecost." In *Many Faces, One Church: Cultural Diversity and the American Catholic Experience*, edited by Peter C. Phan and Dianna Hayes, 13-25. Lanham, MD: A Sheed & Ward Book, 2005.

Sunquist, Scott W. *The Unexpected Christian Century: The Reversal and Transformation of Global Christianity, 1900–2000.* Grand Rapids: Baker Books, 2015.

Tan, Jonathan Y. "Asian American Catholics and Contemporary Liturgical Migration: From Tradition-Maintenance to Traditioning," In *Liturgy in Migration: From the Upper Room to Cyberspace*, edited by Teresa Berger. Collegeville: Liturgical Press, 243–257, 2012.

_____. *Christian Mission among the Peoples of Asia.* Maryknoll, NY: Orbis Books, 2014.

_____. "Pope Francis's Preferential Option for Migrants, Refugees, and Asylum Seekers," *International Bulletin of Mission Research* 43 no. 1 (2019): 58-66. DOI: 10.1177/2396939318801794.

_____. "The Implications of Transient Migration and Online Communities for Changing the Church in Asia," In *Changing the Church: Transformations of Christian Belief, Practice, and Life*, edited by Mark D. Chapman and Vladimir Latinovic, 183-190 New York: Palgrave Macmillan, 2021. DOI: 10.1007/978-3-030-53425-7_21.

Turner, Victor. *Dramas, Fields, and Metaphors.* Ithaca, NY: Cornell University Press, 1974.

Tweed, Thomas A. and Stephen Protheto, ed. *Asian Religions in America: A Documentary History.* New York: Oxford University Press, 1999.

United Nations High Commissioner for Refugees. "Asylum-Seekers." UNHCR, 2016. http://www.unhcr.org/asylum-seekers.html.

————. "Resettlement." UNHCR, 2016. http://www.unhcr.org/resettlement.html.

United Nations, *International Migration Report 2017*. New York: United Nations, 2017.

————. "UNHCR - Refugee Statistics." UNHCR. Accessed January 17, 2021. https://www.unhcr.org/refugee-statistics/.

USA for UNHCR, "What Is a Refugee," 2016. http://www.unrefugees.org/what-is-a-refugee/.

Vimalasekaran, Peter. "Strategies for Reaching Refugees." In *Scattered and Gathered: A Global Compendium of Diaspora Missiology*, edited by Sadiri Joy Tira and Tetsunao Yamamori, 207–20. Regnum Studies in Mission. Oxford: Regnum Books, 2016.

Van Gennep, Arnold. *The Rites of Passage*. Chicago, IL: University of Chicago Press, 1960. Translated by Monika Vicedom and Gabrielle Caffee.

VanThanh, Nguyen and John M. Prior, eds. *God's People on the Move: Biblical and Global Perspectives on Migration and Mission*. Eugene, OR: Pickwick Publications, 2014.

————. *What Does the Bible Say About Strangers, Migrants, and Refugees?* New York: New City Press, 2021.

Villafane, Eldin. *The Liberating Spirit: Toward a Hispanic American Pentecostal Social Ethic*. Grand Rapids: Eerdmans, 1993.

Waltke, Bruce K. *An Old Testament Theology: An Exegetical, Canonical, and Thematic Approach*. Grand Rapids, MI: Zondervan, 2007.

Walls, Andrew F. "Mission and Migration: The Diaspora Factor in Christian History," *Journal of African Christian Thought* 5, no. 2 (Dec 2002): 3-11.

————. *The Missionary Movement in Christian History: Studies in the Transmission of Faith*. Maryknoll, N.Y. Orbis Books, 1996.

Wan, Enoch, ed. *Diaspora Missiology: Theory, Methodology, and Practice*. Portland, OR: Institute of Diaspora Studies, 2011.

Wan, Enoch, and Anthony Casey. *Church Planting among Immigrants in US Urban Centers: The "Where", "Why", And "How" of Diaspora Missiology in Action*. Portland, OR: Institute of Diaspora Studies, 2014.

Wan, Enoch, and Thanh Trung Le. *Mobilizing Vietnamese Diaspora for the Kingdom*. Portland, OR: Institute of Diaspora Studies, 2014.

Wan, Enoch and Anthony Casey. *Church Planting among Immigrants in US Urban Centers.* Portland: Institute of Diaspora Studies, 2016.

Welsh, Jennifer. *The Return of History: Conflict, Migration, and Geopolitics in the Twenty-First Century.* Toronto: House of Anansi Press, 2016.

Wuthnow, Robert. *America and the Challenges of Religious Identity.* Princeton, NJ: Princeton University Press, 2005.

Yong, Amos. "The In/Migrant Spirit: De/Constructing a Pentecostal Theology of Migration,:" edited by Peter C. Phan and Elain Padilla. *Theology of Migration in the Abrahamic Religions. Christianities of the World.* New York: Palgrave/Macmillan, 2014.

Yosso, Tara J. Whose Culture has Capital? A Critical Race Theory Discussion of Community Cultural Wealth. *Race, Ethnicity and Education 8,* no. 1. (2006): 69–91.

Made in the USA
Middletown, DE
28 March 2022